BILL O'REILLY'S

LEGENDS & LIES

BILL O'REILLY'S
LEGENDS & LIES

THE REAL WEST

WRITTEN BY DAVID FISHER

Henry Holt and Company
New York

Henry Holt and Company, LLC
Publishers since 1866
175 Fifth Avenue
New York, New York 10010
www.henryholt.com

Henry Holt® and ⊞® are registered trademarks of Henry Holt and Company, LLC.

Distributed in Canada by Raincoast Book Distribution Limited
Library of Congress Cataloging-in-Publication Data is available
ISBN: 978-1-62779-507-4

Henry Holt books are available for special promotions and premiums.
For details contact: Director, Special Markets.

First Edition 2015

Interior Design by Nancy Singer
Endpaper map by Jeffrey L. Ward

Photo research and editing provided by Liz Seramur, with assistance from Nancy Singer,
Emily Vinson, and Adam Vietenheimer

Jacket art credits: Background and title logo courtesy of FOX NEWS CHANNEL;
Denver Public Library, Western History Collection/Bridgeman Images; Chappel, Alonzo
(1828–87) (after)/Private Collection/Ken Welsh/Bridgeman Images; Private Collection/
Peter Newark Western Americana/Bridgeman Images; Private Collection/Bridgeman
Images; Universal History Archive/UIG/Bridgeman Images

Interior art credits appear on pages 293–94.

Printed in the United States of America

10 9 8 7 6 5 4 3 2 1

CONTENTS

DANIEL BOONE
1734–1820

KIT CARSON
1809–1868

WILD BILL HICKOK
1837–1876

BLACK BART
1829–?

BASS REEVES
1838–1910

DAVID CROCKETT
1786–1836

GEORGE ARMSTRONG
CUSTER
1839–1876

JESSE JAMES
1847–1882

BILLY THE KID
1859–1881

DOC HOLLIDAY
1852–1887

BUTCH CASSIDY
1866–1908

BUFFALO BILL AND
ANNIE OAKLEY
1846/1860–1917/1926

BILL O'REILLY'S

LEGENDS & LIES

INTRODUCTION

Pace High School
Miami, Florida
August 1971

The classroom was filled with bored faces. About forty of them. All staring at a young history teacher fresh out of college who, at age twenty-one, was just a few years older than his students. What had I gotten myself into?

My initial task was to get these teenagers interested in things that had happened in America hundreds of years ago, events they thought had little or no meaning in their current lives.

It wasn't easy.

While I taught, I learned. There was a way to spread historical information around so that the urchins would not nod off. But it involved energy and thought, not just standing there pontificating. I learned back then that in order for people to enjoy history, you have to make it come alive in a vivid way. My students were taught to put themselves into the historical fray by visualizing themselves in the action. Those who did that learned about America in an unforgettable way.

Enter this book, *Legends & Lies*. It is based upon my high school teaching techniques that cut through the clutter to tell amazing stories. Want specifics? How about this: Evidence suggests that the real Lone

Ranger was a black man! You'll ride with him through a series of harrowing adventures that few Americans know about.

What you will read in this book is the truth about some very famous people. It's not always pretty, and it's definitely not the stuff they taught you in school. No, these pages are filled with facts and personalities, many of them disturbing. But we have made them all real people on the page because they were real people in life. Folks who did extraordinary things. A guy like Kit Carson, traveling thousands of miles through the freezing Rocky Mountains and then over the scorching-hot Arizona desert. At least Carson had a horse—the bandit Black Bart was afraid of horses and actually walked from Illinois to Montana! Don't believe me? Read the book. Walk alongside him.

America has a tendency to glamorize its past, creating myths instead of reporting truth. Let's take the Old West, for example. Our image of that time is John Wayne, Marshal Matt Dillon in *Gunsmoke*, and maybe a squinting, grizzled Clint Eastwood mowing down bad guys in a dusty town. But the truth about the West is far different from *Rio Bravo* or *Stagecoach* or *The Good, the Bad and the Ugly*. This was a place where brutality ruled, and life expectancy was measured in months. If you lived to be forty, you were way ahead. Some famous western men and women were both heroes and villains, split personalities. The dangers they faced were unrelenting.

Did you know that some Indians were more civilized than the settlers they encountered? But other Native Americans would torture in ways that are nearly inconceivable. Some outlaws, such as Butch Cassidy and Black Bart, were almost noble in their outlook. Some lawmen, such as Pat Garrett, were not. It is these stories that we will relate to you in this book, and after reading them, you will know the truth about America's lively and unique past. You will have also learned about some lies that still circulate today. Debunking falsehoods is a major theme here.

As in my previous history books, *Killing Lincoln, Killing Kennedy, Killing Jesus,* and *Killing Patton*, we will put you on the scene as historical events unfold. You will be in the room and on the trail with Jesse James, Wyatt Earp, Wild Bill Hickok, and many other legendary figures. You will vividly see these men live and sometimes die. While reading this book, you will experience history rather than be numbed by it. Some say that after reading the Killing series, they understand the towering figures in history in a unique way. Each of those books has sold millions of copies.

When I engaged my students all those years ago, I painted a verbal picture for them of times past. Billy the Kid, for example, was a lot like they were, a confused teenager who chose the wrong road and paid the ultimate price. Or did he? There's always a bit more to the story if you dig deep enough. In *Legends & Lies*, you will see that the Kid's fate may have turned out far differently than many believe or the press reported.

And that's the fun of these pages. We dig deep, uncovering facts that illuminate the legends and debunk the lies that have somehow become folklore. History can be thrilling, and America's past is full of tremendous characters whose exploits can enrich our own lives today. It took me a while to convince my students of that, but I did it, and my history classes rocked, according to their own reviews (conducted each year at the school's behest).

Now it's your turn, and as a plus, there's no homework! Enjoy the exciting journey, and thanks for reading the book!

Bill O'Reilly
January 2015

DANIEL BOONE

Traitor or Patriot?

As Daniel Boone approached his log cabin one October day in 1778, carrying fur and meat to take his family through the winter, he probably guessed something was wrong. Keenly perceptive and attuned to the rhythms of nature, he would have sensed the discord. His family came out to greet him, followed almost immediately by several stern-looking men. As Boone dismounted, one of them handed him a subpoena. Another man stepped forward, unrolled a scroll, and announced, "Daniel Boone, you are hereby formally charged with treason and shall face a court-martial . . ."

No one embodied the spirit of the frontier more than Daniel Boone, who faced and defeated countless natural and man-made dangers to literally hand cut the trail west through the wilderness. He marched with then colonel George Washington in the French and Indian War, established one of the most important trading posts in the West, served three terms in the Virginia Assembly, and fought in the Revolution. His exploits made him world famous; he served as the model for James Fenimore Cooper's Leatherstocking Tales and numerous other pioneer stories. He was so well known and respected that even Lord Byron, in his epic poem *Don Juan*, wrote, "Of the great names which in our faces stare, The General Boon, back-woodsman of Kentucky, Was happiest amongst mortals anywhere . . ."

And yet he was accused of treason—betraying his country—the most foul of all crimes at the time. What really happened to bring him to that courtroom? And was the verdict reached there correct?

Daniel Boone was born in Pennsylvania in 1734, the sixth child of Quakers Sarah and Squire Boone. His father had come to America from England in 1713. The Boones were known as thrifty, prosperous people. His cousin, James Boone, had a knack for numbers and eventually became known as "Boone, the Mathematician." But Daniel Boone did not find comfort in the classroom or with books. He had enough schooling to know how to sign his name, but his real education was learning the skills of survival on the frontier: He became an expert hunter, tracker, trapper, marksman, and trailblazer. It was said that no Indian could aim his rifle,

Born in 1734 in Birdsboro, Pennsylvania, Daniel Boone was the seventh of twelve children.

find his way through a pathless forest, or search out game better than young Daniel Boone. He was hard to pin down to any one place; he always loved being on his own, away from the clatter of the cities.

When Squire Boone was "disowned" by the Quaker meeting for allowing his children to "marry out of unity"—meaning to marry non-Quakers—he moved his family to North Carolina. The Boones had only just settled there when the French and Indian War began in 1754. Young Daniel Boone served as a wagoneer in British major Edward Dobb's North Carolina militia. He marched with Lieutenant Colonel George Washington under the despised General Braddock in his disastrous effort to capture Fort Duquesne. When Braddock was killed in the Battle of the Wilderness, Washington took command and began building his heroic reputation. During the war, Boone first heard tell of a place the Indians called the Dark and Bloody Ground, a paradise that some people called Kentucke. An Indian trader named John Finlay had actually been there and was determined to get back. At that time, very little about the lands south of the Ohio River was known to the British, and Boone listened to these stories with excitement, his heart making the decision that he would go there.

A small group of extraordinarily courageous men risked their lives exploring and settling the American frontier. They were people who felt an urgent pull to see what lay beyond the next mountain and depended on their skills, wits, and sometimes just plain luck to reach the next summit. They were most at home in foreign and wild places, living off God's bounty. Many of these early American pioneers are forgotten, but through hundreds of years of American history, Daniel Boone has stood for them all.

It took Boone twelve more years to finally get to Kentucke, and by that time he had married his neighbor's daughter, Rebecca Bryan, and they'd had four children, in addition to taking in several nieces and nephews. He'd also explored the area called Florida (he reportedly bought land near Pensacola but elected not to settle there), as well as the unspoiled wilderness of the Alleghenies, the Cumberlands, and the Shenandoah Valley. In 1851, author Henry Howe described Boone's arrival in Kentucke, writing that his party, "after a long and fatiguing march, over a mountainous and pathless wilderness, arrived on the Red River. Here, from the top of an eminence, Boone and his companions first beheld a distant view of the beautiful lands of Kentucky. The plains and forests abounded with wild beasts of every kind;

Thomas Cole's *Daniel Boone Sitting at the Door of His Cabin on the Great Osage Lake, Kentucky,* 1826

deer and elk were common; the buffalo were seen in herds and the plains covered with the richest verdure . . . this newly discovered Paradise of the West." Daniel Boone was the first settler to set his eyes and bestow a name on many of the now familiar features of Kentucky. Like many frontiersmen of the time, as Boone explored, he carved his name into the trees to show he had been there, and a beech tree on the Watauga River in Tennessee still bears the inscription D. BOON CILLED A. BAR ON TREE IN THE YEAR 1760.

His first time in Kentucke, he stayed only long enough to know that he'd found the open spaces in which he wanted to raise his family. He returned in 1769 with five other men, blazing the first trail from North Carolina into eastern Tennessee. During that expedition, he spent two years there, twice being captured by Indians; the first time, he was set free, the next time, he escaped. As he later wrote, the Indians "had kept us in confinement seven days, treating us with common savage usage . . . in the dead of the night, as we lay in a thick cane-break by a large fire, when sleep had locked up their senses, my situation not disposing me for rest, I touched my companion, and gentle awoke him. We improved this favorable opportunity, and departed, leaving them to take their rest, and speedily directed our course towards our old camp." His companion was his brother-in-law, John Stewart, who had been captured with him both times, but eventually Stewart's luck ran out. While out hunting one day, he was shot by an Indian raiding party and took refuge in a hollowed-out tree, where he bled to death; his body was found there almost five years later.

Boone would spend his winters hunting beaver and otter, and in the spring sell or trade the furs he had collected. In the summers he would farm and hunt deer, gathering meat for the winter and deerskins for trade. The value of these deerskins, or buckskins, fluctuated against the British pound and later the American dollar, and eventually *buck* became an acceptable slang term for "dollar."

Boone also made his clothes from the skins of the animals, and his buckskin shirt and leggings, moccasins, and beaver cap were the accepted dress of the frontiersmen.

In 1773, Boone decided it was time to move his family to Kentucke. He sold his farm and all his possessions and agreed to lead the first group of about fifty British colonists into the new territory. On the journey west, his son James trailed behind, bringing cattle and supplies to the settlements. On October 9, James Boone's small group was camped along Wallen Creek when Indians attacked. They had failed to take the necessary precautions and were defenseless. James and several others were brutally tortured and killed. Although Boone urged the rest of the settlers to push forward, this deadly attack frightened them into returning to civilization in Virginia and Carolina. He had no choice but to go back with them.

Early American history
has been told—and often
exaggerated—by the pen
and the paintbrush. Daniel
Boone's fame as a bear hunter
is depicted by Severino Baraldi
(*above*), while this portrait of
the lone woodsman was painted
by Robert Lindneux.

Boone blazing the trail west in George Caleb Bingham's 1851–52 oil painting, *Daniel Boone Escorting Settlers through the Cumberland Gap*

Boone was not a man who relished a fight, but he never backed away from one, either. In 1774, he led the defense of three forts along Virginia's Clinch River from Shawnee attacks and, as a result, earned a promotion to captain in the militia—as well as the respect of his men. While Boone proved to be one of the settlers' most ferocious fighters, he did understand the reason for the Indians' resistance and perhaps even sympathized with them, admitting that the war against them was intended to "dispossess them of their desirable habitations"— in simpler words, take their land.

His reputation was growing, the word spread by his admirers, who never hesitated to tell stories of his courage, even if some were a bit exaggerated. In 1775, the Transylvania Company, which had purchased from the Cherokees all the land lying between the Cumberland Mountains, the Cumberland River, and the Kentucky River, south of the Ohio, hired Boone to lead the expedition of axmen that carved the three-hundred-mile-long Wilderness Road through three states and the Cumberland Gap. It was this trail that opened up the frontier to the many thousands of settlers who would follow.

When Boone's men finally reached Kentucke, he laid out the town and fort of Boonesborough. During that journey, four men were killed and five were wounded by the increasingly hostile Shawnees. But Boonesborough and Harrodsburg, wrote Henry Howe, "became the nucleus and support of emigration and settlement in Kentucky." The settlers, including Boone's wife and their children, raced to erect fortifications strong enough to resist Indian attacks, and on May 23, 1776, the Shawnees attacked Boonesborough. They were repelled, but they would come back, and everybody knew it.

Less than two weeks later, the Continental Congress, meeting in Philadelphia, signed the Declaration of Independence. It would take more than a month for the settlers to learn of it.

On April 1, 1775, Boone and thirty axmen began construction of Fort Boonesborough, choosing a location in a defensible field "about 60 yards from the river, and a little over 200 yards from a salt lick."

The coming war for independence did not really affect or concern them; they were already too busy fighting a war for their own survival. Boone was not a political man and did not strongly support either the Revolutionaries or the British. That was not a luxury he had time for. Life on the frontier was always a daily life-or-death struggle. Just about a week after the noble document was signed, for example, Boone's daughter, Jemima, and two other young girls were kidnapped by a Shawnee-Cherokee raiding party. He immediately gathered nine men and set off after them.

From all accounts, Daniel Boone was not a man of exuberant emotions. He kept his feelings contained and was respected for his cunning and his steadfast leadership. He was not a man who ever asked another to take a risk in his place. When a task needed to be done, he took the lead. The rescuers pursued the Indians for three days, finally sneaking up on them as they sat by a breakfast fire. Their first shot wounded a guard and alerted the others to escape. Two of the Indians were killed, and the three girls were freed without harm. This kidnapping and rescue later served as an inspiration for James Fenimore Cooper, who included a similar incident in *The Last of the Mohicans*, with the character Hawkeye modeled after Boone.

The Revolutionary War just brushed the frontier, and rather than facing the redcoats, the pioneers fought Native Americans supplied and supported by British forces headquartered in Detroit. It was questionable whether the Indians were actually fighting to protect the Empire or to maintain their own rights to live and hunt on the land. By 1777, Indians were focusing their attacks on Boonesborough, forcing the settlers to stay close to the fort. One afternoon, Boone was outside the perimeter when the Shawnees attacked. As Boone took up his long gun to return fire, a bullet smashed into his ankle and sent him to the ground. He was carried through the closing gate as Indian bullets ripped into the wooden walls.

The constant pressure of attacks kept the settlers confined, and by the end of the year, supplies were running low. In early February, Boone was asked to lead a twenty-seven-man expedition to the Blue Licks, a salt lick located several miles away. It was a very risky mission: Several weeks earlier, three Shawnee chiefs in captivity at Fort Randolph had been killed, and the tribe was seeking revenge. As Boone's men were gathering vital salt, he was alone, hunting for provisions—and he was surprised and captured by a Shawnee war party. More than one hundred warriors were led by Chief Blackfish, a man Boone had met decades earlier while serving in Braddock's campaign. Blackfish apparently respected Boone as the chief of his people and told him he intended to avenge the murders of the three Indian chiefs by killing everyone in the salt-gathering party, then destroying Boonesborough. Boone negotiated with him, finally offering to arrange the peaceful surrender of his men, who would then go north with the tribe. Chief Blackfish agreed.

As this G. W. Fasel lithograph depicts, when Boone's daughter and two friends were kidnapped by Indians in 1776, he tracked them down and rescued them—an episode that served as an inspiration for James Fenimore Cooper's *Last of the Mohicans*.

Boone was reputed to be the young nation's greatest Indian fighter, as shown in this Baraldi painting of an attack on Boonesborough.

Boone led the Shawnees to his hunting party—and when his men saw him with the Indians, they suspected that he had betrayed them and prepared to fight for their lives. "Don't fire!" Boone warned them. "If you do they will massacre all of us." He put his reputation on the line, ordering his men to stack their arms and surrender. In the confusion, some men escaped and hurried back to warn the settlers.

Daniel Boone and the remaining members of the expedition went north with the Shawnees to the village of Chillicothe, where there was great debate on how to treat the prisoners: Some of the braves wanted to kill them, but apparently Boone convinced them otherwise. As the weeks went by, he actually was adopted into the tribe and given the Indian name Sheltowee, or "Big Turtle." He was known to hunt and fish and play sports with the tribe, and there were even some stories that he took a bride. The Shawnees trusted him enough to take him to Detroit, where he met with the British governor Hamilton. But when he returned to Chillicothe, he found more than four hundred fifty armed and painted braves preparing to attack Boonesborough. He feared that the unprepared settlers would be slaughtered. Boone waited for the right opportunity, and in the confusion of a wild-turkey hunt, he managed to slip away.

He raced 160 miles in less than five days, on foot and horseback. He paused only one time for a meal. He reached Boonesborough still dressed in Indian garb, and his warning was met with great suspicion. The men who had escaped the original attack cautioned that he was cooperating with the Shawnees, pointing out that he had lived safely among the tribe for months and that he had returned while many of their relations remained captives. Finally Boone was able to convince the settlers to strengthen their wooden fortifications and, in an effort to prove his loyalty, suggested that instead of waiting for the attack, they take the offensive.

He and his friend John Logan led a thirty-man raiding party to the Shawnee village of Paint Creek on the Scioto River. After a trek of several days, they found it abandoned— meaning the main Indian force, then under the command of the Canadian captain Duquesne, was already on its way to the settlement. The raiding party made it back safely, and the cattle and horses were brought into the fort, which was made as secure as possible. Soon Boonesborough was surrounded by as many as five hundred Shawnee braves. British colors were displayed, and the settlers were told to either surrender, with a promise of good treatment, or fight and face the hatchet. Rather than fighting, Boone asked Captain Duquesne for a parley.

Boone and eight other men met with the Indians in a meadow beyond the settlement's walls. Eventually they reached an agreement: The Ohio River would be the boundary between the settlers and the tribes. As they shook hands, the Indians tried to grab Boonesborough's leaders and drag them away, but carefully hidden sharpshooters opened fire. Boone and his men retreated, and an eleven-day siege began. The enemy made several efforts to break into the fort, but riflemen inside the garrison released a steady stream of accurate fire on anyone who came within range. When the Indian force broke off the attack, thirty-seven braves had been killed and many more wounded, while inside the walls only two settlers had died and two were wounded. The resistance, led by Daniel Boone, had saved the settlement.

But within weeks, Boone was accused of treason. Two militia officers—whose kin had been taken on the salt-lick expedition and were still being held captive in Detroit—claimed he had been collaborating with the Indians and the British. He was accused of surrendering the original expedition at the salt flats, consorting with the British in Detroit in their plan to capture the settlement, intentionally weakening Boonesborough's defense by taking thirty men on the "foolish raid" on Paint Creek, and leaving the fort vulnerable by bringing its leadership outside to negotiate with Blackfish. The penalty for treason was death by hanging.

Boone's trial was held at another settlement, Logan's Station. With few records available, it is difficult to reconstruct events. His accusers were Richard Callaway and Benjamin Logan. Callaway testified, "Boone was in favor of the British government and all his conduct proved it."

Boone insisted on representing himself rather than retaining a lawyer. He testified that both his salt expedition and the settlement were outmanned and outgunned, and neither of them was strong enough to survive a surprise attack. To prevent a massacre, he had been forced to "use some stratagem," telling the Indians "tales to fool them." After hearing his testimony, and perhaps taking into account his good name, the judges found him not guilty—then promoted him to the rank of major.

Boone accepted the acquittal but could not forgive the insult, so he left Boonesborough and founded a new settlement in an area known as Upper Louisiana, which actually was in present-day Missouri. When asked why he'd left Kentucke, he replied, "I want more elbow room." In recognition of his accomplishments, the Spanish governor of that region granted him 850 acres and appointed him commandant. He settled there with his family but couldn't stay settled long.

Perhaps still angry about the false accusations, in 1780 he finally joined the Revolution, acting as a guide for George Rogers Clark's militia as they attacked and defeated a joint British and Indian force in Ohio. In that attack, his brother Ned was shot and killed. Apparently believing they had killed the great Daniel Boone, the Shawnees beheaded Ned Boone and took his head home as a trophy.

This Currier and Ives hand-colored lithograph by Fannie Flora Palmer, *The Rocky Mountains—Emigrants Crossing the Plains*, 1866, illustrates the barren beauty of the frontier—although Palmer never left New York.

A year later, Daniel Boone stood for election to the Virginia Assembly. He would be elected to that body three times.

Two years later, at the Battle of Blue Licks, the then lieutenant colonel Daniel Boone warned his commanding officer that the militia was being led into an Indian trap. He explained that the Indians had left a broad and obvious trail, which was contrary to their

custom and "manifested a willingness to be pursued." Boone believed that "an ambuscade was formed at the distance of a mile in advance" and urged him not to cross the Licking River until the area could be properly scouted or reinforcements known to be marching toward them arrived. But as the commanders debated their strategy, a headstrong young Major McGary ignored Boone's advice and instead mounted and charged the enemy. When he was in the middle of the stream, he paused, waved his hat over his head, and shouted, "Let all who are not cowards follow me!" As the rest of the men cheered and followed, Boone supposedly said, "We are all slaughtered men," but still joined the attack. As pioneer historian Howe described it, "The action became warm and bloody . . . the slaughter was great in the river." When the trap was sprung, as Boone had warned, he fought courageously and helped organize the militia's retreat. Boone himself was in desperate trouble: Several hundred Indians were between him and the main force. Howe wrote, "Being intimately acquainted with the ground, he, together with a few friends, dashed into the ravine which the Indians had occupied, but

which most of them had now left to join the pursuit. After sustaining one or two heavy fires, and baffling one or two small parties, who pursued him for a short distance, he crossed the river below the ford, by swimming, and entering the wood at a point where there was no pursuit, returned by a circuitous route. . . ."

Unfortunately, as he made this miraculous escape, Boone's twenty-three-year-old son, Israel, was shot and became one of sixty men killed in the battle. It was the worst defeat the Kentuckians were to suffer in the long war against the Indians—and it came weeks after the Revolution had ended in the East.

After the war, Boone settled in Limestone, Kentucky, a booming town on the Ohio River. He worked there as the deputy surveyor of Lincoln County, a horse trader, and a land speculator—as well as owning a small trading house.

By the time America became an independent nation in 1783, Daniel Boone was one of its most famous citizens. That fame was magnified a year later during the celebration of his fiftieth birthday, with the publication of historian John Filson's book, *The Discovery, Settlement,*

This fanciful hand-colored lithograph by Henry Schile (c. 1874), *Daniel Boone Protects His Family*, probably best captures the enduring image of the legendary frontiersman.

and Present State of Kentucke, with an appendix entitled "The Adventures of Col. Daniel Boon, One of the First Settlers." The book, published both in the United States and England, was a great success and guaranteed Boone's place in history. A year later, *The Adventures of Colonel Boone* was published by itself, further spreading Boone's fame. The image of Boone exploring the frontier, dressed in deerskin, fighting Indians, stood for all of the men—and women— who settled the West. Although the book supposedly included words that came "out of his own mouth," the sometimes exaggerated tales caused Boone to admit later, "Many heroic actions and chivalrous adventures are related of me which exist only in the regions of fancy. With me the world has taken great liberties, and yet I have been but a common man."

Boone's battles were not yet completely done. The Revolution was over, but the Indians north of the Ohio River had not given up fighting for their land. Battle hardened and desperate, they continued to raid settlements, killing and kidnapping people or stealing their livestock. In 1786, a war party of more than four hundred fifty braves had come into the Cumberland region and announced their intention to kill all the Americans. Mingo, Chickamauga, and Shawnee warriors had raided several settlements and murdered a number of people. In response, Benjamin Logan put together an army of 888 men and rode into the Mad River Valley to find and punish the tribes. Boone served as one of the commanders of the raiding party. Unfortunately, it proved far easier to find innocent Indians than those who had staged the attacks, and Logan's men burned seven villages and destroyed the food supply of mostly peaceful natives. Among those taken prisoner were the Shawnee chief Moluntha, who believed he had made peace with the Americans. When he was brought to see Colonel Logan, he carried with him an American flag and a copy of the treaty he had signed at Fort Finney declaring he would fight no longer. He had proudly honored that agreement. However, while he was there he was accosted by the now colonel McGary—the same officer who had ignored Boone's advice about riding into the Indian trap—who demanded to know if he had been present at the Battle of the Blue Licks. Although Moluntha had not fought in that battle, McGary did not believe his claim and clubbed him to death with a tomahawk. In an incredible twist, Logan adopted the chief's son and raised him to become an honored American soldier.

Boone, too, was greatly chagrined by the vengeance taken on innocent Indians. He brought several Shawnees back with him to Limestone, where he fed and cared for them until a truce could be negotiated and a prisoner exchange arranged. Although he was already in his fifties, quite an old age at that time, he still had one more fight left in him. During a 1787 Indian raid in Kanawha Valley, a settler named John Flinn and his wife were killed, and their young daughter, Chloe, was kidnapped. Boone happened to be nearby and quickly organized a party to pursue the Indians. Boone's men caught up with them and killed them, rescuing the child—who was watched over by Boone for the remainder of his years.

Like many other men of action, Daniel Boone was not especially successful when it came to business, and most of his enterprises eventually failed. He made and lost large amounts of money speculating in Kentucke land, buying and selling claims to vast tracts. For a brief time, he was rich and owned seven slaves, which some believed to be the most of any one master in the entire territory of Kentucke. His common decency was his greatest business flaw, as he was too often reluctant to enforce a claim to the detriment of others. He said he just didn't like the feeling of profiting from another man's loss. The respect he gained was paid for in the dollars he forfeited. Ironically, in 1798, a court in Mason County issued a warrant for his arrest for his failure to testify in a court case, while later that same year, Kentucke honored him by naming a large region of the state Boone County.

But what pressed on him most was a large debt he spent much of his later life repaying: While sleeping in a Richmond tavern on his way to Williamsburg in 1780, he was robbed of twenty thousand dollars in depreciated scrip and land certificates that had been entrusted to him by settlers to purchase supplies and buy land claims from the Virginia government. Although some of the settlers forgave him, he vowed to pay all of them back completely. It took him more than thirty years to do so, which he finally did by selling off most of the lands he had been awarded in 1815 by President James Monroe. After making the final repayment, it was said he was left with fifty cents.

His wife, Rebecca, died in 1813 after nearly fifty-seven years of marriage. She was buried on a knoll along Tuque Creek in Missouri, in the shade of large apple trees that had been grown from seeds Daniel had brought with him from Kentucke.

In spirit, as well as body, Daniel Boone never really left the wilderness, continuing to hunt and fish well into his older years. There is some evidence that he went hunting up the Missouri all the way to the Yellowstone River in his eighty-first year. He spent the last years of his life living in the large stone house his son Nathan had built on the land originally given to Boone by the Spanish in the town of Booneslick, Missouri, where Kit Carson would grow up years later. In 1820, secure in his status as an American hero, he said simply, "My time has come," and died. He was two and a half months short of his eighty-sixth birthday.

In all those years after he had left Kentucke, Boone had rarely, if ever, spoken about the court-martial. Certainly any question about his allegiance had been answered decades earlier when he fought for the patriot cause. That the state of Kentucky had chosen to honor him

The only portrait of Daniel Boone painted from life, Chester Harding's oil painting was done in 1820, only a few months before Boone's death.

by naming a county after him and President Monroe publicly recognized his service to the new country by awarding him a large tract of land settled any doubts about his loyalty. In *The Adventures of Colonel Boone*, the accusations were dismissed without being directly addressed: "My footsteps have often been marked with blood, and therefore I can truly subscribe to its original name [The Dark and Bloody Ground]. Two darling sons, and a brother, have I lost by savage hands, which have also taken from me forty valuable horses, and abundance of cattle."

Near the end of his life, he was able to look back on the many sacrifices he had made to help settle the nation. He said, "Many dark and sleepless nights have I been a companion for owls, separated from the cheerful society of men, scorched by the summer's sun, and pinched by the winter's cold, an instrument ordained to settle the wilderness. But now the scene is changed: peace crowns the sylvan shade."

DAVID CROCKETT

★ CAPITOL ★ HILLBILLY ★

During David Crockett's first visit to Washington, D.C., in 1827, the newly elected congressman from Tennessee was stopped by a man who loudly proclaimed his support for President John Quincy Adams. When Crockett responded angrily, "You had better hurrah for hell and praise your own country," the man demanded to know who was speaking. Crockett stood tall and replied, "I'm that same David Crockett, fresh from the back-woods, half horse, half alligator, a little touched with the snapping turtle; can wade the Mississippi, leap the Ohio, ride upon a streak of lightning and slip without a scratch down a honey locust; can whip my weight in wildcats and, if any gentleman pleases, for a ten dollar bill he may throw in a panther . . ."

Davy Crockett, who lives in American legend as "the King of the Wild Frontier," was celebrated during his lifetime as "the Coonskin Congressman," a backwoodsman who had "kilt bears" and fought Indians, then went to Congress to fight for the rights of the hardworking settlers. He was among the most popular people in the country; his autobiography was so successful that he followed it with two more books. A play based on his exploits entitled *The Lion in the West* was a hit in New York in 1831, and marching bands would often greet him when he arrived in a city. He was so admired, in fact, that a faction of the Whig Party supported him for the presidency before the campaign of 1836.

But instead of going to the White House, on March 6, 1836, Crockett and about one hundred courageous Texans trapped in a century-old mission in San Antonio known as the Alamo were overwhelmed and killed by more than a thousand Mexican troops under the command of General Santa Anna. "Never in the world's history had defense been more heroic," reported an 1851 book entitled *The Great West*. "It has scarce been equaled, save at the Pass of Thermopylae."

Crockett was the rare American who went from the quagmire of American politics to the real battlefields of freedom. People have long wondered—and speculated—how this national hero ended up dying at the Alamo. Others have taken the question even further and wondered if he did actually die there.

David Crockett, as he liked to be called, was a true child of the American frontier. His great-grandparents immigrated to America from Ireland in the early 1700s. His father, John Crockett, was born in 1753 in Virginia and was one of the Overmountain Men—patriots living west of the Appalachians—who fought in the Revolutionary War. Several members of the Crockett family were killed or captured and enslaved by Cherokees and Creek Indians in 1777. Davy Crockett was born in 1786, near the Nolichucky River in Tennessee. As did all children growing up on the frontier, Davy learned how to track, hunt, and shoot fast and straight, and was always comfortable in the backwoods. His father worked various jobs, from operating a gristmill to running a tavern, but struggled to support his family. When David Crockett was twelve years old, he was leased out as a bound boy to settle his father's debt, tending cattle on a four-hundred-mile cattle drive. When he returned home, he was enrolled in Benjamin Kitchen's school—and just four days later, after whupping the tar out of a bully, he took off from home to avoid his father's wrath. His real knowledge came from practical lessons on how to survive on his own in the world.

After spending three years on the trail, finding work wherever it was offered as a hand, a drover, a teamster, and even a hatter, or simply hunting his food when it became necessary, he arrived back at the Crockett Tavern. It has been suggested that his adventures during these years, as he related them in his autobiography, served as a model for Mark Twain's *Huckleberry Finn*. And Twain did acknowledge reading Crockett's tales.

He took several jobs to settle the rest of his father's debts; he worked for six months at a neighbor's tavern, where, he wrote, "a heap of bad company meet to drink and gamble." And when that note was satisfied, he began working for another neighbor, a farmer named John Canady. Crockett spent four years on the Canady farm, staying on for pay long after the debt was settled. During that period, the plain-speaking personality that was to prove so politically appealing years later first began to emerge. Upon meeting a lovely young girl, for example, he wrote that his heart "would flutter like a duck in a puddle, and if I tried to outdo it and speak, it would get right smack up in my throat, and choke me like a cold potato."

It was on the Canady farm that he got his first real taste of book learning, using the money he earned to pay Canady's son for reading lessons, and after several months' hard studying, "I learned to read a little in my primer, to write my own name, and to cypher some in the first three rules in figures."

David Crockett also began growing himself a reputation, not only as a straight talker but also as a straight shooter. The practice in shooting matches at the time was to split a beef carcass into four quarters, with contestants competing separately for each one. Entry was twenty cents a shot. At one of those events, Crockett not only won the whole cow, he also won the "fifth quarter"—the hide, horns, and tallow.

Before his twentieth birthday in 1806, he married and settled on a rented farm with the former Miss Polly Finley, a lovely girl he'd met at a harvest festival. He hunted bear and fowl, trapped forest animals, cleared acreage and planted crops, and fathered two boys, but there was a pull inside him that he couldn't ignore. When war was declared against Great Britain in 1812, most of the Indian tribes sided with the British, believing their victory would end American expansion into the West. Tribes that had lived peacefully with settlers for decades suddenly went on the warpath. In August 1813, a thousand Red Sticks, as Alabama Creek Indian warriors were known, attacked Fort Mims and massacred as many as five hundred people. Crockett answered the call for help, signing up as a scout for Colonel Andrew Jackson's militia army, which was marching south to avenge that attack.

Although Davy Crockett might well have seen it as his duty to fight for his country,

After the largest massacre of settlers in the South at Fort Mims, Davy Crockett volunteered to fight for Colonel Andrew Jackson.

he had other reasons for wanting to go. It's possible he recognized an opportunity to make his name—and perhaps avenge the earlier murders of his kin. His farm was struggling, the money he would earn was desperately needed, and his unique skills would be very valuable during a war and just might secure his future. Polly begged him not to go, but he told her, "If every man would wait till his wife got willing for him to go to war, there would be no fighting done till we all got killed in our own house."

He quickly established himself as a reliable scout—although even he admitted his sense of direction was woefully lacking. Once, while hunting, he realized he was lost, and "set out the way I thought [home] was, but it turned out with me, as it always does a lost man, I took the contrary direction from the right one."

No one knows how a man will react to battle until lead is flying, and Davy Crockett turned out to be a courageous soldier. In early November, General John Coffee, under the command of Andrew Jackson, led about a thousand dragoons in an attack on the Alabama Creek village of Tallushatchee. An estimated two hundred warriors were killed in the brief battle. At the Battle of Talladega a week later, Coffee's men killed an additional 299 Creeks.

But Crockett also learned that war was a lot more complicated than he had anticipated. He found that he admired the courage of his enemies, and whenever it was possible, he avoided confrontations with them. At the same time, he grew to despise Andrew Jackson for the way he treated his men. "Old Hickory" was a brutal leader, who seemed not to care about his troops' welfare. Although Crockett and other scouts did their best to hunt wild game for the militia, because of lack of food and supplies, countless men just got on their horses and rode home. Davy Crockett's enmity toward Jackson that began during this campaign would follow the two men throughout their political careers—and spark Crockett's ride to the Alamo.

Although Crockett earned his reputation as a frontiersman, it was his engaging personality that attracted people to him. He was a great storyteller, with a lively wit and an appealing aw-shucks personality. For many other men, lack of an education might have proved a barrier to a political career, but he learned how to use it to his advantage. Later on, he often reminded voters that he wasn't one of those fancy men from back east who were always changing their minds to please their supporters, but just a regular man trying to do the best he could for his people. His political philosophy wasn't particularly sophisticated: He stood up for what he believed, he didn't seem to care if his positions were popular, and he wasn't afraid to confront the most powerful men in the nation. He articulated his credo this way: "Be always sure you're right, then go ahead."

Colonel David Crockett,
painted by A. L. DeRose,
engraved by Asher B. Durand

Davy Crockett's political career began when his former commanding officer, Captain Matthews, was a candidate for the office of lieutenant colonel of the Fifty-Seventh Regiment of the Tennessee Militia and asked Crockett to run for major. Initially Crockett turned him down, explaining that he'd done his share of fighting, but the captain insisted. Finally, Crockett agreed. Only when it came time to make his campaign speech did he learn that his opponent would be Captain Matthews's son. The meaning was clear to him: Matthews thought that running an unqualified hayseed against his son would guarantee victory. That insult got Crockett fired up, and he decided that if he was going to run, he should run against Matthews himself, for colonel. He stood on a tree stump and "told the people the cause of my opposing him, remarking that as I had the whole family to run against any way, I was determined to levy on the head of the mess."

His audience, presumably delighted by the honesty of this speech, elected him to run the militia. Ironically, he became Colonel Crockett on the campaign trail rather than on the battlefield.

Crockett found that politics fit him well. But he didn't forget where he came from. Consciously or not, he always advertised his frontier background, from the buckskin clothes he wore to the way he spoke to the political positions he supported. His greatest political strength was that ordinary people believed he understood their needs—the key requirement for a populist politician.

His wife Polly had died giving birth to their daughter, and he had remarried—to a woman with an eight-hundred-dollar dowry, so for the first time in his life he didn't have to struggle to earn his keep. After moving to Lawrence County in 1817, he served as a town commissioner and helped draw the new county's borders, then accepted an appointment as the local justice of

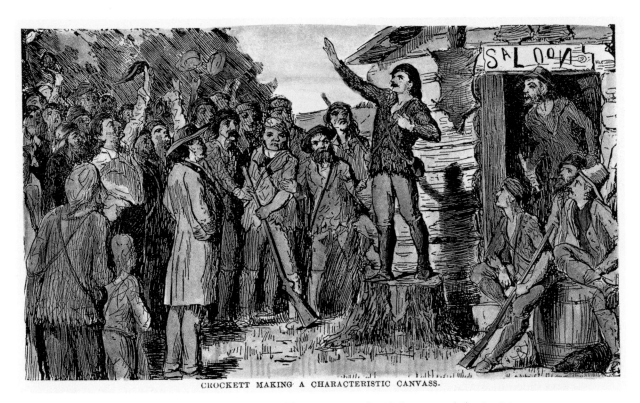

CROCKETT MAKING A CHARACTERISTIC CANVASS.

On the campaign stump, Crockett would sometimes finish his speech by inviting everyone to join him for a drink, leaving his opponent to address a reduced crowd.

the peace. In 1821, his friends and supporters urged him to run for the Tennessee legislature, representing the counties of Lawrence and Hickman. As he remembered, "It now became necessary that I should tell the people something about the government, and an eternal sight of other things that I knowed nothing more about than I did about Latin, and law."

His opponent, he recalled, "didn't think he was in any danger from an ignorant back-woods bear hunter." Crockett stood up on the stump and told people that he had come for their votes, and that if they didn't watch mighty close, he'd get them. In one campaign appearance, he told his listeners the story of a traveler who saw somebody beating on an empty barrel. When asked what he was doing, the man explained that just a few days earlier there had been cider in there and he was trying to get it out. Then Crockett added, "there had been a little bit of a speech in me a while ago, but I believed I can't get it out." The crowd laughed, and as he finished, he told them it was time to wet their whistles and led them to the liquor stand—leaving only a sparse few people to listen to his frustrated opponent.

Crockett won his first election, receiving more than twice as many votes as his rival. Although other members of the legislature referred to him derisively as "the Gentleman from the Cane"—meaning from the uncivilized backwoods—he stood up to the wealthy and powerful. His staunch support for the struggling west Tennessee farmers and local folk made him so popular that a year after his election his constituents presented him with a .40-caliber flintlock with the motto GO AHEAD inscribed in silver near the sight. He named this beautiful hunting rifle Old Betsy, in honor of his oldest sister.

When he was not doing the people's work, he was building a new cabin for his family in the wilds of the Obion River, relying on Old Betsy to keep his family fed and warm. On one hunt, he brought down a six-hundred-pound bear, although he admitted that it took three shots. That he chose to live in the wilderness, where a man survived by his wits rather than his wallet, reinforced his growing reputation as a man of the people. Although he did not intend to stand for reelection in 1823, when a newspaper article appeared to lampoon him, he changed his mind. His opponent, Dr. William Butler, was Andrew Jackson's nephew-in-law. It proved to be one of the most memorable populist campaigns ever run. On the stump, Crockett confessed that his campaign was financed by the raccoon pelts and wolf scalps his children and hunting dogs had gathered, and he reckoned after visiting Dr. Butler's impressive home that he walked on fancier materials on his floor than most people's wives wore on their backs. Crockett wore his buckskin shirt with extra-large pockets—for a twist of tobacky and a bottle of hooch—and won the election by 247 votes.

At this same time, Andrew Jackson's political fortunes were skyrocketing. The military hero, who had defeated the British in the Battle of New Orleans and led the nation to victory in both the War of 1812 and the First Seminole War, was a nominee for the presidency in 1824. Although Jackson won the popular vote, the close election was thrown into the House of Representatives, which chose John Quincy Adams. But Tennessee senator Jackson had established himself as a formidable politician and kept his sights firmly on the White House.

Crockett had aroused Jackson's anger by supporting the candidate running against Old Hickory's handpicked choice for governor in 1821, personally defeating his relation two years later, and backing Jackson's opponent when he ran for the Senate. In fact, Crockett called his vote against Jackson "the best vote I ever gave."

When his supporters urged him to run for Congress in 1825, Crockett accepted their nomination, then lost a woefully underfinanced campaign to the incumbent by 267 votes. But his reputation continued to grow, and it was known that in the winter of 1826, he and his hunting buddies accounted for 105 dead bears. Supposedly he had killed 47 of them himself.

Crockett lived a life of adventure—but one fraught with danger. He almost died twice from malaria, suffered near-fatal hypothermia, and was mauled by a bear. He had cheated death so often that his family refused to believe he had been killed at the Alamo and sent young John Crockett to verify it. Once, while he was earning his living cutting and selling barrel staves, his barge got caught in the rapids and he was trapped in its tiny cabin as it flooded. He struggled to escape through a small window and got stuck, urging rescuers to pull him out no matter what it required, "neck or nothing, come out or sink." Indeed, they got him out, but he suffered serious injuries. Among the rescuers was a wealthy businessman and politician, Memphis mayor Marcus Brutus Winchester, who would take to Crockett and financially support his successful run for Congress in 1827.

Crockett's homespun appeal attracted considerable attention in Washington, even before he arrived there. He was introduced by letter to Henry Clay, "the Great Compromiser," who was preparing to run for the presidency, by Clay's son-in-law, James Irwin, as an uncouth, loud talker, who was "independent and fearless and has a popularity at home that is unaccountable."

Even nearly two centuries ago, a backwoodsman who often dressed in hand-sewn buckskin was considered out of place in the nation's increasingly sophisticated and dignified capital. However, that worked in Crockett's favor politically. Although he belonged to no political party, the Whigs saw great potential in him and helped build on the myths about him that were already spreading. More than a century later, Crockett would be celebrated on television by the Disney company as a man who wrestled alligators and "kilt him a bear when he was only three," but the foundations of his legend were laid not in Hollywood but while he was in Congress.

In Congress, Crockett never wavered from his support for the rights of the poor. During his first term, he opposed a land bill because it might result in squatters being driven off their farms, pointing out, "The rich require but little legislation. We should at least occasionally legislate for the poor." Although he had ended up supporting Andrew Jackson in Old Hickory's victorious run for the White House in 1828, he didn't hesitate to fight hard against him—as well as other members of the Tennessee delegation—when the land bill again was proposed in 1830. He answered to a higher power than Washington politicians, he explained: the people who put him in office; the kind of people whose children "never saw the inside of a college, and never are likely to do so."

Crockett was becoming a problem for Jackson. He was an extraordinarily popular

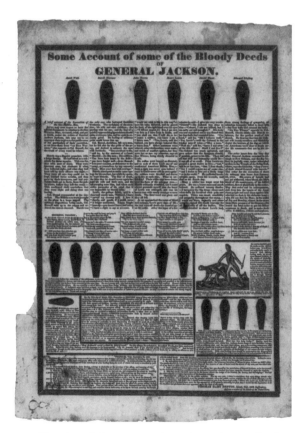

Crockett's biggest political rival was Andrew Jackson, seen in this 1860 portrait by D. M. Carter, who was charged with extraordinary "bloody deeds" in this 1828 "coffin" handbill.

politician who too often opposed him. Their biggest fight came when Jackson introduced the Indian Removal Act in 1829, which proposed granting to the tribes the unsettled lands west of the Mississippi River, where they would be taught "the arts of civilization," in exchange for their land within existing state borders. Jackson believed this separation of whites and Indians was the only way to ensure peace and was the most humane way of dealing with the Indian problem. Crockett opposed him; he had lived among Indians his whole life and believed they should be left in peace on their own lands. Describing it as "a wicked, unjust measure," he voted against it and said bitterly, "I gave a good honest vote, and one that I believe will not make me ashamed on the day of judgment." The bill passed, but the Cherokee chief sent a letter to Crockett thanking him for his vote.

When Crockett stood for reelection in 1831, Jackson personally recruited a man named William Fitzgerald to run against him. It was going to be a difficult campaign for Crockett because the majority of people in his district had supported the Removal Act. Fitzgerald ran a dirty campaign, accusing Crockett of being a violent drunk and a gambling man who cheated on his wife. His men would post signs advertising a Crockett appearance that Crockett knew nothing about—but when he failed to show up, he was the one who was blamed. The tensest moment of the campaign came during a debate in Nashville. As the *Nashville Banner* reported,

> Fitzgerald spoke first. Upon mounting the stand he was noticed to lay something on the pine table in front of him, wrapped in his handkerchief.
>
> He commenced his speech. . . . When Fitzgerald reached the objectionable point, Crockett arose from his seat in the audience and advanced toward the stand. When he was within three or four feet of it, Fitzgerald suddenly removed a pistol from his handkerchief and, covering Colonel Crockett's breast, warned him that a step further and he would fire.
>
> Crockett hesitated a second, turned around and resumed his seat.

The episode caused a stir, but Jackson was well liked in Tennessee, and Crockett lost the election. To pay off all his campaign debts, he had to sell his land, and with the assistance of someone who knew how to spell, a man named Matthew St. Clair Clarke, he "wrote" *The Life and Adventures of Colonel David Crockett of West Tennessee*, one of the first campaign biographies. It marked the beginning of his transformation from David Crockett to Davy Crockett, King of the Wild Frontier. It described his life-threatening adventures and his good character while vilifying Andrew Jackson—and was an immediate success. Two years later, after he defeated Fitzgerald to regain his seat in Congress, his official autobiography was published—partially to correct some of the taller tales told in that first book—and caused such a great stir that a segment of Whigs began suggesting he would be the perfect candidate to succeed Jackson in the White House.

Ironically, considering his feelings about Jackson—in 1833 he told reporters, "Look at my neck and you will not find any collar with a label, 'My Dog, Andrew Jackson'"—he actually helped the president survive the first presidential assassination attempt in American history. On the afternoon of January 30, 1835, an unemployed house painter named Richard Lawrence, who believed he was King Richard III, approached Jackson as he left the capitol, drew his pistol and, at point-blank range, pulled the trigger. Incredibly luckily for the president, the gun misfired. The sixty-seven-year-old Jackson began hitting his attacker with his cane. Crockett and several other men leaped on Lawrence and dragged him to the ground. In the melee, the madman managed to pull a second pistol from under his coat and fire at Jackson from inches away—and that gun also misfired! Thanks to Crockett, several other men, and amazing good fortune, the president's life was saved—although no one ever has been able to figure out why either gun, much less both of them, misfired. Lawrence spent the rest of his life in an asylum.

To reinforce his growing reputation, Crockett "authored" another book, *A Narrative of the Life of David Crockett, written by Himself,* and for the only time in his life visited the Northeast, on what arguably was one of the first celebrity publicity tours. He traveled from Baltimore to Philadelphia by steamboat and train, the first time he had ridden on the latter. The Whigs had gathered a large, enthusiastic crowd to greet him when he arrived in Philadelphia, which he described as "the whole face of the earth covered with people." From there he went to New York, where, once again, delighted crowds turned out to see him. He spent an evening at the theater and toured the roughest area of the city, a pro-Jackson slum known as Five Points. It was so filthy, he remarked, that the people there were "too mean to swab hell's kitchen," a phrase that later coined the nickname for an uptown slum. When he reached Boston, again the welcoming crowds turned out, and he toured Faneuil Hall and visited various factories. He dined at the leading restaurants and sipped champagne "foaming up as if you were supping fog out of speaking trumpets."

Although his congressional district had been gerrymandered by the pro-Jackson legislature in 1833, he had still managed to win that election. But the frontier was moving westward, and Tennessee was being settled by people who didn't know Crockett and instead were vocal in their admiration for President Jackson. In the congressional election of 1835,

Crockett's opponent, Adam Huntsman, who had lost a leg in the Creek War, made Crockett's inability to get a land bill passed by Congress in three terms a major issue in the campaign. Huntsman was supported by both President Jackson and Tennessee's Governor Carroll and beat Crockett by 230 votes.

During the campaign, Crockett had promised several times to move to Texas if he was defeated or if Jackson's vice president, Martin van Buren, was elected president. What probably surprised everyone was that this was a campaign promise Crockett intended to keep. On November 1, 1835, dressed in his hunting suit and wearing a coonskin cap, he gave Old Betsy to his son John Wesley Crockett and, following the trail blazed by his friend Sam Houston, set out for Texas with three friends, telling his constituents, "Since you have chosen to elect a man with a timber toe to succeed me, you may all go to hell and I will go to Texas."

Many have speculated on the real reasons he went to Texas. *Texas* is an Indian word, meaning "friends," but for hundreds of years it had been unsettled by whites. The territory had been claimed by France and Spain, then became Mexico's when it won its independence from Spain in 1821. The Mexican government initially had welcomed American settlers to the territory, believing they would control the Indians living there. But by 1826, the Anglos wanted to rid themselves of Mexican control and establish an independent state that they intended to name Fredonia. The leader of the original settlers, Stephen Austin, went to Mexico City to petition for recognition as a separate Mexican state, with the right to form its own legislature. Instead, he was arrested and thrown into a dungeon.

But the spirit of independence had caught hold. In 1835, seventeen thousand of the twenty thousand people living in Texas were Americans. Austin returned to Texas after spending eight months in prison and immediately began forming militias to fight for Anglo rights under the Mexican constitution. Mexican leader Santa Anna threatened an invasion to quell the uprising. The Texas War for Independence began at the battle of Gonzales in October 1835. A month later, Texas declared its independence, naming Sam Houston its commander in chief. It was a situation ripe for heroics.

Davy Crockett did not go to Texas to die at the Alamo but rather to live in a country he described in a letter to his children as "the garden spot of the world. The best land and the best prospects for health I ever saw, and I do believe it is a fortune to any man to come here." There obviously were many reasons for him to leave Tennessee: He had been defeated by the Jacksonians and abandoned by the Whigs; he was separated from his wife; he was in debt and had no source of income; and for a man who had spent much of his life pursuing adventure, he lacked any current challenges. It also was the right place to reestablish his reputation:

The Alamo, Midnight, lithograph by Frank Callcott

Many people had begun wondering if all the attention and publicity had changed him. His exploits had been so obviously exaggerated that some doubted there was much truth to any of them. And it was not in his nature to back away from a fight.

It's impossible to know what his expectations were when he rode to Texas. Although it's clear that he intended to become a land speculator and perhaps make "a fortune yet for my family, bad as my prospect has been," some historians believe he planned to become involved in the politics of the new republic, maybe even run for president. He did write that he expected to be elected to the planned constitutional convention. When he learned the provisional government was offering 4,600 acres of good growing land to any man willing to fight for Texas's freedom, he announced, "As the country no longer requires my services, I have made up my mind to go to Texas. I start anew upon my own hook, and may God grant that it be strong enough to support the weight that may be hung upon it."

When he finally reached Nacogdoches in January 1836, he received a "harty [*sic*] welcome to the country," which included a cannon salute and invitations to social events held in his honor. In Nacogdoches, with sixty-five other men, he volunteered with the Texas Volunteer Auxiliary Corps, taking an oath to fight for six months in return for 4,600 acres. Before signing the oath, he insisted the word *republican* be inserted to ensure he would not be obliged to serve a dictatorship. In early February, provisional government president Sam Houston ordered him to lead a squad of expert riflemen to reinforce San Antonio de Bexar.

Until the preceding December, San Antonio had been occupied by more than a thousand Mexican soldiers. But after a five-day battle, the Mexican army had been defeated and had surrendered all property, guns, and ammunition to the Texans. The furious Santa Anna was determined to demonstrate to the settlers that resistance to Mexican rule was futile by retaking San Antonio—whatever the cost. He made it clear that there would be no quarter given, no prisoners taken; this would be a lesson the Texans would never forget. When 1,800 Mexican troops arrived in San Antonio on February 23, the 145 Texans—among them Davy Crockett—moved into the fortified mission called the Alamo.

Historians have been studying—and debating—the details of the battle for the Alamo for years without reaching agreement as to precisely how it unfolded. Apparently Sam Houston initially told his commander in San Antonio, Colonel William B. Travis, to destroy the mission and withdraw, believing his troops lacked the manpower and supplies necessary to defend it. Had Travis been able to comply with those instructions, most of the garrison could have survived, but he allowed his men to vote on whether to stay—and rather than retreat, they elected to stay and fight. When Santa Anna arrived and demanded their surrender, Travis responded with a cannon shot.

The Alamo was a small fortress, protected by limestone-block walls eight feet high and about three feet thick. Santa Anna's army immediately began bombarding the mission, his artillery moving closer each day. On the twenty-fifth, an estimated three hundred Mexican troops crossed the San Antonio River and reached a line of abandoned shacks less than one hundred yards from the walls. It was an important strategic position from which to launch an assault; the Texans had to dislodge them. While the Alamo's cannons and Crockett's marksmen provided cover, a small group of volunteers reached the shacks and burned them down.

Travis pleaded for reinforcements, warning that his troops were running out of ammunition and supplies. On the twenty-sixth, 420 men with four artillery pieces set out from the fort at Goliad to relieve the garrison. When this force was unable to successfully ford the San Antonio River, they turned back, although about twenty men volunteered to try to reach the Alamo.

"The enemy . . . treated the bodies with brutal indignation." They were thrown onto a pile and burned. The remains are believed to be in this casket in San Antonio's San Fernando Cathedral.

Little is known about what was going on inside the Alamo during the siege, although one of the few survivors of the battle, a woman named Susanna Dickinson, wrote that Davy Crockett had entertained the garrison with his violin and storytelling. In records found after the massacre, Colonel Travis wrote of observing Crockett everywhere in the Alamo "animating men to do their duty." It was also reported that Crockett had killed five Mexicans in succession as they tried to fire a cannon at the walls, and some claimed that he came within a whisker of killing Santa Anna, who had wandered into rifle range. There is some evidence that Crockett had managed to sneak out through Mexican lines to locate the small band of reinforcements waiting at Cibolo Creek and guide them into the Alamo. Several months after the battle, the *Arkansas Gazette* reported, "Col. Crockett, with about 50 resolute volunteers had cut their way into the garrison through the Mexican troops only a few days before the fall of San Antonio." The meaning of that is clear, and it erases any doubts about his courage and

Fuerte del Alamo

a Entrada
b Habitaciones de Oficiales
c Cuerpo de Guardia
d Comandancia de Artillería
e Cuartel de Artillería
f Cuarteles
g Parque
h Foso interior
i Caballero alto
j Batería a barbeta
k Batería atronada
l Fosos exteriores

Batería del Ejército Mexicano

ALAMO

VILLITA

Río   de   San   Antonio

BEJAR

Campo Santo

Camino de Río Grande

"Remember the Alamo" was the battle cry that led Sam Houston's troops to victory at the Battle of San Jacinto six weeks later—and Americans have never forgotten the sacrifices made there. *Above*, a map of the Alamo based on Santa Anna's battlefield map; *opposite, top left*, Newell Convers Wyeth's *Last Stand at the Alamo*; *top right*, an imagined Crockett fighting his last battle; *bottom*, William H. Brooker's engraving *Siege of the Alamo, March 6, 1836*

THE LAST STAND AT THE ALAMO.

THE ALAMO FLAG

SIEGE OF THE ALAMO. MARCH 6, 1836.

his integrity: Crockett had made his way out of what appeared to be a hopeless situation and could have escaped. Instead, he fought his way back inside to make a final stand with his men.

Santa Anna's army, which had been reinforced and numbered four thousand troops, attacked before dawn on March 6, advancing, according to Henry Howe in *The Great West*, "amid the discharge of musketry and cannon, and were twice repulsed in their attempt to scale the walls." Susanna Dickinson later testified that when the attack began, Crockett had paused briefly to pray, then started fighting. After a fierce battle, Mexican troops breached the north outer walls. Although most of the defenders withdrew to the barracks and chapel, Crockett and his men stood in the open and fought. They fired their weapons until they were out of ammunition, then used their rifles as clubs and knives until they were overwhelmed.

It isn't known how Davy Crockett died. There are several conflicting reports. A slave named Ben, who also survived the battle, claimed he had seen Crockett's body surrounded by "no less than 16 Mexican corpses," including one with Crockett's knife still buried in it. Henry Howe reported, just fifteen years after the battle, that "David Crockett was found dead surrounded by a pile of the enemy, who had fallen beneath his powerful arm." Most historians believe he was killed by a bayonet as he clubbed attackers with his rifle. He was forty-nine years old.

As happens often when heroes die without witnesses, alternative stories have persisted. One claims that Crockett and several other men either surrendered or were captured and brought before Santa Anna, who ordered their immediate execution. The purported eyewitness to that, a Mexican lieutenant named José Enrique de la Peña, supposedly wrote in a diary, found and published almost one hundred fifty years later, that Crockett had been executed, and "these unfortunates died without complaining and without humiliating themselves before their torturers."

There were only three survivors: Susanna Dickinson and her young child and the black slave, Ben. "The enemy," wrote Howe, "exasperated to the highest degree by this desperate resistance, treated the bodies with brutal indignation." Although there were some reports of mutilation, it is generally agreed that the bodies were thrown onto a pile and burned. The number of Mexicans who died in the attack is estimated at between six hundred and sixteen hundred men. Texans were shocked by the massacre. Almost immediately, "Remember the Alamo" became the rallying cry of the Texas army of independence. Less than two months later, on April 21, General Sam Houston's army captured Santa Anna at the Battle of San Jacinto, and the Republic of Texas was born.

The legend of Davy Crockett grew even larger after his death. A book entitled *Col. Crockett's Exploits and Adventures in Texas . . . Written by Himself* was published the summer after his death and, while clearly a work of fiction, served to reinforce his heroic sacrifice. Another story circulated claiming that Crockett was last seen standing at his post swinging his rifle as Mexican troops poured through a break in the walls. The memoir of Santa Anna's personal secretary, Ramón Martínez Caro, published in 1837 in Mexico, reported, "Among the 183 killed there were five who were discovered by General Castrillón hiding after the assault. He took them immediately to the presence of His Excellency who had come up by this time. When he presented the prisoners, he was severely reprimanded for not having killed them on the spot, after which he turned his back upon Castrillón while the soldiers stepped out of their ranks and set upon the prisoners until they were all killed." Although this was purportedly an eyewitness account, there is no direct evidence that Crockett was one of these men.

Crockett became a symbol of the spirit of Texas and America, a man who willingly gave his life for freedom. His last known words, written to his daughter weeks before his death, have often been quoted: "I am rejoiced at my fate. I would rather be in my present situation than be elected to a seat in Congress for life. Do not be uneasy about me, I am with my friends . . . Farewell, David Crockett."

His son John Wesley Crockett served two terms in Congress and finally was able to pass an amended version of the land bill that his father had initially introduced. Like so many others, he spent years trying to uncover the facts of his father's death—but in his lifetime no reliable witnesses stepped forward.

More than one hundred twenty years later, the larger-than-life character Davy Crockett, the King of the Wild Frontier, was introduced to a new generation of young people in a television series—coonskin cap, tall tales, and all—that captivated the nation and had millions of Americans singing his praises, saluting his courage, and romanticizing the frontier way of life.

KIT CARSON

Duty Before Honor

any years later, in the warmth of his own memories, Kit Carson would describe what happened at the rendezvous in Green River as an "affair of honor." Although few mountain trappers took much note of the year, Carson put it at the summer of 1835. For those men, who mostly lived in small roaming bands, a rendezvous was an important event. Hundreds of mountain men and natives from local tribes would camp together for a month or, as he wrote in his autobiography, "as long as the money and credit of the trappers last" to trade goods and tales. Coffee, sugar, and flour, then considered luxuries, sold for two dollars a pint, and ordinary blankets for as much as twenty-five dollars apiece. There were daily contests, including shooting, archery, and knife and tomahawk throwing; there was fiddling and dancing; there was drinking and revelry; and, naturally, there was gambling and brawling. The laws of these camps were whatever the strongest men could enforce, and arguments often were settled with rifles at twenty paces. Among the people at this particular meeting on the Green River in Wyoming was an especially disagreeable French Canadian trapper named Joseph Chouinard, who was said to be "exceedingly overbearing" and who, "upon the slightest pretext . . . was sure to endeavor to involve some of the trappers in a quarrel." Other trappers avoided him, until one day he violently grabbed a beautiful young Arapaho woman named Singing Grass. Holding tightly on to her arms, he began kissing her and rubbing himself against her.

That was finally enough for Kit Carson. He was small in stature, no more than five feet four, but large in courage. Brandishing his hunting knife, he warned Chouinard to let go of the Indian woman. "I assume the responsibility of ordering you to cease your threats," he said, "or I will be under the necessity of killing you."

It was a challenge Chouinard could not turn down. He released the girl and angrily walked off toward his own lodge. Minutes later, the two men faced each other on horseback, as knights had done hundreds of years earlier. The French Canadian carried a rifle; Kit Carson was armed with a single-barrel dragoon pistol. At the mark, they raced toward each other. When they were only a few feet apart, both men fired; Carson's shot ripped

Kit Carson earned his reputation among mountain men when he stood up to the bully Chouinard at the 1835 rendezvous, as seen in this 1858 woodcut.

into Chouinard's right forearm, throwing off his aim so that, as Carson later recalled, "[H]is ball passed my head, cutting my hair and the powder burning my eye. . . . During our stay in camp we had no more trouble with the bully Frenchman."

As the trappers cheered him, Carson walked off with Singing Grass.

Christopher Carson was born in Madison County, Kentucky, on Christmas Eve 1809, the eleventh of fifteen children. It was the same year Abraham Lincoln was born, the year in which James Madison succeeded Thomas Jefferson as president of the seventeen newly United States. His father was a celebrated hunter and farmer who had fought in the Revolution. Within a year of Kit's birth, his father moved his family to the frontier settlement of Cooper's Fort in Boonslick Country, Missouri. This was considered the edge of the civilized nation. Most of the land stretching from there all the way to the Pacific Ocean was wilderness, with occasional settlements inhabited by the native peoples who were fighting to protect their territory, their food sources, and their way of life. It took great skill and daunting courage to survive in these dangerous lands. Those who took the risk were the mountain men, the trappers, the explorers, and the soldiers who went into the unknown in search of adventure. As the author Henry Howe wrote in his classic volume *The Great West* more than one hundred fifty years ago, "From the Mississippi to the mouth of the Colorado, from the frozen regions of the North to Gila in Mexico, the beaver trapper has set his traps in every stream. Most of this country, but for their daring enterprise, would be, even now, a terra incognita to geographers. . . . These alone are the hardy pioneers who braved the way for the settlement of the western country."

Carson was loosely related to the legendary frontiersman and trailblazer Daniel Boone—Boone's daughter was married to Carson's uncle—and there is no doubt that Boone served as young Kit Carson's role model. Missouri had been part of the 1803 Louisiana Purchase—bought for about four cents an acre—and quickly became the jumping-off place for expeditions going west, where life was a constant battle for survival against nature—and the native tribes. Carson became a man in that wilderness, learning how to track and shoot and, when necessary, fight Indians.

Carson's father died when Kit was only nine years old; some histories report that he was killed by Indians, while others claim that a large branch from a burning tree fell on him. His mother remarried, but Kit never got along with his stepfather. When he was fourteen years old, his stepfather apprenticed him to a harness and saddle maker named David Workman, during which time Kit heard the exciting stories told by mountain men returning from the West, stories that captured his imagination. After his second year, he couldn't wait any longer. "[B]eing anxious to travel for the purpose of seeing different countries," he ran away, joining a wagon-train expedition to the Rocky Mountains. Workman placed a notice in the newspaper, offering a one-cent reward for the return of his apprentice.

During the next years, Carson tasted adventure, working as a cook for trapper and fur trader Ewing Young, as a teamster in the copper mines near Rio Gila, and as an interpreter along the Chihuahua Trail into Mexico. He'd dropped out of school before learning to read or write, but he learned to speak Spanish and eight Indian languages from a mountaineer named Kincard. He trapped beaver, traded furs, and, when it became necessary, fought Indians.

His first recorded battle with Indians came in 1829, when one of Ewing Young's trading parties was attacked by Navajos. Young was determined to get vengeance and organized his own raiding party, which trailed the Indians to the head of the Salt River and waited. When the Navajos spotted a small band of trappers, they attacked—and rode into Young's ambush. His men—young Kit Carson among them—opened fire and killed fifteen Indians.

A rendezvous near Green River, Oregon, about 1835

Eventually Carson would become one of history's most renowned Indian fighters, but he acquired this reputation only out of necessity. The mountain men lived by a warrior's code that required an eye for an eye, a scalp for a scalp. When one member of your tribe was killed, that score had to be settled. A warrior who showed great courage in battle, who got close enough to physically touch his enemy, was said to be "counting coup," and this was the highest honor he could achieve. Carson recounted one story in which he was awakened by a Blackfoot brave counting coup—literally prodding him with a knife. The band of Indians had snuck into camp to steal horses. Carson kicked him away, scrambled to his feet while grabbing his own knife, and fatally stabbed his attacker.

In 1839, Carson led a party of forty-three mountaineers in an attack on the Blackfeet who had been raiding their camp. They charged into the Blackfeet village, quickly killing ten warriors. The battle raged for more than three hours. During the action, a mountaineer named Cotton was trapped beneath his horse after it was shot from underneath him. Six warriors raced forward to take his scalp. Carson leaped from his saddle, steadied his hand,

and shot the leader through his heart. Three more Indians were shot down by other shooters before they could reach cover, enabling Cotton to get loose and make his way to safety.

Kit Carson believed totally in the warrior's code—but he also spent many years living peacefully among the tribes. After his encounter with Chouinard, he took Singing Grass as his wife and settled in her village. When Singing Grass died giving birth to their second child, he married a Cheyenne maiden named Making-Out-Road. He was considered an honored guest in the lodges of the Arapahos, Cheyennes, Kiowas, and Comanches. Even his favorite horse was proudly named Apache. He lived so easily among the tribes that he once remembered, "For many consecutive years I never slept under the roof of a house or gazed upon the face of a white woman. . . . My rifle furnished nearly every particle of food on which I lived."

Carson had earned a fine reputation as a hunter and trapper, becoming known as "the Monarch of the Prairies" and "the Nestor of the Rocky Mountains," Nestor being a mythical Greek king known for his bravery. His word was said to be "as sure as the sun comin' up," and his skills enabled him to hire on in the 1840s as "hunter to the fort," meaning he was responsible for supplying all the food for the forty-man garrison at Bent's Fort, the only trading post on the Santa Fe Trail between Missouri and Mexico. Ultimately, though, Carson and his fellow trappers proved so proficient at their trade that by the time of the last rendezvous in 1840, the beaver had been hunted almost to extinction.

Yet during his years on the frontier, as Charles Burdett wrote in his *Life of Kit Carson*, "his curiosity, as well as care to preserve the knowledge for future use, led him to note in memory every feature of the wild landscape, its mountain chains, its desert prairies . . ." and prepared him to play a very special role in the settling of the West.

The concept of Manifest Destiny, the dream of a nation that stretched across the continent from the Atlantic to the Pacific, was beginning to take hold. At his inauguration in 1845, President James K. Polk prophesized, "It is confidently believed that our system may be safely extended to the utmost bounds of our territorial limits, and that as it shall be extended the bonds of our union, so far from being weakened, will become stronger . . ."

Kit Carson proved to be extraordinarily important in the fulfillment of that dream. In 1842, after sixteen years on the frontier, he brought his four-year-old daughter, Adaline, to live with his sister in St. Louis, where she could receive the proper education he never had. From St. Louis he boarded the first steamboat at work on the great Missouri River, intending to return to his family homestead. Also on that boat was Lieutenant John C. Frémont of the Army Corps of Topographical Engineers, who coincidentally was looking to hire an experienced guide to lead him to Wyoming, where he was to survey the South Pass, the most

Kit Carson (*left*) and John Frémont came from completely different backgrounds, but their adventures introduced America to the possibilities of the great West.

popular route across the Continental Divide, and measure the height of the mountains. After introducing himself to Frémont, Carson explained, "I have been some time in the mountains and I think I can guide you to any point there you wish to reach." After making inquiries, Frémont hired Carson to guide the expedition at a salary of one hundred dollars a month.

The two men hardly could have been more different. While the rough-hewn Carson had never learned to read or write, Frémont was a polished, ambitious mathematics teacher who was married to the daughter of powerful United States senator Thomas Hart Benton. Senator Benton, the political champion of Manifest Destiny, apparently had helped his son-in-law get his army commission, then convinced Congress to support his explorations.

The twenty-eight-man party that would eventually make both Frémont and Carson national heroes departed St. Louis on June 10, 1842. Several of Carson's closest friends had joined the expedition, mountain men he respected and trusted, men he wanted to have by his side in a fight. When they reached Fort Laramie, Wyoming, they learned that almost a thousand Sioux had attacked a party of trappers and Snake Indians and were still in the region.

Carson and Frémont would save each other's lives
as they fought Indians, outlaws, Mexicans, and the
elements to survey the western wilderness.

The expedition was advised to turn back or risk being massacred. Frémont refused, replying
that his government had directed him to perform a certain duty and he intended to do so. If
he perished in the effort, he was confident his government would avenge his death. Carson
admired the Southerner's fortitude and courage, and that helped cement their friendship.

The expedition accomplished each of its objectives, and Frémont's beautifully written
reports, which were reprinted in newspapers throughout the country, thrilled Americans with

their vivid descriptions of a magnificent landscape and vast regions waiting for settlement. Frémont was celebrated as "the Pathfinder," and Kit Carson was credited as his trusted scout. While Frémont returned to Washington to lay plans for a second expedition, Kit Carson married for the third time—his second wife having left him to join the migration of her tribe—this time to a Mexican, Senora Josefa Jaramilla, with whom he would have three children. To appease her family he agreed to convert to Catholicism.

Frémont and Carson's second expedition, intended to map the remainder of the Oregon Trail, began in the summer of 1843 and eventually brought them in sight of the magnificent Cascade Range. During their return journey, they became snowbound in the Sierra Nevada and faced starvation. Food was so scarce that their half-starved mules "ate one another's tails and the leather of the pack saddles," and Frémont gave his men permission to eat their dogs. Somehow Carson managed to scrounge enough food for them to survive. During the trek through the deep snow, Frémont and Carson left their party to scout for a path over a raging, icy river. As Frémont wrote, "Carson sprang over, clear across a place where the stream was

Josefa Jaramilla-Carson with Kit Carson Jr.

compressed . . ." but when Frémont tried to follow, his moccasins slipped on an icy rock and he fell into the river. "It was some few seconds before I could recover myself in the current, and Carson, thinking me hurt, jumped in after me, and we both had an icy bath."

After spending the winter at Sutter's Fort in California, the expedition set out for home. To get there, they had to go through the Mojave Desert. In addition to heat and thirst, they had to endure several Indian attacks. After Indians stampeded their livestock, Carson took off after them. As Frémont later described it, "Carson may be considered among the boldest. . . . Two men, in a savage desert, pursue day and night an unknown body of Indians into the defiles of an unknown mountain—attack them on sight, without counting numbers, and defeat them in an instant."

As they made their way out of the Mojave, they encountered a Mexican man and boy, survivors of an Indian attack. They had been ambushed by an estimated thirty Indians, they said; two men had been killed in the attack, their two female cooks had been captured, and twenty horses had been stolen. Carson and his friend Richard Godey volunteered to go after the captured women. The two men tracked the Indians for two nights and found them at dawn. They silently crawled into the camp, hiding among the stolen horses. When the horses stirred, alerting the Indians, Carson and Godey had no choice but to attack. They raced into the camp. Carson raised his rifle and shot the leader dead. Godey's first shot missed, but his second shot killed his target. The Indians hesitated to respond, believing the two men must be the point of a much larger group waiting in ambush.

Carson and Godey recovered fifteen horses and then began searching for the captured women. Instead, they found the bodies of the two Mexican men who had been killed, staked to the ground and mutilated. In response they "took the hair" of the Indians they had shot, honoring the counting-coup tradition.

Frémont's reports transformed Kit Carson into a frontier legend, the brave tracker who saved the expedition in the snowbound mountains, then practically single-handedly attacked and defeated thirty wild Indians. While the true story was amazing enough, reporters and dime novelists exaggerated it even further, attributing to Kit Carson all the ideal traits—humility, loyalty, and bravery—characteristic of this new country. The first of these "blood and thunders," as these books were known, *Kit Carson: Prince of the Gold Hunters*, told the fictional story of Carson rescuing a kidnapped young girl from the Indians. Carson, who didn't know how to read, had to have these stories read to him.

Frémont's third expedition left St. Louis in the summer of 1845, initially intending to map the source of the Arkansas River. But when the expedition accomplished this objective, he continued on to California, which was still Mexican territory, to support the growing number of American settlers there who wanted to join the United States. The superior number of Mexican troops forced Frémont to go north, making camp at Klamath Lake, Oregon. One night in May 1846, as the party slept, Indians crept into camp and killed Carson's friend Basil Lajeunesse with a single hatchet blow to his head. In the ensuing battle, two more of Frémont's men were killed. Several attackers also died and, as Frémont later reported, the enraged Carson continued to pummel the body of one of them, beating his face into pulp.

THE YOUTH'S COMPANION HISTORIC MILESTONES

KIT CARSON ·· HUNTER AND TRAPPER ·· IMPLACABLE FOE OF HOSTILE INDIANS BUT FRIEND AND PROTECTOR OF THOSE THAT WERE PEACEFUL ·· TRAIL MAKER · PATHFINDER · GUIDE ·· INCOMPARABLE SCOUT AND LOYAL AND EFFICIENT SOLDIER ·· THE LAST OF THE OLD FRONTIERS-MEN AND ONE OF THE GREATEST

For more than a century, *The Youth's Companion* was one of the country's most popular magazines for children. This heroic illustration was published in about 1922.

That wasn't enough to satisfy him, though; to avenge Lajeunesse's death, he led an attack on a Klamath tribe fishing village where 150 braves lived. When Carson's rifle misfired during the battle, a Klamath warrior took aim at him with a poisoned arrow. Frémont acted instantly to save his life—"he plunged the rowels of his spurs deep into his horse" and trampled the enemy warrior. By the end of the day, in what became known as the Klamath Lake Massacre, most of the Indians had been killed and their village had been burned to the ground. Only later was it discovered that this tribe probably was not involved in the initial attack.

Coincidentally, on the day of the massacre, President Polk called on Congress to declare war on Mexico. Frémont's mapping party was almost instantly transformed into a fighting force called the California Battalion. Carson was given the rank of lieutenant. Returning to California, Frémont led a successful insurrection and declared himself military governor of the new American territory. Carson was dispatched to Washington, D.C., to inform President Polk of the victory, a cross-country journey he promised to make in sixty days. His planned route would take him through Taos, where he hoped to spend at least a brief time with his wife, whom he hadn't seen in more than a year. But when he was only days from home, he encountered General Stephen Kearny and his Army of the West, which had successfully seized New Mexico for the United States, and was en route to California. Kearny ordered Carson to turn around and guide him to San Diego and to send Frémont's dispatches to President Polk with another rider. Although he was only one long ride from his wife, he responded, "As the General thinks best," and joined his troops.

By the time Kearny's one hundred dragoons got to California, the situation there had changed drastically. The Mexicans had counterattacked, and Frémont was besieged by Californios, Mexican troops carrying eight-foot-long lances. Kearny clearly underestimated the Mexican troops when he launched an attack on the village of San Pasqual. By the end of the second day of fighting, almost fifty of Kearny's vastly outnumbered Americans had been killed or wounded, and the survivors were trapped on a hilltop without sufficient food, water, or ammunition. If they were not quickly reinforced, they would face annihilation. During the night, Kit Carson and Navy Lieutenant Beale removed their shoes and silently slipped through enemy lines, coming so close to being caught that Carson later claimed that "he could distinctly hear Lt. Beale's heart pulsate." Knowing they could not risk using the trails, the two men ran, walked, and crawled almost thirty miles barefoot through the sagebrush and cactus of the rocky terrain, the prickly pears digging into their bare feet. They raced through two nights without food or water until they finally reached American lines in San Diego. Carson had chosen the more difficult terrain to cover so arrived after Lieutenant Beale. Kearny's troops

When General S. W. Kearny's troops were surrounded and greatly outnumbered by Mexican forces, Carson and Navy Lieutenant Beale crawled through enemy lines, then ran almost thirty miles barefoot to save the besieged soldiers.

were preparing to make a final, desperate attempt to break out when the two hundred American reinforcements sent by Carson and Beale reached them. The Mexican army withdrew and the remnant of Kearny's battalion was saved. It took Lieutenant Beale more than a year to recover fully from this experience.

When the war ended, Commodore Stockton, who had been involved in the American revolt, declared Frémont governor of California. Six weeks later, General Kearny, claiming to be acting on government orders, charged Frémont with insubordination, a serious military offense, and named himself acting governor. Frémont immediately dispatched Carson to Washington to plead his case before President Polk. While in the capital, Carson stayed in Frémont's home, choosing to sleep outside on the porch rather than in a stuffy bedroom. Frontiersman Kit Carson was a sensation in Washington, though there was little about his physical appearance that reflected his exploits. The blood-and-thunder books had depicted him as a giant, America's first action hero, so people were greatly surprised that in the flesh this living legend actually was a small, stoop-shouldered, bowlegged, and freckled man, and that he responded to questions with simple, often one-word answers and spoke in a voice "as soft and gentle as a woman's." His appearance was so different from expectations that one man who had traveled a long distance to meet the great Indian fighter looked him up and down and said, "You ain't the kind of Kit Carson I am looking for." In fact, Carson's fame was so great across the country that there was a lively business in Kit Carson imposters.

The real Kit Carson was not impressed by his own celebrity. In fact, after making four more trips across the country as President Polk's personal courier, Carson happily mounted up and headed home.

At this point in his life, Carson and one of the men he'd traveled with, Lucien Maxwell, decided to build a real homestead in the Rayado valley, about fifty miles east of Taos. "We had been leading a roving life long enough and now, if ever, was the time to make a home for ourselves," he explained. "We were getting old and could not expect much longer to continue to be able to gain a livelihood as we had been doing for many years. . . . We commenced building and were soon on our way to prosperity."

It was impossible for him to stop adventuring, though, and he continued to accept commissions from the government. He led other survey teams into the Rockies; he drove

The 1847 Battle of Buena Vista was one of the bloodiest fights of the Mexican-American War. More than 3,400 Mexican troops and 650 Americans under the command of General Zachary Taylor were killed or wounded before Santa Anna withdrew in the night.

a herd of 6,500 sheep from New Mexico to the markets of California, where they sold for $5.50 per head; and at times he pursued Indians and outlaws. Not long after he had settled down with his third wife, "Little Jo," he learned that a Jicarilla (Apache) Indian raiding party had attacked a small group riding toward Santa Fe, killing merchant James White and another man and taking his wife, daughter, and a black female slave captive. The Jicarillas had then killed the child with one blow of a tomahawk and thrown her body into the Red River. Carson couldn't let this stand. He saddled up and joined the posse headed by an army major. They tracked the Indians for twelve days over harsh terrain. In camps along the way they found scraps of Mrs. White's dress and some of her possessions. When they finally found the Indian band with their captives, Carson wanted to attack immediately, but the major insisted that they instead parley with them and try to arrange a trade for the women. Carson was furious, knowing that the Indians had no interest in talk, but he was a man who followed orders. As the major waited, a single rifle shot rang out from the Indian camp, striking that officer squarely in the chest. In an incredible coincidence, only minutes earlier he had taken off his buckskin gauntlets and put them in his breast pocket. The buckskin had saved his life.

The outnumbered Indians scattered, leaving behind their belongings, but the major's order to charge came too late. They found Mrs. White's body and determined "her soul had but just flown to heaven." She had been shot through her heart with an arrow only minutes earlier. Then Carson found something he would never forget. According to his biographer,

> Among the trinkets and baggage found in the [Indians'] camp there was a novel, which described Kit Carson as a great hero, who was able to slay Indians by scores. This book was shown to Kit and, he later wrote, "It was the first of the kind I had ever seen . . . in which I was made a great hero, slaying Indians by the hundreds. . . . I have often thought that perhaps Mrs. White, to whom it belonged, read the same and knowing that I lived not very far off, had prayed to have me make an appearance and assist in freeing her. I consoled myself with the knowledge that I had performed my duty."

The ride home had been difficult. The posse was caught in a blizzard and one of their men froze to death. Later Carson learned that the Jicarilla had been caught in the same storm. And he shed no tears when he learned that without the furs and blankets that they had been forced to leave behind in the camp, many of them had frozen to death as well.

Sometime in 1849, Carson was told about a plot to murder two merchants. A man appropriately named Fox had hired on to guide the merchants on a trip to buy goods they

Kit Carson fought Indians, then went to Washington to fight for those same peoples, but his actions eventually caused him to be reviled by the tribes of the Southwest.

would use for trade. To accomplish that, they were carrying a large sum of money. In fact, Fox intended to kill them on the trail and then leave the bodies in the wilderness. Fox made the mistake of trying to enlist a shady character living in Rayado to help him. This man turned down the offer and, when Fox went back out on the trail, told the story to the local army post commander. When Carson learned of it, he gathered a small posse and raced almost three hundred miles through Indian territory to catch up with the party, arriving just in time to save the two merchants. Although they offered Carson a substantial reward, he refused to accept even one penny and instead took Fox back with him to jail.

As the American frontier moved steadily westward, Indian resistance to the settlers increased. The pioneers lived in fear of sudden and deadly attacks. Few people dared leave a settlement without first making careful preparations. It would be impossible to determine how many encounters Kit Carson had with the tribes, but it is accurate to state that precious few men could match that number. He had come to be known as the greatest Indian fighter in the West. No man was more qualified or better prepared to deal with the tribes, whether the encounter required words spoken over a shared peace pipe or the skilled use of a rifle, knife, or hatchet.

In 1865, Kit Carson, the nation's most famous Indian fighter, told a congressional committee, "I came to this country in 1826 and since then have become pretty well acquainted with the Indian tribes, both in peace and at war. I think, as a general thing, the difficulties arise from aggressions on the part of the whites."

But Carson avoided violence when possible. For instance, in the summer of 1851 he went east to St. Louis to visit his daughter and buy provisions for the winter, and on his way back, a few miles after crossing the Arkansas River, he encountered a band of Cheyennes. Carson could not have known these Cheyennes were on the warpath; a chief had been flogged by an American officer and they were out for revenge. Carson knew his party was too small and ill equipped to outrun them; he ordered the wagons to stay close and told his men to have their rifles ready. The Indians' war party shadowed them for more than twenty miles. When the caravan made camp for the night, Carson invited the advance party to join him for a talk and a smoke.

These young braves did not recognize Carson. Although they would have recognized his name, they would not have known what he looked like. So they certainly did not suspect that this white man spoke their language. As the pipe was passed, the Indians began speaking to each other in the Sioux language, so that if any of the white men escaped this trap, the Sioux would be blamed for the attack. It was not an unusual ruse. But as they continued smoking into the night, they eventually resorted to their own tongue. Finally they revealed their plan: When the pipe was next passed to Carson, he would have to lay down his weapon to take it, and at that moment they would attack and kill him. Then they would kill the other members of the party.

Carson understood every word, and he waited. When it was his turn, rather than taking the pipe, he grabbed his rifle and stood in the center of the circle, ordering his men to ready their weapons. The Cheyennes were stunned. Speaking to them in their own language, Carson demanded to know why they wanted his scalp. He had never been guilty of a single wrong to the Cheyennes, he said, and in fact their elders would tell them that he was a friend. Finally he ordered them out of his camp, warning that anyone who refused to leave would be shot and that if they returned, they would "be received with a volley of bullets."

Carson knew his threat would not stop the Indians indefinitely, but it would buy time. At the darkest point of that night, he took a young Mexican runner aside and instructed him to run as fast as possible to Rayado and return with soldiers. Their lives depended on him, he whispered. The boy was long gone by sunrise. It was said that young runners could cover more than fifty miles in a day. Almost a full day passed before the Cheyennes reappeared. They were wearing their war paint. As their braves approached, Carson warned them that a scout had been sent ahead for help. If they attacked, he admitted to them, the Cheyennes would suffer large casualties but eventually they would win. He knew that. But he had many friends among the soldiers and they would know which people had committed this crime "and would be sure to visit upon the perpetrators a terrible retribution."

Indian scouts found the boy's footprints, but with his long lead time they knew he could not be caught. Reluctantly, the war party withdrew. Two days later an army patrol under the command of Major James Henry Carleton arrived to escort Carson's party safely to Rayado.

As ruthlessly as Kit Carson often fought against the Indians, he also fought for them. In the early 1850s, he became the Indian agent—the government's representative to the tribe— for the Mohauche Utes, or Utahs, and several Apache tribes. While the Apaches continued to fight, initially the Utes remained at peace with the white man. Carson worked for the best interests of the tribe and at times fought doggedly with officials in Washington. He even requested permission to live with the Utes on their reservation, which was denied. Utes came almost daily to his ranch for food and tobacco, which he had paid for himself and happily supplied to them. He was so respected by the tribe that he became known as "Father Kit," and General Sherman once remarked, "Why his integrity is simply perfect. They [the Utes] know it, and they would believe him and trust him any day before me."

Unfortunately, when many Utes died from smallpox after receiving blankets from the government's Indian supervisor, the tribe joined the Apaches on the warpath. Eventually this uprising was smothered, but Carson's relationship with the tribes of New Mexico never completely recovered. The days when the Indians had freely roamed the plains were ending. During the gold rush, more than a hundred thousand people flocked to the West, and the Indians were pushed off their traditional lands onto reservations. Carson watched this clash of civilizations from his ranch and eventually began to believe that the two peoples could not live together peacefully and that it was best for the Indians to live far away from the white settlers.

In 1868, Carson led a delegation of Utes to Washington, where he negotiated the "Kit Carson Treaty" that guaranteed peace, territory, and government assistance to the tribe.

By 1860, the issue of slavery had raised passions in the West, although in that region slaves were mostly Mexican and Indian. While many people in New Mexico sympathized with the Confederacy, Carson remained loyal to the Union. When the Civil War began in 1861, he was appointed a colonel in the First New Mexico Volunteer Infantry. Years earlier, young Kit Carson had walked into the wilderness to live by wit and skill, and finally civilization, or at least the shadow of it, had caught up with him. He moved his family to Albuquerque and went to war.

Carson's first engagement was the 1862 battle of Val Verde, in which both Union and Confederate troops suffered large casualties but neither side declared victory. After two days' hard fighting, the Union troops withdrew and the Rebels made a wide swing around the garrison at Fort Craig and proceeded up the Rio Grande toward Albuquerque and Santa Fe. After that battle, Kit Carson spent the rest of the war once again fighting Indians. His commanding officer for much of that time, coincidentally, was General James Carleton, the same man who while a major had rescued Carson's caravan from the Cheyennes. After the Confederate attempt to capture New Mexico had been repulsed, Carleton took aim at the Indian tribes—in particular, the Navajos. Navajo raiding parties had taken advantage of the war to become a serious threat to settlers, a threat that Carleton, who didn't share Colonel Carson's respect for the native tribes, was determined to remove.

In 1862, Carleton ordered the Mescalero Apaches moved from their lands in the Sacramento Mountains to newly constructed Fort Sumner and the Bosque Redondo, the Round Forest, on the Pecos River. He issued an order: "All Indian men of that tribe are to be killed whenever and wherever you can find them. . . . If the Indians send in a flag of truce say to the bearer . . . that you have been sent to punish them for their treachery and their crimes. That you have no power to make peace, that you are there to kill them wherever you can find them."

Carson was appalled. He had lived his life with honor, and now he was being forced to choose between disobeying a direct order, which would mean facing a court-martial, and committing despicable acts. No one knows what went on his mind, but he might well have realized that even if he refused the order, the man who replaced him would not—and that man probably would not understand the tribes as he did. While he accepted the command to force the Apaches into confinement, he refused to follow the rest of General Carleton's orders. Instead he met with the elders of the tribe and convinced them to surrender. Within a few months, he brought four hundred Apaches to Bosque Redondo.

The Mescalero campaign was simply the beginning. Carleton then gave Carson command of two thousand troops and ordered him to capture the Navajos and imprison them on the

During his campaign against the Navajos, Carson's commanding officer, the brutal general James Carleton, told his troops that Indians "must be whipped and fear us before they will cease killing and robbing the people."

same reservation as their enemy, the Apaches. "You have deceived us too often," Carleton warned the Navajos, "and robbed and murdered our people too long, to trust you again at large in your own country. This war shall be pursued against you if it takes years, now that we have begun, until you cease to exist or move. There can be no other talk on the subject."

That was too much for Carson. He resigned his commission, stating, "By serving in the Army, I have proven my devotion to that government which was established by my ancestors. . . . At present, I feel that my duty as well as happiness directs me to my home and family and trusts that the General will accept my resignation."

The reason for what happened next will never be known, but the result has caused the name Kit Carson to be reviled by the tribes of the Southwest from that time forward in history. Carleton somehow convinced Carson to change his mind. Some historians believe General Carleton gave him assurances that once the Navajos were on the reservation they would be allowed to live peacefully. It also is true that Carson had come to believe that Indians and settlers could never live peacefully together and urged their separation. He may well have believed that by carrying out this policy he actually was ensuring the safety of both the Native Americans and the new Americans. Whatever the cause, Carson agreed to round up the Navajos.

Copyright 1904
By E.S. Curtis
x 1013

By the turn of the nineteenth century, the Navajos, here crossing Canyon de Chelly in northeastern Arizona, had settled peacefully on this land, as negotiated by Carson.

Rather than standing and fighting the army, the Indians dispersed and fled into the hills. The army retaliated by burning their crops and orchards, their cornfields and bean patches, their fruit trees and melon fields. Guards were posted by sources of salt and water, and Carleton authorized a fee to be paid to soldiers for each Indian animal they captured or killed. The army invaded the Navajos' main hunting grounds and camp, Canyon de Chelly, and destroyed it, burning it as completely as Sherman would level Atlanta. Without a single major battle being fought, almost ten thousand Navajos surrendered to Carson's troops. It was the largest number of Indians ever captured, and back east it added to the legend of Kit Carson.

In April 1864, the army led these captives on a forced march of more than three hundred miles to Fort Sumner. Hundreds of Indians died on "the Long Walk," as it is known in tribal history. Although Carson was not riding with his troops, as their commander he was responsible for their actions. Captives died from sickness, starvation, and exposure to the cold. Some of those who could not keep up were shot by soldiers. When they reached the reservation, conditions were not much better. Many more of the native peoples died during their four years of captivity. Eventually the Apaches escaped and disappeared into the hills, while the Navajos, after signing a treaty in 1868 with General Sherman, were moved to a portion of their traditional lands, where they have remained.

For his service, Kit Carson was promoted to the rank of general.

In late 1864, General Carson was sent to west Texas with 325 soldiers and 75 Ute scouts to subdue the Indians there. Kiowas, Comanches, and Cheyennes were known to be in that area. Carson headed toward the ruins of Adobe Walls, which he remembered from his scouting days two decades earlier. On November 25, his troops attacked a Kiowa village estimated to include 176 lodges. But the scouts failed to discover that this was one of the smallest of many villages in the area. The Kiowas fled from the attack but began gathering a massive Indian force. Within hours, about fourteen hundred warriors attacked. It was similar to the situation in which General Custer would find himself a few months later. One of the men with Carson later described the initial counterattack, writing that the Indians charged "mounted and covered with paint and feathers . . . charging backwards and forwards . . . their bodies thrown over the sides of their horses, at a full run, and shooting occasionally under their horses." Carson's men dug into the ruins of Adobe Walls. Unlike Custer, Carson had brought with him twin howitzers, big guns, and used them to his advantage. But he was greatly outnumbered. Backfires and the howitzers kept the Indians at a distance until Carson was able to effect a retreat. Carson suffered 6 dead and 125 wounded, while the tribes suffered many times that. Both the army and the tribes declared victory, the Kiowas calling it "the time when the Kiowas repelled Kit Carson."

When fifty-nine-year-old Kit Carson died in May 1868, he had become among the most famous and respected men in the nation.

At the end of the Civil War, Carson was given command of Fort Garland, in the Colorado Territory. It was the proper choice, wrote General John Pope, because "Carson is the best man in the country to control these Indians and prevent war. . . . He is personally known and liked by every Indian . . . no man is so certain to insure it as Kit Carson."

When he finally left the army in 1867, he resumed fighting to protect the Utes, whom he had long embraced as friends. Although his health was failing, he returned to Washington with several chiefs to negotiate a fair treaty, which guaranteed to that tribe peace, territory, and assistance. Carson and the Ute chiefs met with President Grant, and eventually a treaty was signed. Then he went home to be with his wife Josefa and their seven children. It was time for him to rest.

He had become one of the most honored men in American history. More than fifty blood-and-thunder novels had been written about him; Herman Melville compared him to Hercules in his novel *Moby-Dick*. He had been instrumental in the creation of an America that would eventually reach from ocean to ocean. But now he was suffering. In 1860, in the San Juan Mountains, he had been leading his horse down a steep hill when the animal slipped and fell on him; Carson became entangled in the lead rope and was dragged for some distance. The internal injuries he suffered caused chest pains, a persistent cough, and breathing difficulty, which plagued him for the rest of his life. In April 1868, Josefa died giving birth to his eighth child. Some believe his spirit died with her. Within weeks he was in bed in the quarters of the assistant surgeon general of the army, just outside Fort Lyon, Colorado. He had been diagnosed with a heart aneurysm, an enlargement of an artery, also believed to have been caused by that fall. As a legendary scout, he knew what lay ahead. Several times coughing attacks threatened his life, and the surgeon, H. R. Tilton, saved it by giving him chloroform. He wrote his will and made arrangements for his children. On May 23, almost exactly one month after his wife's death, Kit Carson smoked his pipe, ate his favorite meal, and lay down. Late in the afternoon, as the doctor read to him, he suddenly called out, "Doctor, compadre. Adios," and died.

Applying our moral standards to a man who lived in and helped shape a different time in our history is an impossible chore. Perhaps the only conclusion to reach is that by his courage and character he helped create this nation. Upon his death, an army officer who had served with him wrote what is perhaps the most fitting description: "Kit was particular to himself. No such combination ever existed in a man before . . . he united the courage of a Coeur de Leon, the utmost firmness, the strongest will and the best of common sense. He could weep at the misfortunes or sufferings of a fellow creature, but could punish with strictest rigor a culprit who justly deserved it."

BLACK BART

Gentleman Bandit

The Wells Fargo & Company stagecoach was rumbling down the rugged Siskiyou Trail in November 1883, making about ten miles an hour. As the stage slowed to begin the steep climb up Funk Hill, not far from the aptly named copper-mining town of Copperopolis, a man dressed in a long white linen duster and a bowler hat, his face covered with a flour sack with holes cut out for his eyes and mouth, similar sacks covering his feet, and holding a double-barreled twelve-gauge shotgun, stepped out from behind a rock onto the trail. The driver, Reason McConnell, immediately began reining in his team. He knew instantly what was going on: He was being held up by the most famous stagecoach robber in the West, Black Bart.

The robber blocked the coach wheels with rocks to prevent the driver from making a run for it, then ordered McConnell to throw down the strongbox, a big, green, locked wooden box with metal bands around it, which often carried gold or coins from miners. On this trip, the Wells Fargo stage was transporting 228 ounces of silver and mercury amalgam, worth about four thousand dollars, and five hundred dollars in gold dust and coins. McConnell replied that he couldn't throw down the box because the company had begun bolting it to the floor inside the stage to prevent robberies. Black Bart told the driver to climb down from his seat, then made him unhitch the horses and walk them down the hill. By the time McConnell was several hundred yards down the trail, the robber was hacking at the box with an ax.

What Bart did not know was that McConnell had been carrying a passenger, nineteen-year-old Jimmy Rolleri, whom he had dropped at the bottom of Funk Hill to do some hunting while the stage made the difficult climb. Rolleri was planning to catch up at the other end. McConnell found Rolleri and told him the stage was being robbed. The two men hustled back up to the top of the hill just in time to see the robber Black Bart climbing out of the stage lugging the strongbox. Grabbing Rolleri's rifle, McConnell began firing. Once! Twice! He missed. Missed again! Bart raced for the thicket. Rolleri reclaimed his rifle and fired into the undergrowth. Twice more. This time, the robber stumbled. He was hit. He regained his footing

71

and disappeared into the thick brush. The two men followed cautiously, knowing an armed and wounded bandit was dangerous. They pursued a trail of bloody droplets until it disappeared. Once again, Black Bart was gone.

But this time he had made a mistake.

Between 1875 and 1883 the mysterious rogue known across the nation as Black Bart, "the Gentleman Bandit," held up twenty-eight Wells Fargo stagecoaches in northern California. His pattern never varied: He robbed only Wells Fargo coaches, he was always alone, he never fired a shot or made threats, and he always escaped on foot.

When the stagecoach robber Black Bart was finally identified and arrested by detective James B. Hume in 1883, he turned out to be a most unlikely suspect. The story begins in John Sutter's sawmill, on the south fork of the American River in northern California, when Sutter's partner, James Marshall, discovered a few flakes of gold. That marked the beginning of the American gold rush, and during the next seven years more than three hundred thousand men caught gold fever and rushed to the area to find their fortunes. Among them was twenty-one-year-old Charles Bowles, who had been born in Norfolk, England, and brought to America as a young child. Bowles and his two brothers had left their home in upstate New York and crossed the continent to pan for gold. At just about the same time, young James Hume and his brother left their home—coincidentally also in upstate New York—carrying with them the same dreams as Bowles. The difference was that Charles Bowles failed completely—and both of his brothers died in the effort—while Hume was able to eke out a living from his claim.

By 1860, Bowles had married and was living on a small farm in Illinois. In 1862, he volunteered with the 116th Illinois Regiment and ended up serving for three years under General William T. Sherman in the March to the Sea. Although many soldiers served in the cavalry, that was not the right assignment for him: "Whistling Charlie," as he was known, was evidently afraid of horses. He apparently served with valor, seeing action in numerous battles, including the bloody Battle of Vicksburg—where he reportedly was seriously wounded—and by the time he was discharged in 1865 he had risen to the rank of lieutenant.

Like so many other soldiers who came home from the war, he found it difficult to return to life on the farm. In 1862, miners working Grasshopper Creek in Montana made a major strike. At the end of the war, a second gold rush began, and once again Bowles couldn't resist it. Apparently he set out on foot for the West, covering as many as forty miles a day, walking all the way to Montana. When he finally got there, he staked a claim and began panning along a creek. On occasion he would write letters to his wife, but he eventually stopped writing, and after several months without any contact at all, she concluded that he had died.

That misconception might have marked the beginning of Charles Bowles's life of grand deception—and retribution. There is much about Bowles that isn't known, but historians have been able to put together a plausible explanation for his hatred of Wells Fargo & Company. To work his claim in Montana, he built a wooden contraption known as a "tom," a device able to separate nuggets from rocks and sand. But, as with most forms of panning, it required a steady flow of water. His claim was promising, and eventually two men approached him and offered to buy the property. When he rejected their offer, they purchased the land above him and shut off the flow of water, making his claim worthless. Apparently these men were affiliated in some way with Wells Fargo, which had been buying substantial amounts of land around mining towns. Bowles considered their depriving him of water an act of economic war and set out to get even. One way or another, he was going to get his gold.

James Hume, after earning a decent living, also turned to the world of crime—but he took the side of the law and became a detective. In the early 1860s, he was appointed city

Under the name Black Bart, Charles Earl Bowles committed twenty-eight stagecoach robberies between 1875 and 1883—without a single person being injured.

marshal and chief of police of Placerville, California, a gold rush settlement better known as Hangtown. At that time, little "detection" actually occurred. It was extremely difficult to connect a person to a crime through the use of evidence: It would be several decades before law enforcement appreciated the value of fingerprints, for example. And photography was a recent invention of little use to detectives. In most cases, witness testimony comprised almost all the evidence.

But Hume set out to change that. He was among the very first detectives known to carefully explore crime scenes, searching for clues. He dug buckshot out of animals and walls to be used for comparisons. He analyzed footprints. He searched for connections between the smallest pieces of evidence and a suspect. In 1872, his stellar reputation earned him the job of Wells Fargo's first chief detective. Hume was comfortably settled into his job when the bandit who would become known as Black Bart struck for the first time.

Wells Fargo had been founded in San Francisco in 1852, offering both banking and express services to miners. It used every possible means of transportation—stagecoach, railroad, Pony Express, and steamship—to carry property, mail, and money in its many forms across the West, and by 1866 its stagecoaches covered more than three thousand miles from California to Nebraska. Their famous green strongboxes, usually carried under the driver's seat, weighed as much as 150 pounds and often held thousands of dollars' worth of gold dust, gold bars, gold coins, checks, drafts, and currency. The long, hard, and isolated trails these coaches traveled made them desirable prey for bandits. In 1874, the Jesse James Gang committed its first stagecoach robbery, getting away with more than three thousand dollars in gold, cash, and jewels, a fortune at that time.

The legend of Black Bart began at the summit on Funk Hill on July 26, 1875, when a man stepped out from behind some rocks and ordered driver John Shine to halt. The bandit was dressed in a linen coat, had a bowler on his head, and, Shine noticed, wore rags on his feet to obscure his footprints. When the coach stopped, the robber shouted loudly to other members of his gang, "If he dares shoot give him a solid volley, boys!" Looking around, Shine saw what appeared to be the long barrels of six rifles pointing at him from behind nearby boulders. Shine didn't argue; he tossed down the strongbox, which contained about two hundred dollars—the equivalent of about four thousand dollars today—and warned his ten passengers to stay quiet. According to the legend, one panicked woman threw her purse out the window, but rather than taking it, the bandit handed it back to her, explaining, "Madam, I do not wish to take your money. In that respect I honor only the good office of Wells Fargo."

Black Bart sent the coach on its way. The last time Shine saw him, he was on the ground, breaking the chest open. The driver stopped his coach at the bottom of the hill and walked back to retrieve the broken box. The robber was gone without a trace—but Shine was shocked to see that the rest of his gang hadn't moved from their positions behind the rocks. Curious, he moved closer and discovered that the "rifles" were actually sticks that had been placed there.

With the proceeds from this robbery, Charles Bowles settled in San Francisco, where he lived under the name Charles Bolton. It was the perfect disguise: He was hiding in plain sight, enjoying the life of a city gentleman. He lived in grand hotels, dined daily at fine restaurants, and dressed to fit the role. Perfectly groomed, he carried a short cane and favored diamonds in his lapel. He was welcome among the swells of the city. When asked, he described himself as a mining engineer, a profession that required him to take frequent business trips.

No one ever figured out that each of those trips coincided with another stagecoach robbery. In fact, there was not a lot of sympathy for Wells Fargo. Many people believed it was just another big company taking advantage of hardworking people. Some stagecoach robbers were glamorized; they were seen as brave bandits robbing the rich and . . . well, robbing the rich.

Bowles often waited months before staging another heist. Later he claimed that he stole only "what was needed when it was needed." Those robberies took careful planning: Because he was afraid of horses, he couldn't ride, so he had to walk to the scene and then walk away

Black Bart's success in robbing Wells Fargo stagecoaches eventually led the company to offer a reward—and when that failed, the company hired private detective Harry Morse, "the Bloodhound of the West," to track down the bandit.

after the job was done. The robberies almost always took place on the uphill side of a mountain, because the horses had to slow to pull the load. And although no one knew it at the time, the rifle he carried was old and rusted and probably wouldn't have fired even if he had loaded it, which he did not.

The second robbery took place more than five months after the holdup on Funk Hill. Once again, the driver reported a lone holdup man, with three armed accomplices hiding among the rocks. When investigators arrived at the scene, they found the sticks still in position.

Almost eighteen months passed before Bowles's next crime. In the interim, he had accepted a teaching position in Sierra County. At that time the school year was only about three months long, and that job probably provided an acceptable diversion for him. Supposedly he was well liked by his students; he was known for reciting poetry and quoting Shakespeare, especially *Henry V*.

When not robbing stages, Bowles lived as a socialite in San Francisco.

At first, Detective Hume was so busy with other matters that he took little notice of these sporadic holdups. But that changed after Black Bart's fourth crime, on October 2, 1878. His method hadn't changed, but for the first time he left a clue. Investigators found a poem in the broken strongbox:

> *I've labored long and hard for bread,*
> *For honor and for riches*
> *But on my corns too long you've tread*
> *You fine-haired sons-of-bitches*

It was signed *Black Bart, the P o 8*.

A day later another stage was robbed. Once again a poem was left at the scene:

> *Here I lay me down to sleep*
> *To wait the coming morrow*
> *Perhaps success, perhaps defeat*
> *And everlasting sorrow*

> *Yet come what will, I'll try it once*
> *My conditions can't be worse*
> *And if there's money in that box*
> *'Tis money in my purse*

Once again, it was signed *Black Bart, the P o 8*.

The audacity of the robber who left poems at the scene quickly attracted the attention of newspaper editors and dime novelists, and Black Bart, the Gentleman Bandit, captured the fancy of the American public. All this publicity naturally brought him to the attention of James Hume. Wells Fargo's analysis of the handwriting suggested a man who had long been employed in clerical work. An eight-hundred-dollar reward was posted for information leading to his capture, and detectives confidently announced he would soon be brought to justice. But the robberies continued without indication that detectives were closing in.

In 1880, Hume finally made an arrest in the case, but it was quickly discovered that the man they arrested actually had the perfect alibi—he had been in prison when several of the robberies occurred.

I rob the rich to feed the poor
Which chardly is a sin,
A widow ne'er knocked at my door
But what I let her in,
So blame me not for what I've done
I dont deserve your curses
And if for any cause I'm hung
Let it be for my verses

Black Bart
The po8

The fact that Black Bart left his own poems, signed "the P o 8," at the scenes of his crimes attracted national attention—although his reason for doing so was never determined.

In fact, no one had the slightest idea why this bandit left poems at these crime scenes, nor why had decided to call himself Black Bart, nor even what his signature, "the P o 8," meant. Only years later was it revealed that the name had been taken from a dime novel published in 1871 entitled *The Case of Summerfield*. The book, which had been reprinted in the *Sacramento Union* soon after its initial publication, featured a robber named Black Bart, a villain who dressed all in black, had long, wild, black hair, and robbed Wells Fargo stagecoaches. Supposedly the story was based on the true exploits of Captain Henry Ingraham's Raiders, a group of Confederate soldiers who robbed Wells Fargo's Placerville stage of as much as twenty thousand dollars to purchase uniforms for new recruits—and left a receipt for the theft. There is some evidence that James Hume was involved in tracking down those soldiers and arresting them. If it was true that Hume was involved in that case, then Bowles might have picked that name to taunt him: *You caught them but you can't catch me.*

Bowles never revealed the meaning of his signature, "the P o 8." Some historians believe it meant simply "the poet," honoring Bowles's love of poetry, while others suggest it referred to "pieces of eight," meaning booty taken by pirates, and was meant to honor the greatest pirate of the Caribbean, Bartholomew "Black Bart" Roberts, who captured more than four hundred ships before being killed in battle.

For more than a century, criminologists have debated why Black Bart left the poems. Maybe the best explanation is that he wanted people to know that he had outsmarted the great Wells Fargo; he wanted to rub the company's nose in the dirt trails used by their stages. At the same time, he apparently took pride in the fact that no one ever got hurt during his holdups. He was the perfect gentleman robber: He was unfailingly polite, he never took anything from passengers, and he never used foul language. In fact, to reassure their passengers, Wells Fargo issued a statement pointing out that "[he] has never manifested any viciousness and there is reason to believe he is averse to taking human life. He is polite to all passengers, and especially to ladies. He comes and goes from the scene of the robbery on foot; seems to be a thorough mountaineer and a good walker," then added, "[I]t is most probable he is considered entirely respectable wherever he may reside." Although that statement may well have calmed passengers, it also helped to make Charles Bowles's Black Bart into a romantic legend.

It was after his fifth robbery that authorities discovered their first real lead. Investigators found out that following the holdup, a stranger on foot had stopped at a farm and paid for a meal. The farmer's teenage daughter described him as having "[g]raying brown hair, missing two of his front teeth, deep-set piercing blue eyes under heavy eyebrows. Slender hands in conversation, well-flavored with polite jokes." It wasn't much, but for the clue-collecting Hume it was a beginning.

The robberies continued through the early 1880s. Several stagecoach drivers reported actually having pleasant conversations with the bandit during the holdups. In 1881, for example, Horace Williams asked him, "How much did you make?" to which he replied, "Not very much for the chances I take."

That so many people considered this thief a hero continued to rankle Detective Hume, and he committed considerable resources to the job of catching the elusive robber. He hired the sixty-man detective agency run by the renowned San Francisco detective Harry Morse, "the Bloodhound of the West," and assigned that company to work on this case. Hume also personally visited the sites of many robberies and diligently scoured the area, looking for the smallest clues. At several of the locations, Hume's team found the robber's abandoned camp, which indicated he had waited there patiently, sometimes for several days, for the stage to arrive.

Bowles's first close call came near Strawberry, California, in July 1882, when he attempted the biggest job of his career. The Oroville stage was carrying more than eighteen thousand dollars in gold bullion, although it isn't known whether he was aware of that. But perhaps because that

gold was on board, Hume had assigned a shotgun-armed guard to ride next to the driver. Black Bart suddenly appeared in the middle of the trail and took hold of the horse, which bolted, and the coach ran off the road. The robber's attention was diverted, so he failed to see armed guard George Hackett lift his shotgun and let loose a volley. The buckshot lifted Bowles's bowler off his head, grazing his scalp. Bowles had no desire—or ability—to shoot back; instead, he disappeared into the brush, leaving his bloodied hat lying in the dirt. The robbery had failed, but he had escaped. By the time a posse got there, he was long gone and had left no other evidence.

Bowles continued to lead two completely different lives: one in San Francisco, where he was Charles Bolton, a man of leisure and wealth, a socialite who slept comfortably on clean sheets and was always welcomed in the better establishments of the city; the other in the wilderness, where he camped alone as he waited for the next stage, sleeping on the hard ground, confronting the elements, eating sardines out of tin cans. Although he subsisted mostly on his ill-gotten gains, he did invest some money in several small businesses that apparently returned a small profit.

It probably isn't accurate to claim that Hume pursued Black Bart with the same diligence and ferocity with which Victor Hugo's classic Inspector Javert hunted for Jean Valjean, but his pursuit lasted more than eight years. Hume was head of investigations for a large company and responsible for solving many cases, but clearly this was the big one. From his investigations he began to develop a theory that was considered radical at the time—criminals will often return to the scene of their crimes. This was especially true of Black Bart, who required a specific set of circumstances for his crimes to succeed: Because he was on foot, he couldn't pursue a stage, so he needed a secluded place where the stage was already moving slowly and thick foliage nearby through which he could make his escape without fear of pursuit. There were only a limited number of such locations, which made Hume believe he was destined to use the same site more than once.

And indeed, Black Bart's end came in the place where he had begun, the summit of Funk Hill. On November 3, 1883, driver Reason McConnell and Jimmy Rolleri pegged four shots at the bandit. Although the first three shots missed, the fourth shot nicked Bowles's hand. The robber ran about a quarter of a mile, then stopped and wrapped a handkerchief around his knuckles to stem the bleeding. He hid the four thousand dollars he'd grabbed in a rotten log and kept the five hundred dollars in coins, put his rifle inside a hollow tree, and made his walkaway. He covered the hundred miles back to the city in three days, then went by train to Reno to lie low for several more.

Hume and Morse rode to the scene of the crime as quickly as their horses would take them. The driver McConnell was certain he'd hit the robber; he'd heard him yelping. The two detectives carefully searched the entire area and eventually found several items that had been left behind in haste, including a derby hat, size 7¼; a tin of supplies, including sugar, coffee, and crackers; a belt; a binocular case; a magnifying glass; a razor; two flour sacks—and a bloodied handkerchief with the laundry mark "F.X.0.7."

A century later, the DNA in the blood might have enabled Hume to identify his man, but in 1883, something much less scientific caught his attention—the laundry mark. In those days, many men had at most only two shirts or handkerchiefs, and few workingmen could afford to send them out to a laundry to be cleaned. Certainly, few common stagecoach bandits sent their shirts out to be laundered. Clearly Black Bart was not the type of holdup man Hume had imagined him to be. From that clue, Hume deduced that Black Bart was living in a big city, and the only big city within walking distance was San Francisco.

Harry Morse's men began visiting each of the more than ninety laundries in San Francisco, trying to associate "F.X.0.7" with a specific person. It took more than a week, but eventually

Thomas Ware, the proprietor of the California Laundry on Stevenson Street, only a few blocks from the Wells Fargo office, identified the laundry mark. The handkerchief belonged to one of his better customers, he said, a Mr. Charles E. Bolton, the mining engineer who lived at the Webb House, a hotel on Second Street.

When Morse investigated further, he found that people spoke highly of this Charles Bolton. He was "an ideal tenant," his landlady explained, "so quiet, so respectable and punctual with his room rent." He was a fine fellow, others said.

Morse assigned several detectives to stake out the hotel. About a week later his men spotted the nattily dressed Mr. Bolton emerging from his rooms. They noted that he appeared to have a wound on his hand. Morse took charge: One afternoon, as his suspect sauntered down the street carrying a fancy cane, Morse successfully made his acquaintance. He had been told that Bolton was a mining engineer, he explained, then asked for his assistance. He had in his possession several pieces of ore that needed to be identified. Perhaps Mr. Bolton would be so kind as to do so?

Remembering this event years later, the detective Morse wrote, "One would have taken him for a gentleman who had made a fortune and was enjoying it. He looked anything but a robber."

Perhaps sensing a business opportunity, Bowles agreed and walked with Morse to the nearby Wells Fargo office, completely unaware that the man who had spent the past eight and a half years trying to capture him was waiting there. It was there that James Hume introduced himself to Charles Bowles and arrested him for the robberies committed by the bandit Black Bart. Bowles by this time had perfected his acting skills and appeared genuinely surprised by the accusation, continuing to insist that a mistake had been made, that he was a fifty-six-year-old mining engineer named Charles Bolton. The handkerchief? Perhaps he'd dropped it and the real Black Bart had picked it up. But any doubt that another mistake had been made was erased after Morse searched his rooms. There he found letters written in the same hand as the two poems left by Black Bart, as well as several shirts bearing the laundry mark "F.X.0.7."

Bowles was taken to Stockton and arraigned. Although he continued to maintain his innocence, at one point he did ask if a man who confessed to a robbery and returned all the proceeds might avoid going to prison. That wouldn't be possible, he was informed, but it was probable that a judge would look kindly upon a man who confessed to his robberies and had never hurt a soul. Finally Bowles/Bolton/Black Bart confessed—to the final robbery. He took authorities to the top of Funk Hill and handed over all the loot.

His arrest took place while San Francisco's newspapers were fighting for circulation, and they all wanted Black Bart's story. Late one night, *Examiner* reporter Josiah Ward got into Bowles's cell. He watched as Bowles entertained a series of visitors, including his landlady, who dabbed the prisoner's eyes as he cried. Eventually Bowles agreed to be interviewed. Ward's article reported him as saying, "I never drink and I don't smoke. All my friends are gentlemen and I never associated with other than gentlemen. I can't claim to be perfect. They do say I will rob a stage occasionally. But no one can say that I ever raised my hand to do any harm. I merely carried a gun to intimidate the driver. As for using it—why for all the gold that road ever carried I would not shoot a man."

In the middle of November, Bowles was convicted of only one robbery—the final job—and sentenced to six years in San Quentin prison. While he was imprisoned, the dime novel *The Gold Dragon; or, The California Bloodhound: The Story of PO8, the Lone Highwayman* was published, adding to his nationwide fame. He never admitted in court that he was Black Bart; he never confessed to another robbery or returned any of the stolen money. It was never determined exactly how much he stole, with estimates ranging between twenty thousand and one hundred thousand dollars, or about three million dollars in today's money.

He was released in January 1888, an event covered by all the newspapers. He had served four and a half years and was released for good behavior. His eyesight was failing, he said, and he had gone deaf in one ear. Asked by a reporter if he intended to return to his "profession," he smiled and said, "No, gentlemen. I'm through with crime." When another reporter followed up by asking if he might write more poetry, he shook his head. "Now, didn't you hear me say that I am through with crime?"

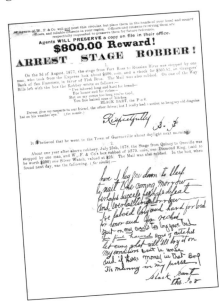

Detective James Hume, who established Wells Fargo's own special-agent operation, relentlessly pursued the famous stage robber for eight years.

Wells Fargo agents followed him for several weeks as he moved from town to town, but in February he walked out of the Palace Hotel in Visalia and was never seen or heard from again.

Or was he? In November later that year, a Wells Fargo stagecoach was held up by a masked highwayman in a manner reminiscent of Black Bart. After he escaped, a poem was found:

> *So here I've stood while wind and rain*
> *Have set the trees a-sobbin*
> *And risked my life for that box,*
> *That wasn't worth the robbin.*

The note was sent to Detective Hume for examination. He compared it to the original poems known to have been written by Bowles and announced that this holdup was committed by a copycat.

However, for several years, rumors of Bowles's activities and whereabouts continued to surface. William Randolph Hearst's *San Francisco Examiner* claimed that after a few robberies in northern California, Wells Fargo had agreed to give Bowles some sort of "pension" in exchange for his promise to never rob another stage, with the figure varying between $125 and $250 a month.

Although the company firmly denied having struck any deal, it did continue to list the newly released "Bolton" as a suspect in several stage holdups, describing him as "a thorough mountaineer, a remarkable walker, and claims he cannot be excelled in making quick transits over mountains and grades," concluding that he was "a cool self-contained talker with waggish tendencies; and since his arrest . . . has exhibited genuine wit under most trying circumstances."

Other stories of his fate speculated that he lived the rest of his life in luxury in Mexico or New York or St. Louis with the proceeds he had secreted from his life of crime. A thief arrested outside Kansas City was identified by local authorities as Black Bart, but one of Hume's men identified him as a different Wells Fargo robber who had served time in Folsom Prison. That same detective claimed he had discovered what had actually happened to Bowles—he had sailed to Japan on the *Empress of China* and was living there happily. One newspaper reported he had been killed holding up a stage from Virginia City to Reno and had been buried in a shallow grave at the side of the road. Detective Hume once said he'd heard that Bowles died while hunting game in the high Sierra. He was supposedly seen in the Klondike after the gold strike of 1896 in the Yukon. Reporter Josiah Ward wrote that Bowles had indeed been hired by Wells Fargo—to ride shotgun on stages, and eventually "saved and bought a ranch where he abode in peace and quiet until he died." Finally, in 1917, *The New York Times* printed the obituary of Civil War veteran Charles E. Boles [*sic*], although no mention was made of another career. If that was Black Bart—and there is no compelling evidence to either confirm or deny that—he would have been eighty-eight years old.

Perhaps it's appropriate that his fate remains unknown; the Gentleman Bandit Black Bart had effectively escaped again, living out the rest of his life in obscurity. No one would ever break his record of twenty-nine stagecoach robberies. Henry Ford introduced his Model T in 1908, thus putting an end to the profession of stagecoach robber forever.

After serving four years and two months in San Quentin, Black Bart was released and supposedly disappeared—although a year later, Wells Fargo issued his last Wanted poster, accusing him of committing two more robberies.

THE DIME NOVELS

The image of the rip-roaring, hard-riding, two-fisted, straight-shooting cowboy, standing up for Old West justice against villainous varmints was initially the creation of small paper books known as dime novels. Although the real skills and courage of the men who tamed the American frontier could often be awe inspiring, these very popular novels successfully turned these men into the near superheroes that have become a staple of popular culture.

There has always been something magical about the exploits of these brave men, but beginning with the minstrel shows and popular music of the mid-1800s, their feats of derring-do were greatly exaggerated. P. T. Barnum might have been the first to exploit the fascination with the frontier, when he presented live Indians as a curiosity at his New York City museum in the 1840s. But the real effort to make the West wilder began in June 1860, when *Malaeska, the Indian Wife of the White Hunter* was published by the New York printing firm Beadle and Adams.

Technological advances in printing in the 1840s had made it possible to inexpensively produce numerous copies of a book. Cheap and easily carried, dime novels were extremely popular among Civil War soldiers looking for any diversion, and soon people everywhere were seeking them out.

The initial success of Beadle's books caused competitors to rush to publish their own, which often were stories that previously had been

THE **BUFFALO BILL** STORIES

A WEEKLY PUBLICATION   DEVOTED TO BORDER HISTORY

No. 184.   Price, Five Cents.

BUFFALO BILL'S NAVAJO ALLY
OR THE WAR WITH THE CAVE-DWELLERS

BY THE AUTHOR OF "BUFFALO BILL"

Buffalo Bill and the chief of the Cave-Dwellers struggled on the edge of the precipice, locked in deadly embrace, while the brave Navajo, tomahawk in hand, kept the other Indians at bay.

Although inexpensive "yellow-backed" paper books had been published earlier, dime novels—and the nickel or "half-dime" novels that followed—generally were published as numbered volumes in series that featured recognizable characters. More than 40,000 different titles were published, many of them by Beadle and Adams, who warned potential authors, "We prohibit what cannot be read with satisfaction by every right-minded person—old and young alike."

serialized in three-penny dailies or story newspapers. Although these books were called dime novels, some of them sold for a nickel or less. The character of the virtuous cowboy fighting vicious Indians and ruthless outlaws grew out of the early stories of heroic frontiersmen, in particular, James Fenimore Cooper's Leatherstocking Tales. To compete, authors had to continuously up the ante, putting their characters into increasingly dangerous situations and then giving them the almost superhuman skills needed to survive for another book. These sensationalized action-adventure stories often were based extremely loosely on real events and used real names—and turned men and women such as Buffalo Bill, Wild Bill Hickok, Bat Masterson, Calamity Jane, and even Belle Starr into American celebrities.

These books were the original pulp fiction, written to be devoured in one gulp and quickly forgotten. Millions of copies were sold. Edward Judson, writing as Ned Buntline, could write a book in a few days and published more than four hundred of them, transforming Buffalo Bill into a legendary figure. The most successful dime novelist was probably Edward Ellis, whose *Seth Jones; or, the Captives of the Frontier*, sold six hundred thousand copies in six languages.

By the time dime novels disappeared early in the twentieth century, the character of the valiant cowboy defeating evil at the last possible moment was forever enshrined in our culture and had become the symbol of the Old West recognized throughout the world. The movies picked it up from there, and the rest has become history!

WILD BILL
HICKOK

Plains Justice

In the settling heat of an early summer evening, at six o'clock on the twenty-first of July, 1865, Wild Bill Hickok stood calmly in the center of the Springfield, Missouri, town square, his Colt Navy revolvers resting easy in a red sash tied around his waist, their ivory handles turned forward. About seventy-five yards away, the gambling man Davis K. Tutt stepped out of the old courthouse, where he'd been settling some fines. The two men stared at each other. Even at that distance, Wild Bill could see the old Johnny Reb Tutt slowly pull a gold watch out of his vest pocket and glance nonchalantly at the time—the very watch that Hickok had warned him not to display. Hickok yelled to him, "Don't you cross the square with my watch!" Tutt responded by slipping the watch back into his pocket and stepping out into the middle of the square. Neither man was the type to back down from a challenge. They faced each other: Dave Tutt turned to his side; Wild Bill squared his shoulders and stood facing straight ahead. For a few seconds, nothing happened. Then they went for their guns.

This story of the first showdown in the Old West has been carried by the winds for one hundred fifty years, and in all that time the details tend to get a bit murky. According to legend, the two men had met the night before at the Lyon House Hotel, where Tutt had demanded that Hickok settle a $35 debt. Hickok insisted that he owed the man only $25, but until the debt could be settled, Tutt took Hickok's gold watch as collateral. Hickok accepted the deal but warned Tutt not to embarrass him by flaunting that watch in public. There was nothing wrong with losing at the table and paying your debts, he knew, but he was not a man who stood by quietly when held up for ridicule.

Legend has it that Tutt wasn't too interested in the correct time when he pulled it out of his vest; he was instead calling Hickok's bluff.

But others claim that the real reason for this feud was lady troubles. Some said that when Hickok had a falling-out with a woman he was courting named Susannah Moore, Dave Tutt had taken advantage of the situation and waltzed in between them. In response, Hickok had struck up a relationship with Tutt's sister. Whatever the reason, there was bad blood between the two men and it was going to end that afternoon. Contrary to the movies and TV Westerns, quick-draw showdowns on main streets were very rare. This was the first one, and it appears that a lot of the townspeople turned out to watch it.

Most reports claim that both men pulled their guns evenly, but, rather than firing wildly, they took their time to aim—then fired simultaneously, their respective volleys sounding like a single shot. "Tutt was a famous shot," said an observer, known in those parts as Captain Honesty, "but he missed this time; the ball from his pistol went over Bill's head . . . Bill never shoots twice at the same man, and his ball went through Dave's heart."

Tutt shouted to bystanders, "Boys, I'm killed!" then fell dead.

After he'd fired, Hickok whirled to face Tutt's men, who were standing nearby and looked ready to draw. "Put up your shootin' irons," he warned, "or there'll be more dead men here."

They reluctantly put down their weapons. And the legend of Wild Bill Hickok, "the Prince of Pistoleers," already well established, began to grow. James Butler Hickok was the most famous gunslinger of the Old West; a man known to be reluctant to shoot, but when it became necessary, his draw was "as quick as thought" and his aim was always true. He was the man boys grew up wanting to become; a man of courage and honor whom other men proudly stepped aside for, then bragged they'd met; a man of such grace and bearing that he made women swoon. The fetching Libbie Custer, General Custer's widow, with whom Hickok may have dallied, wrote of him,

> Physically, he was a delight to look upon. Tall, lithe and free in every motion, he rode and walked as if every muscle was perfection, and the careless swing of his body as he moved seemed perfectly in keeping with the man, the country and the time in which he lived. . . . [H]e carried two pistols. He wore top-boots, riding breeches and dark blue flannel shirt, with scarlet set in front. A loose neck handkerchief left his fine firm throat free [and] the frank, manly expression of his fearless eyes and his courteous manner gave one a feeling of confidence in his word and in his undaunted courage.

Fame sometimes has a lot of sharp edges and has to be handled carefully. Hickok's reputation as a deadly gun followed him throughout his life, wherever he traveled, and brought with it some heavy challenges. And some people wonder if, on his last day, it was that fame that caused his demise.

In his lifetime, Hickok became the embodiment of all the virtues attributed to the great

This was the image of the gunfighter Wild Bill Hickok that thrilled Americans: "'Wild Bill' Hickok (1837–76) demonstrates his marksmanship with his Colt Navy model revolver."

men who fought to settle the West, a man who stood up for what was right. He was born in 1837, in the frontier town of Homer, Illinois. His parents, William Alonzo and Polly Butler Hickok, were abolitionists who risked their lives by turning their home into a station on the Underground Railroad. The Hickok family often hid slaves in cubbyholes dug out under their floorboards and, when necessary, carried them to the next station in their wagon. It was said that the Hickoks provided for dozens, maybe even hundreds, of escaping slaves.

Even as a young man, Hickok was known to be a sure shot, and when he was still a teenager he rode with the Jayhawkers, an antislavery militia fighting in the Kansas Territory. There he became known as Shanghai Bill because of his height and his slim frame, but the name didn't stick. It was there that he purportedly first met his lifelong friend William Cody,

a twelve-year-old boy who years later would gain fame as Buffalo Bill, but who was then scouting for the army. The way Cody told the story, he was being bullied by some local toughs and Hickok stepped into the situation and walked him out.

William Hickok's legend had its origins in the summer of 1861 at the Pony Express station in Rock Creek, Nebraska. Speculation abounds concerning what actually happened there, and over time the tales have gotten taller. The twenty-four-year-old Hickok had been driving freight wagons and coaches along the Santa Fe Trail for Russell, Majors, & Waddell, the parent company of the Pony Express, until he got into a tussle with a bear; when his shot ricocheted off the bear's head, Hickok rassled it and cut its throat, but not before that bear inflicted some serious damage. While recuperating, Hickok did odd jobs at the relay station, tending to horses and wagons for station manager Horace Wellman. Hickok lived with Wellman and Wellman's wife, Jane, in the station's small cabin, which had been built on land Wellman purchased from a local rancher named David C. McCanles. McCanles was an ornery fellow, who insisted on derisively calling Hickok "Duck Bill," supposedly a reference to his large, narrow nose and protruding lips—and another name that didn't stick. Naturally, being made fun of did not sit well with Hickok. One day McCanles showed up at the station with his son, Monroe, and two members of his gang, demanding his land back because Wellman was late on his payments. But, once again, another version of the story says that the real reason McCanles showed up concerned the affections of a young woman who had taken a liking to Hickok.

McCanles stood outside the cabin and began haranguing Hickok and the Wellmans, possibly ordering them off his land. A blanket had been hung inside the cabin, most likely to provide some privacy, and both Hickok and Wellman stepped behind it. One of them—it never was quite clear which—took a Hawken rifle off the wall and fired once through the blanket into McCanles's chest; he fell dead on the ground. McCanles's men, James Woods and James Roberts, went for their guns. Woods rushed the cabin, but Hickok pulled his Colt and wounded him, allowing Jane Wellman to finish him off with her sharpened garden hoe. Hickok fired again through the door, this time hitting Roberts, who stumbled off into the woods. Hickok pursued him and came out alone. Monroe McCanles ran off untouched.

Civilization was coming to the West, and three dead men now required a legal hearing. Four days after the shoot-out, Hickok and Horace Wellman were on trial. McCanles had

꘎ This was the first published image of Wild Bill Hickok, Alfred Waud's lithograph, as it appeared in *Harper's Magazine*, 1867.

come to Nebraska from North Carolina, so, in addition to being a bully, he was thought to be pro-Confederate. Wellman and Hickok claimed they had been defending company property, and the circuit judge agreed with them. But as soon as the verdict was rendered, Hickok packed his saddlebags and left Rock Creek to join the war. The first battle of the Civil War, First Bull Run, had just begun at Manassas, Virginia.

By 1867, stories of derring-do in the West were thrilling readers in the big cities. In February of that year, journalist George Ward Nichols published a long, illustrated article entitled "Wild Bill" in the popular *Harper's New Monthly Magazine*. In this wildly exaggerated article, McCanles showed up at the station with his gang of "reckless, blood-thirsty devils, who would fight as long as they had the strength to pull the trigger." By the time the shooting ended, Hickok had dispatched McCanles and ten of his men. The hair-raising story introduced a fighting man to a post–Civil War American public searching desperately for a hero. Nichols created a larger-than-real-life character, a living legend, Wild Bill Hickok. "You would not believe that you were looking into the eyes that have pointed the way to death to hundreds of men," he wrote. "Yes, Wild Bill with his own hands has killed hundreds of men. Of that I have no doubt. He shoots to kill as they say on the border."

Hickok wasn't the first Wild Bill, but when the name finally fell to him, he quickly became the one and the only. Another story that helped build his legend occurred when he enlisted in the Union army and was tasked with spying on the Rebels, scouting, and acting as a provost, or military policeman. One night he came upon a large group of troublemakers, probably fueled by drink, roughing up a bartender outside a saloon. There had been a fair fight, which the bartender had won, but the toughs came back with friends. They had dragged the bartender outside and were beating on him, threatening a hanging. Hickok didn't hesitate, putting himself between the bartender and the mob. "How 'bout we make this a fair fight," he said, glaring at them with his steel-blue eyes. Two men reached for their guns. But before they could clear their holsters, Hickok had drawn both his ivory-handled revolvers and had both men in his sights. They stopped and took their hands away from their weapons. Hickok nodded appreciatively, pointed his guns over their heads, and shot out a kerosene light. "That'll be enough," he was reported to have said. And as the crowd began dissipating, a woman called out, "My God, ain't he wild!"

Wild Bill could indeed be a wild man: He drank, he brawled, he loved the cards and the ladies and treated them both with respect; he could be a gentleman or a cold-blooded shooter, depending on the occasion. He wasn't just passing through life, he was taking thrilled Americans with him on his adventures as the cowboys and gunslingers and lawmen fought to tame the Wild West.

Hickok's exaggerated exploits quickly made him a living legend. In this Hays City brawl, Sheriff Hickok supposedly faced fifteen Seventh Cavalry soldiers—killing two of them and shooting several more.

His legendary skills as a horseman and sure shot served him well during the Civil War. While many fighting men preferred to carry a long gun, Hickok was a pistoleer. He became well known for carrying two ivory-handled Colts, tucked handles-out into a sash or wide belt, which enabled his quick draw. Gunslingers were particular about the way they drew their weapons; a split second could mean the difference between life and death, and Hickok favored the lightning-quick cross-draw in which he'd reach across his body with both hands and pull out his guns. It was a unique style and required a hard twist of the wrist. Some said he'd based it on the technique used by military officers to draw their swords, but others believed it was his lifelong choice from early on. It was also during the war that he became known for wearing a broad-brimmed hat, his long, drooping mustache, and flowing hair.

More stories about Wild Bill's Civil War exploits circulated: During one battle he worked as a sniper and supposedly shot thirty-five men. Hickok himself years later told a story of working as a spy behind Confederate lines at the Battle of Westport, an important fight that took place near where Kansas City now stands. Apparently a skirmish broke out across the Sugar Creek River, with the Union and Confederate troops close enough to see the expressions on their enemies' faces. One of the bluecoats suddenly recognized Hickok behind gray lines. "Bully for Wild Bill!" he shouted, catching the attention of a Rebel sergeant, who suddenly realized there was a spy in the ranks. He reached for his pistol, but Hickok beat him to the draw and drilled him in the chest; then, as Hickok remembered it, "As he rolled out of his saddle, I took his horse by the bit and dashed into the water as quick as I could. . . . The minute I shot the sergeant our boys set up a tremendous shout, and opened a smashing fire on the Rebs who had commenced popping at me. But I had got into deep water, and had slipped off my horse over his back, and steered him for the opposite bank by holding onto his tail with one hand, while I held the bridle rein of the sergeant's horse in the other hand." Wild Bill then crossed the river to safety.

After that escape, Hickok delivered his intelligence to General Curtis, information that may well have aided the Union troops in their victory at what became known as "the Gettysburg of the West" and ended with the Rebels being driven out of Missouri.

Hickok's bravery and success as a scout attracted the attention of Union commanders, and when the war ended, General William Tecumseh Sherman employed him as a guide to take his party to Fort Kearny, Nebraska. He also scouted in the West for General Winfield Scott Hancock and Lieutenant Colonel George Armstrong Custer. In Custer's 1874 book, *My Life on the Plains*, he wrote of Hickok, "Of his courage there could be no question. His skill in the use of the rifle and pistol was unerring. His deportment was entirely free of bravado. . . . His influence among frontiersmen was unbounded, his word was law, and many are the personal quarrels and disturbances which he had checked among his comrades. . . . I have a personal knowledge of at least half a dozen men whom he has at various times killed, others have been seriously wounded—yet he always escaped unhurt in every encounter."

The great respect in which Hickok was held made him the perfect lawman. His presence alone, often without a word or warning spoken, was known to quiet a combustible situation. At the end of the war, he raised his right hand and became a US deputy marshal at Fort Riley, Kansas, while also hiring on as a scout in the Indian Territory for George Custer's Seventh Cavalry. The Indian tribes were seen as an obstacle to the spirit of Manifest Destiny, the belief that America would someday stretch across the continent from the Atlantic to the Pacific, as ordained by God. Agreements were reached with several tribes, granting them reservations, but other tribes decided to stand and fight for their traditional lands. In May 1867, while based in Fort Harker, Kansas, Hickok reported being attacked by a large Indian

Rincon train station, New Mexico, 1883

band, successfully driving them off by killing two of them. Two months later, he led a patrol in pursuit of Indians who had attacked a homestead near the fort and killed four men. Although some stories claim Wild Bill's patrol returned to the fort with five prisoners after killing ten more, others say they returned to Fort Harker without ever having seen an Indian.

Hickok worked out of Hays City, Kansas, and as US deputy marshal tracked down deserters, horse and mule thieves, counterfeiters, and everyone else who ran afoul of the law. In 1868, he worked with his old friend, then government detective William F. Cody, to transport eleven Union deserters from Fort Hays to Topeka for trial.

After the fanciful *Harper's* article spread Hickok's fame throughout the West, he was faced with the downside of being a legend: He had to live up to it every day. People expected to see him regularly perform the kind of feats they'd read about. There was also the continual threat of yet another lowlife trying to earn his spurs by standing up to Wild Bill Hickok.

In 1869, Hickok won a special election to finish the term of the sheriff of Ellis County and marshal of Hays City. Hays needed him. It was a boomtown built out of the tumbleweeds to be the jumping-off point for teamsters carrying freight brought by the Kansas Pacific railroad from back east down to all the towns along the Smoky Hill and Santa Fe Trails. An endless stream of land speculators, tradesmen, storekeepers, and clerks, and sometimes their families, came roaring into town, followed by the buffalo hunters, the cattlemen, the adventurers, the Civil War veterans, and all the others looking for a place to stay a night or settle for a time. To satisfy these transients' social needs, twenty-three saloons and gambling dens were built practically overnight, and the prostitutes and the card sharks and the cattle rustlers and the con artists followed the money. Within a year or so, Hays City had become the largest city in northwest Kansas—as well as the wickedest. It was a lawless place. One writer even referred to it as "the Sodom of the plains."

Hickok quickly made his presence known. As author and historian Lieutenant Dan Marcou explained, "He would not walk down the sidewalk, he would walk down the middle of the street, his eyes were always searching. He was looking for trouble and when he found it he rushed in. His trademark entry to a saloon was to slam the saloon doors open all the way to the wall, both to let it be known he was there and make certain no one was hiding behind them. Then he announced his presence and, in most cases, Wild Bill coming through the door was all that was necessary."

Trouble came to Hays City in all kinds of ways, and Hickok always responded. As one young mother wrote in a letter, she had entrusted her baby to a friend for a few moments so she could get her chores done, but somehow this man's attention wandered, and when she looked out from the shop, she was stunned to see her child crawling in the dusty street as horses and wagons whizzed by. Almost simultaneously she saw Hickok race into the street and rescue the baby—and, after making sure the child was safe, pummel the man responsible.

Hickok was not a man to draw his guns easily, but when it became necessary he was the fastest draw around. In the summer of 1869, a drunken cowboy named Bill Mulvey came bursting out of Tommy Drum's Saloon and began shooting out lamps and windows. Hickok tried to calm him down peacefully, but Mulvey somehow got the drop on him. Thinking quickly, Hickok looked over Mulvey's shoulder and yelled, "Don't shoot him in the back, he's drunk!" Mulvey hesitated—just long enough for Wild Bill to draw his gun and drill the cowboy in his chest.

Only weeks later, a drunken teamster named Sam Strawhun and about eighteen of his buddies began shooting up John Bittles Beer Saloon. Strawhun had been chased out of town several weeks earlier after attacking a member of the town's Vigilance Committee, a group

Martha Cannary, the fabled Calamity Jane, circa 1895

of citizens trying to bring order to Hays City. He'd come back with vengeance on his mind and was heard to promise, "I shall kill someone tonight, just for luck." Hickok managed to get Strawhun and his men out into the street, then collected their beer mugs, which he brought back inside. Strawhun followed, looking for a fight; he threatened to tear up the place. "Do it," Hickok was said to warn, "and they will carry you out."

Strawhun went for his gun. Hickok was faster, drawing his Colts and putting two bullets into Strawhun's head before he could pull the trigger. At the inquest, a jury determined that Hickok had been trying to restore peace and that his actions were justifiable. Although the local newspaper wrote, "Hays City under the guardian care of Wild Bill is quiet and doing well," two killings in only a few months stirred the town, and in the next election Hickok was defeated by his own deputy, Peter Lanihan. Some questions about misconduct and irregularities were raised during the election.

After that, Wild Bill drifted in and out of Hays City, sometimes working with Lanihan to enforce the law. From all reports, Hickok enjoyed all the delights of the place and could often be found sitting back against the wall at a poker table in one of its many saloons. He was also known to enjoy the company of the dance-hall girls, although stories that he dallied there with Martha Jane Cannary, who gained her own fame as the sharpshooting Calamity Jane, probably aren't true. The two legends crossed paths in Hays City, but there is no evidence they ever were involved romantically.

Hickok's stay in Hays City ended abruptly in July 1870, when he was confronted by Jeremiah Lonergan and John Kyle, two privates from Custer's Seventh Cavalry. Animosity between Hickok and the troopers from Fort Hays had been building for a long time. Some of the veterans still resented the fact that Hickok had been paid as much as five dollars a day as a scout during the war while they were doing tougher duty and earning substantially less. More recently, it seemed as if every time they rode into town to blow off some steam, Hickok was waiting there to restrain them. With Lonergan, though, it was personal. His military career had been marked by both desertions and courage, and at some point he'd lost a tussle to Hickok. Lonergan and Kyle reportedly had been drinking the night they decided it was high time to deal with Wild Bill. Witnesses say Hickok was leaning against Tommy Drum's bar, quite probably having enjoyed several whiskeys himself. The saloon was filled with other troops from Custer's command when the two soldiers came in. Lonergan apparently came up behind him and, without one word of warning, grabbed hold of his arms and slammed him down to the floor. The two men wrestled, and when the fight turned in Hickok's favor, Kyle pulled his .44 Remington pistol, put the barrel into Hickok's ear, and squeezed the trigger.

Longhorn cattle drive from Texas to Abilene, Kansas

The gun misfired.

Before Kyle could load a dry charge, Hickok managed to get one hand free, pulled out his Colt, and fired it, his first shot hitting Kyle in the wrist. Kyle's gun clattered to the floor. Hickok fired again, this time striking Kyle in the stomach. As Kyle fell, mortally wounded, Wild Bill got off another shot, his bullet smashing into Lonergan's knee; Lonergan screamed and rolled off Hickok. Wild Bill knew he had only seconds before other cavalrymen in the area heard about the fight and came to settle the score, so he scrambled to his feet and dived through the saloon's glass window. He went back to his rented room to retrieve his Winchester rifle and at least one hundred rounds of ammunition. If a fight was coming, he was going to be ready for it. He walked up to Boot Hill, the cemetery and the highest point in the town, and took his position, waiting for them to come.

Fate had smiled on Wild Bill Hickok. This was the closest he had come to being killed in his career, and his life had been saved only because the black powder cartridges used by Kyle's Remington were notorious for absorbing moisture, causing them to jam. Kyle was considerably less fortunate; he died in the post hospital the next day, joining the growing list of outlaws and troublemakers brought to final justice by Wild Bill Hickok. History records no legal hearings held about this matter, but clearly Wild Bill understood that Hays City was no longer a safe place for him.

Each of these tales was reported in the newspapers back east, where readers were riveted by the adventures of brave Americans taming the Wild West. The stories piled up as competing newspapers and the publishers of the popular dime novels fought for readers, and as a result Wild Bill Hickok became one of the best-known men in America. Some said he was even more famous than the president of the United States.

Hickok's celebrity brought him to the attention of the town elders in Abilene, Kansas, known to be the rowdiest cow town in the West. Abilene had suddenly and unexpectedly found itself in need of a new marshal when Tom "Bear River" Smith was shot and nearly decapitated with an ax during a dispute with a local cattle rancher. For Hickok, Hays City was fine preparation for Abilene.

Abilene was the railhead at the end of the Chisholm Trail. Cowboys drove their herds all the way up from San Antonio, and from there the cattle were shipped back east. But it was a difficult place to pursue a civilized life. The citizens lived in fear each time a large herd arrived. The Texas cowboys, after months on the trail and with a payoff in their pockets, intended to have fun—and there were plenty of disreputable men and fancy women anxious to help them do it. Neither side was about to let the honest citizens stop them. So in April 1871, Abilene mayor Joseph G. McCoy offered Hickok a badge and $150 a month, plus 25 percent of the fines received from the people Hickok arrested.

Hickok began by offering some strong advice to potential troublemakers: "Leave town on the eastbound train, the westbound train, or go North in the morning"—"North" meaning Boot Hill, and no one doubted his words. Hickok and his three deputies began cleaning up the town by closing down the houses of ill repute and warning the saloon keepers against employing card sharks and con men. He stood up to the bullies and the drunkards and enforced ordinances against carrying guns in town. He employed all the legal powers given to him, and if at times he found it necessary to exceed those boundaries, nobody much objected—and it didn't seem that anyone defied him twice. Mayor McCoy once said, "He was the squarest [most honest] man I ever saw."

As always, Hickok backed down from no man. Among the gunslingers who came to town was the outlaw John Wesley Hardin. While working along the Chisholm Trail, he supposedly killed seven men, and then between one and three more in Abilene, before Hickok pinned on the badge. Hickok finally confronted the eighteen-year-old Hardin—although at that time the marshal had no knowledge that he was a wanted man—and ordered him to hand over his guns for the duration of his stay in town. Many years later, Hardin bragged in his autobiography that he'd offered them to Hickok butt-end first and then, as the marshal moved to take them, employed the "road agents spin," in which he twirled the guns in his own hands, ready to fire them. That statement is tough to believe, as that's an old trick and Hickok certainly would have known about it, and Hardin never made the claim until long after Hickok's death. The more likely story is that he simply handed them over.

At some point much later, while trying to get some shut-eye in his apartment at the American House Hotel, Hardin became irate because his roommate's loud snoring was making that impossible—so he fired several shots through the wall into the next room to get the man's attention. Unfortunately, one of those bullets hit the man in the head, killing him instantly. When Hickok responded to reports of gunfire in town, Hardin climbed out a window and hid in a haystack, later writing, "I believed that if Wild Bill found me in a defenseless condition he would take no explanation, but would kill me to add to his reputation." Instead of standing up to the marshal, Hardin stole a horse and hightailed it out of town.

Hickok also found time to do some courting. Only a few months after he moved to Abilene, "the Hippo-Olympiad and Mammoth Circus," starring the beautiful Agnes Thatcher Lake, came to town, and Hickok took up with the leading lady. Agnes Lake was a well-known dancer, tightrope walker, lion tamer, and horsewoman, who had toured Europe and even spoke several languages. Wild Bill was smitten but was convinced that she would eventually return to the East Coast.

Until that time, another gal, Jessie Hazell, the proprietor of a popular brothel, had held his attention. But the "Veritable Vixen," as the successful businesswoman was known in Abilene, instead had returned the affection of another suitor, Phil Coe. Coe was a gambler who co-owned the Bull's Head Tavern with gunfighter Ben Thompson. Even before their romantic competition, Hickok and Coe had built a strong dislike for each other. Not only had Hickok's rules been bad for Coe's business, but the marshal had embarrassed Coe by personally taking a paintbrush and covering the Bull's Head's finest advertisement: a painting of a bull with a large erect penis that adorned the side of the building. In response, Coe reportedly promised that he was going to kill Hickok "before the frost," claiming that he was such a sure shot that he could "kill a crow on the wing."

The famous story goes that when Hickok heard that, he replied, "Did the crow have a pistol? Was he shooting back? I will be."

This feud finally erupted into gunplay on the cool night of October 5. It is generally agreed that Coe, who might have been drunk, announced his intentions by firing several shots into the air, in violation of the law. Hearing the shots, Hickok told his close friend and deputy, Mike Williams, to stay put while he investigated. Wild Bill found Coe and a large number of his supporters waiting for him in front of the Alamo Saloon. Coe told the marshal he'd fired at a stray dog. Hickok responded by ordering Coe and his men to hand over their guns and get out of town.

This was the moment Coe had been waiting for. Hickok was alone on a dark street, completely surrounded by men who hated him and his laws. Coe fired twice; both shots missed. Hickok returned the fire and he did not miss. Both shots hit Coe in the stomach.

Suddenly, from the corner of his eye, Wild Bill saw another man with a revolver charging at him out of the shadows. He whirled and fired twice more. The man went down in the dirt. It was probably only seconds later that Hickok realized that he'd killed his deputy, Mike Williams, who had heard the four shots and come running to stand with him.

Hickok turned on the mob, reportedly warning, "Do any of you fellows want the rest of these bullets?" They saw the anguish and the anger on his face and drifted away. Williams's body was carried into the Alamo and laid on a billiard table. It was said that Hickok wept.

After that night, he was a changed man. He'd spent his life killing men who had deserved it, but this was different. He had reacted too quickly and his friend had paid the ultimate price. There were so many things Wild Bill Hickok was good at, but finding a way to forgive himself was not among them. His anger had been unleashed; it seemed like he was out of control. Within months the town had turned on him; a newspaper editorial declared that "gallows and penitentiary are the places to tame such blood thirsty wretches as 'Wild Bill.'" In December, Abilene relieved him of his duties, and Wild Bill Hickok rode out of town.

His prospects were limited. Because of his work, and that of others like him, the West had become considerably less wild. He'd worked his way out of a job. He returned to Springfield and set out to earn his keep gambling. Historians report that he drank too much and won too little. It was there that Buffalo Bill found him.

The one thing Hickok had left was his reputation. People would pay to see him—pay a lot. He had dipped his toe into show business earlier, partnering with Colonel Sidney Barnett of Niagara Falls, New York, to produce a show called *The Daring Buffalo Chase of the Plains*, but the buffalo did not like being roped and the show had failed. Meanwhile, the showbiz bug had bitten Buffalo Bill Cody, who was producing *Scouts of the Plains; or, On the Trail*, a

Legends (*from left*) Wild Bill Hickok, Texas Jack Omohundro, and Buffalo Bill Cody in an 1874 promotional photo for Cody's show *Scouts of the Plains*

Hickok spent one winter performing in Cody's
show, and when he went back out west, Cody
and Texas Jack Omohundro each gave him five
hundred dollars and a pistol, urging him to
"make good use of it among the Reds."

precursor to his famous *Wild West Show*. He offered Hickok a fair salary to star in the show.
Hickok had little choice but to accept the offer.

Hickok apparently was terrible onstage. Worse, he knew it and was said to spend much
of his time between performances presiding over a card game and a stream of liquor bottles.
Legend has it that while the show was playing in New York City he walked into a poolroom
to find a fair game. The players didn't recognize him and began making fun of his long hair
and western clothes. There was no one left standing when he walked out the door. Later he
explained, "I got lost among the hostiles."

Few doubt that Hickok could have spent the rest of his days trading on his fame, earning
a living simply by showing up and telling his stories to awed crowds in the concert saloons
and variety halls of the new entertainment called vaudeville. But that wasn't right for him; he
never quite embraced or fully accepted his celebrity. Perhaps that was due to his personality,
which always chose action over words, or to his knowledge that so many of the tales written
about him had been exaggerated or simply made up. He had accomplished a great deal, but
no one could have done all the things with which he was credited.

Finally he could take it no more and left Cody's show, going back out west where he
belonged, eventually settling in Cheyenne, Wyoming, in 1876. His reasons for landing in
Cheyenne aren't known, but one may have been that Agnes Lake was staying there with

friends. It was the first time they'd seen each other since Abilene, though they had continued to correspond through the years. They took up quickly, though, and were married within months. The local newspaper noted, "Wild Bill of western fame has conquered numerous Indians, outlaws, bears and buffalos, but a charming widow has stolen the magic wand . . . he has shuffled off the coil of bachelorhood."

Hickok still needed to figure out how to earn a living. His once-legendary eyesight appeared to be diminished and his bankroll was thin. Two years earlier, an expedition led by General Custer had discovered gold in the Dakotas, setting off a gold rush. Shortly after his marriage, Hickok gathered a group of men and set out for the Black Hills. Although people generally believe that he was going there to prospect, there also is the possibility that he was hoping to be hired on as marshal of the boomtown of Deadwood, giving him a chance to relive the great days of his life and to tame one last town.

Deadwood was no different than all the other towns that sprang up to support gold strikes. Money came hard, and the law was whatever the toughest men in town decided it was. Hickok mined during the day and played cards at night, trying to win enough of a stake to bring Agnes out there. He wrote to his new wife often, promising her, "We will have a home yet, then we will be so happy." But there were also signs that he sensed real danger around him, and in his last letter to her he promised, "Agnes darling, if such should be we never meet again, while firing my last shot, I will gently breathe the name of my wife, Agnes, and with wishes even for my enemies I will make the plunge and try to swim to the other shore."

Some historians believe Hickok was resigned to his fate and had even predicted it, supposedly telling a friend, "I have a hunch that I am in my last camp and will never leave this gulch alive . . . something tells me my time is up. But where it is coming from I do not know."

On August 2, 1876, Hickok strolled into Nutter and Mann's Saloon, looking for a game of poker. Historians have speculated that he went to the saloon directly from a local opium den. Three men he knew were seated around a table, the only empty chair facing a wall. Hickok never sat with his back to a door; he wanted to see trouble when it walked in. Sitting in the available seat made it impossible for him to watch the rear entrance. He twice asked the other players to change seats with him, but both requests were refused. That these men felt comfortable turning down the great Hickok is an indication of how far his stock had fallen. Only a few years earlier, almost everyone would gladly have given up his seat for an opportunity to play cards with the famous Wild Bill Hickok. Reluctantly Hickok sat down in that chair and put his chips on the table.

The night before, he had played poker with a former buffalo hunter and gambler, Jack

McCall, known as Crooked Nose Jack; Hickok had cleaned him out, then offered him some money for breakfast. Some saw that as an insult. But McCall was back the next day, standing at the bar when Hickok walked into Nutter and Mann's. If they acknowledged each other at all, no one ever spoke of it. Wild Bill's game of five-card draw had been in progress for some time when McCall got up from his bar stool and walked past Hickok toward the back door—then stopped suddenly about three feet away from him and turned. Hickok had been winning and had just been dealt a pleasing hand—black aces and black eights. He had discarded his fifth card and was waiting for his next card—legend claims it was the jack of diamonds—when McCall suddenly pulled out his double-action Colt .45 six-shooter, shouted, "Damn you! Take that!" and fired one shot into the back of Hickok's head at point-blank range. The bullet tore through his skull, emerging from his cheek and striking another player in the wrist. Wild Bill Hickok died instantly.

McCall reportedly pulled the trigger several more times, but his gun failed to fire. It was later determined that all six chambers were loaded, but only one bullet fired—the shot that killed Hickok. McCall raced outside and jumped on his horse, but his cinch was loose and the saddle slipped. He ran into a butcher's shop, where he was quickly captured by the sheriff.

A satisfactory explanation for the assassination has never been found. McCall might have been avenging the "insult" from the previous night. But during his trial, he claimed that Hickok had killed his brother and he was avenging that shooting, although there is no evidence that he even had a brother. There were rumors that he had been paid to assassinate Hickok, and there is always the possibility that he simply wanted to kill the famous Wild Bill.

A trial was held in Deadwood the next day, and McCall, claiming he was entitled to avenge his brother's death, was acquitted. The local newspaper derided the verdict, suggesting, "Should it ever be our misfortune to kill a man . . . we would simply ask that our trial may take place in some of the mining camps of these hills."

McCall left town. When he reached Yankton, capital of the Dakota Territory, he was arrested once again. His acquittal in the first trial was set aside because Deadwood was not yet a legally recognized town. McCall was tried a second time—and during this trial it was suggested that he had been hired to commit the killing by gamblers who feared that Hickok, "a champion of law and order," was about to be appointed town marshal. This time the jury convicted McCall, and he was sentenced to death. He was hanged on March 1, 1877.

The cards Wild Bill Hickok were holding when he was shot, black aces and eights, have been forever immortalized in poker lore as the famed "dead man's hand."

Since Hickok's death almost one hundred fifty years ago, a question has remained

ASSASSINATION OF WILD BILL (J. B. HICKOK) BY JACK McCALL, AT DEADWOOD CITY, D. T.

During the assassin Jack McCall's first trial, Hickok was described as a "shootist," who "was quick in using the pistol and never missed his man, and had killed quite a number of persons in different parts of the country."

unanswered: Why did he agree to take a seat with his back to a door? No one will ever know for sure, but since that fateful day, many have wondered if Hickok was simply tired of life. In many ways, he had become a captive of his fame: Although he no longer was capable of living up to it, the great expectations remained. Wild Bill might well have moved to Deadwood, a wild place where reputations didn't hold much water and where what mattered was only what happened yesterday, to escape his own legend. But on that fateful August day in 1876, it finally caught up with him.

At his death, he was credited with thirty-six righteous shootings. And his friend Captain Jack Crawford, who had scouted the trails of the Old West with him, probably described him best when he recalled, "He was loyal in his friendship, generous to a fault, and invariably espoused the cause of the weaker against the stronger one in a quarrel."

UP AND DOWN TOWNS

As tens of thousands of settlers raced to find their fortunes in the West, countless boomtowns suddenly burst out of the sagebrush. Many of these towns, which usually were dirty, poorly built, and often lawless, existed for only a brief time, until the mines gave out, the cattle drives ended, or the railroad crews set down somewhere else; then they quickly became ghost towns. But whether a town struggled on or ceased to exist, the events that took place there—and their subsequent appearance in numerous movies and TV shows—made the names Dodge City, Deadwood, and Tombstone legendary.

Dodge City, Kansas, came into existence in 1871, when a rancher settled there to run his operation. Originally named Buffalo City, until someone discovered there already was a place by that name, it was perfectly located just a whisker west of Fort Dodge and near the Santa Fe Trail and Arkansas River. It boomed a year later, with the coming of the Santa Fe railroad and the opening of the first saloon. The railhead allowed cowboys to ship buffalo hides and, within a few years, longhorn cattle driven up on the Chisholm Trail from Texas to points north and east. Then they would stay awhile to brush off the trail dust and spend their earnings. "The streets of Dodge were lined with wagons," wrote one city elder. "I have been to several mining camps where rich strikes had been made, but I never saw any town to equal Dodge." "The Queen of the Cow Towns," as it was called, offered a wide choice of saloons—including the famous Long

Branch—gambling dens, brothels, and even, for a brief period, a bullring. The hardest men in the West—cowboys off the trail, buffalo hunters, bull whackers, and muleteers—would ride in rich, ready for a good time, and ride out a few days later poor but happy. For a time, Dodge really was as wild as its legend. It welcomed more gunslingers than any other city, and

Dodge City's Long Branch Saloon, which was built in 1874 and burned down in 1885, probably is best remembered as Miss Kitty's place, where Marshal Matt Dillon would "set a spell" in the TV series *Gunsmoke*. The saloon was the center of entertainment in western towns. In addition to serving "firewater," it might feature professional gamblers playing faro, Brag, three-card monte, poker, and dice games, or dancing, billiards, or even bowling. Many of them never closed, and a few didn't even have a front door.

several of the great lawmen tried to calm it down, among them Wyatt Earp, Bat Masterson, and Bill Tilghman. But it was actually the Kansas state legislature that caused Dodge's demise, when it extended an existing cattle quarantine across the state in 1886 and shut down the end of the trail. With that, the fast money disappeared, and most of the population realized it was time to "get out of Dodge."

Deadwood, South Dakota, sprang up almost overnight after gold was discovered, first by General Custer in the Black Hills, then quickly by a miner in Deadwood Gulch in 1875. Because by treaty this was Indian land, the army tried to keep out the prospectors, so it took tough men to settle it. Fortunes were made, mostly by the saloon keepers, gamblers, opium dealers, and ladies of the evening, who had followed the gold diggers. Its reputation as a lawless town was sealed when Wild Bill Hickok was shot in the back of the head there in 1876, and for a while, Deadwood averaged one murder per day. Hickok and Calamity Jane had ridden in together as guards escorting a wagon train bringing prostitutes and gamblers from Cheyenne, and both of them were buried on Deadwood's Boot Hill. Only three years later, in 1879, a massive fire destroyed almost three hundred buildings; by that time, new gold claims were pretty much played out, people were ready to move on to the next boomtown, and Deadwood settled down.

Miners pulled the modern-day equivalent of almost $1.5 billion in silver from the mines near Tombstone, Arizona, between 1877 and 1890, and within a few years, its population exploded, from about one hundred

After being founded in 1879 when silver was discovered nearby, in less than seven years, the town of Tombstone grew from one hundred people to fourteen thousand. An 1886 fire destroyed the expensive pumping plant, and the population dwindled to a few hundred, turning it into a ghost town. It exists today as a tourist destination, the once-wild city where the legendary gunfight at the O.K. Corral took place.

to fourteen thousand. It got its name because its founder, Ed Schieffelin, had been warned that the Apaches didn't cotton much to prospectors and that the only thing he'd find in the hills there was his own tombstone. For several years, there were few more dangerous towns on the frontier; "the town too tough to die," as it was known, was close enough to the Mexican border for rustlers to use as their base of operations. Eventually there were more saloons, gambling houses, and brothels there than in any town in the

Southwest. When the Cowboys gang met the Earp brothers at the O.K. Corral, Tombstone's place in history, and in the movies, was ensured.

Numerous other violent boomtowns eventually became ghost towns. Canyon Diablo, Arizona, for example, was created when railroad workers had to wait for a bridge to be built, and within months fourteen saloons and ten gambling houses faced one another on Hell Street. The first sheriff was dead five hours after he pinned on his badge, and none of the five men who followed lived more than a month. When the bridge was finally completed ten years later, most people got on the train and left.

Gold was discovered in Bodie, California, in the Sierra Nevada in 1859, and before the vein dried up a decade later, the population had grown to ten thousand people. There is a long list of towns that boomed briefly, from Fort Griffin, Texas, to Leadville, Colorado (originally known as Slabville). However, throughout the country, it was believed that "the roughest, toughest town west of Chicago" was Palisades, Nevada, which had more than a thousand showdowns, bank robberies, and Indian raids in about three years in the mid-1870s. Although no one is quite sure how it began, each day as the railroad arrived, townspeople would stage a fake showdown or holdup and getaway for the benefit of the "dudes" from back east. Apparently this was done for entertainment rather than profit, as no money changed hands. The terrified passengers, who were never let in on the joke, would tell stories of their encounters with outlaws to newspapers back home. The stories were printed or otherwise passed along, allowing Palisades to gain its notorious reputation.

BASS REEVES

★ The Real Lone Ranger ★

On Monday night, January 30, 1933, racing to the unmistakable beats of Rossini's *William Tell* Overture, a new hero rode into American cultural history.

American families struggling through the Great Depression gathered around the radio every night for a few hours of escape and entertainment. On that winter's night, they were introduced to a remarkable character who would take Americans with him on his adventures into the next century. In a mellifluous voice resonating with awe, the announcer introduced the Superman of the Old West:

> A fiery horse, with a speed of light—a cloud of dust, a hearty laugh, The Lone Ranger is perhaps the most attractive figure ever to come out of the West. Through his daring, his riding, and his shooting, this mystery rider won the respect of the entire Golden Coast—the West of the old days, where every man carried his heart on his sleeve and only the fittest remained to make history. Many are the stories that are told by the lights of the Western campfire concerning this romantic figure. Some thought he was on the side of the outlaw, but many knew that he was a lone rider, dealing out justice to the law abiding citizenry. Though the Lone Ranger was known in seven states, he earned his greatest reputation in Texas. None knew where he came from and none knew where he went.

And then, as thunder boomed in the background, the story began: "Old Jeb Langworth lived alone in his small shack just outside the wide open community of Red Rock. One evening as he was watching the coffee boil and the bacon sizzle in the pan, and thinking of how snug his cabin was, with the storm raging outside, there came a knock on the door . . ."

A masked man riding the range with his trusty sidekick, the Indian brave Tonto, protecting the weak, righting wrongs, and dispensing Old West justice with his blazing guns, the Lone Ranger was the perfect hero.

No one knew his real name or where he came from, only that he left his calling card, a silver bullet, when he uttered his famous parting words, "Hi-Yo, Silver—away!" then disappeared into the wilderness until the next episode. The Lone Ranger eventually became one of the most iconic figures in American media, a star of radio, television, movies, novels, and comic books.

But what has been almost completely forgotten is that the character of the Lone Ranger was likely based on the life of a real person, whose true story is even more incredible than the fictitious adventures of the masked man.

Bass Reeves was a black American, born into slavery in Crawford County, Arkansas, in 1838, but came of age in Grayson, Texas. He was the property of William S. Reeves, but apparently early in his life was given to Reeves's son George. While growing up, Bass Reeves never learned to read or write, but his mother taught him the Bible, and he was known to recite verses from memory. He was such a good marksman that his master entered him in shooting contests. When George Reeves eventually became the county sheriff and tax collector, he undoubtedly was pleased to have his sharpshooting servant at his side. Unfortunately, the history of black men in America around that time is difficult to reconstruct. Reeves would later claim to have fought in the Civil War battles of Chickamauga and Missionary Ridge under Colonel George Reeves and earned his freedom on the battlefield, but another story claims that he attacked his master when they argued over a card game and knocked him out, a crime punishable by death in Texas, so he was forced to flee into Indian Territory. Whatever the truth about his early years, Bass was twenty-two years old in 1863 when Abraham Lincoln issued the Emancipation Proclamation and he became a freeman.

He eventually settled in the Indian Territory, which included present-day Oklahoma, and lived there peacefully among the tribes, the white squatters, and the white criminals escaping justice. He learned to speak the languages of "the five civilized tribes" (the Choctaws, Chickasaws, Seminoles, Creeks, and Cherokees) and gained a reputation as a skilled tracker, horseman, and deadeye shot—both right- and left-handed, and with both pistols and long guns. Bass Reeves was a big man, described as being six feet two and a muscular two hundred pounds, with a big, bushy mustache and piercing eyes that could a freeze a man before he made a foolhardy move. At first, as a freeman, he made his living working on farms, but his knowledge of the Territory "like a cook knows her kitchen," as he once put it, enabled him to become a trusted guide and interpreter for the US marshals riding that range.

At the time, it was well known that "There is no God west of Fort Smith." Indian Territory was one of the most dangerous places in the world. The murder rate rivaled that of the worst cities in the country; people were killed over anything from a horse to a coarse

The Lone Ranger became one of America's most popular characters. In addition to 2,956 radio shows, he was the protagonist of motion pictures and animated features, books, a syndicated comic strip and comic books, 221 half-hour television episodes, and even a video game.

word. The outlaw Dick Glass once killed a man in a dispute over an ear of corn. It was once estimated that out of the twenty-two thousand white men living in the Territory, seventeen thousand were criminals on the lam. While tribal courts had jurisdiction over the Indians, white criminals had to be taken to Fort Smith, Arkansas, or Paris, Texas, for trial. The only law enforcement was the few US deputy marshals working out of Fort Smith. There often wasn't a lawman to be found within two hundred miles, leaving plenty of room for vigilante justice.

It was a good place for a freeman, because it might have been the most racially and ethnically integrated area in the United States. Few people had the time or the inclination for racism. Everybody pretty much lived together and suffered equally. Even the outlaw gangs were integrated. Dick Glass, for example, who ran one of the most vicious gangs in the

Territory, was himself half-black and half–Creek Indian, and his gang consisted of five black men, four Indians, and two white men.

Bass Reeves was living on his own farm in Van Buren, Arkansas, with his wife, Jinnie, their three children, his mother, and his sister in 1875, when President Ulysses S. Grant appointed Judge Isaac Parker to bring law and order to the Western District of Arkansas. This included all of western Arkansas and the Indian Territory, seventy-four thousand lawless square miles. It was considered a safe place for every type of criminal on the prairie to hide out: the murderers, rapists, cattle robbers, and thieves; the bootleggers selling to the Indians; and the con men. Parker, who was to gain fame as "the Hanging Judge," was given permission to hire two hundred new deputies. Having heard that Reeves could speak the Indian languages and had often assisted marshals, he offered him a permanent position as a US deputy marshal. Legend has it that when Reeves was asked by a family member why he was willing to risk his life enforcing "white man's law," he replied, "Maybe the law ain't perfect, but it's the only one we got, and without it we got nuthin'."

The United States Marshals Service was founded in 1789, created in the Judiciary Act by the First Congress. It was established to be the law-enforcement arm of the federal judicial system. US marshals, and the deputies they legally appointed to assist them, were empowered to serve the subpoenas, summonses, writs, warrants, and other legal documents issued by the

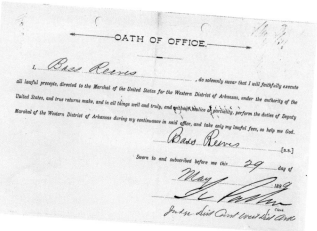

Judge Issac Parker appointed Bass Reeves a deputy US marshal in 1879. In the Hanging Judge's twenty-one years on the bench, he tried 13,490 cases—and saw seventy-nine people hanged.

federal courts, make all arrests, and handle prisoners anywhere in the country. Unlike local law enforcement, their jurisdiction was not limited by borders. They were paid for the work they did, meaning they earned a fee for each wanted man they brought to justice. But it was incredibly dangerous work. More than 130 deputies were killed in the Territory before Oklahoma became a state in 1907.

Although Reeves was not the first black US deputy marshal, he quickly became the best known, and several of his characteristics would later come to be associated with the Lone Ranger. In those days, when a deputy went out on the trail after outlaws, he would take a wagon (in which to bring back the fugitives he caught), a cook, and a posse man (a deputy who would work with him). Reeves's posse man was often an Indian from the tribal Lighthorse, which is what the five tribes called their mounted police force. Although Reeves worked with many different Indian officers, apparently there was one man that he chose to ride with whenever possible. His name is lost to history, but he in all probability served as the model for the Lone Ranger's faithful sidekick, Tonto. Also, later in Reeves's fabled career, he was known for giving a silver dollar to those people who helped him, which obviously is close to the concept of the Lone Ranger leaving a silver bullet.

Among the many virtues the Lone Ranger shared with Reeves was a great sense of fair play and a desire to bring 'em back alive. Almost immediately after accepting the job, Reeves's respect for the law became clear. According to legend, one afternoon out on the trail he spotted a group of men holding a lynching party and rode over to them. Lost to history is whether the prisoner was a horse thief or a cattle thief, but apparently he'd been caught dead-to-rights and the penalty for that crime was well known. The suspect was sitting on a horse, his hands tied behind his back, a noose around his neck. When Reeves was told what had happened, he showed the group his badge and explained that in this part of the world, he was the law and he intended to take this man back to Fort Smith. Sitting tall on his own horse, showing his two pistols and complete confidence, he presented a figure nobody seemed anxious to challenge. He cut the noose and rode away with the suspect. As far as he was concerned, that man's fate needed to be in the hands of Judge Parker, not a mob out on the prairie. Nobody dared try to stop him.

He also believed in bringing prisoners back alive, although he didn't hesitate to shoot when it became necessary. During a tense confrontation with a horse thief named John Cudgo, he laid out his philosophy. In 1890, Reeves went to Cudgo's spread on the Seminole Nation to arrest him for larceny. The two men had known each other for almost a decade. As Reeves approached Cudgo's house, the outlaw suddenly popped out from beneath his front

Bass Reeves (*far left*) had served as a deputy marshal for twenty-eight years when this "family photo" was taken in 1907—the year Oklahoma entered the Union and instituted the Jim Crow laws that forced him to end his federal law-enforcement career.

porch, holding his Winchester. Reeves ordered him to surrender and he refused, warning that no marshal was taking him back to Fort Smith—especially not Reeves. He then asked Reeves to send his posse men away so that the two of them might talk. When the men were gone, Cudgo cocked his rifle and said he wanted to be allowed to die in the house he'd built, trying to provoke Reeves into shooting him. Reeves shook his head and told him, "Government law didn't send me out here to kill people, but to arrest them." Hours later, Cudgo surrendered without a single shot being fired.

As for his integrity, few tasks could possibly be more difficult for a lawman than having to arrest his own son, and that was the situation Reeves faced in 1902 when his son Bennie was accused of fatally shooting his wife when he caught her cheating on him. After the murder, Bennie Reeves had fled into the Territory. When the district marshal initially gave the warrant to another deputy, Reeves supposedly insisted that he be the man to serve it, explaining, "There's no sense in nobody else getting hurt over my son. I'll bring him in." He tracked Bennie to a small town. Nobody knows what took place between the two of them, but Reeves brought his son to justice. Bennie Reeves was convicted of the crime and sentenced to life imprisonment at Fort Leavenworth, Kansas, but was released for good behavior after ten years.

Reeves also arrested his own minister for selling whiskey. Reeves himself served as a deacon of his church in Van Buren, Arkansas, and it was said that some nights while on the trail he would chain captured fugitives to a log and preach the Gospel to them, asking them to confess their sins and repent.

Bass Reeves served as a US deputy marshal for thirty-three years. Although the precise number of men he tracked down and brought to justice isn't known, he is credited with more than three thousand arrests. The number of men he shot or killed also isn't known, although newspapers reported that he had killed twenty men. Outlaws used to say that drawing on Bass Reeves was as good as committing suicide. Whatever the number, by the time he retired he had become a legend, and songs were being written about him. It was said that when the famous outlaw Belle Starr heard that Reeves had been given the warrant for her arrest, she actually walked into Fort Smith and surrendered.

Just like the Lone Ranger, Reeves would travel light and move as quickly as possible. Because he couldn't read the warrants, when getting ready to go out on the trail he would have someone read as many as thirty of them to him. He would memorize each one, including the crime and the description of the wanted man, and was said to have perfect recall. He usually traveled with a wagon driven by his cook, one posse man, and a long chain. He often traveled with two horses; if he had to work in disguise he didn't want his good riding horse attracting attention. His posse would stay on the trail for several weeks, sometimes months, and the wanted men he captured would be chained to the rear axle of the wagon, usually in pairs, until he'd caught his fill and decided to bring them all back to Judge Parker's court. Other deputies were bringing in five or six men at a time; on one trip Reeves returned with sixteen

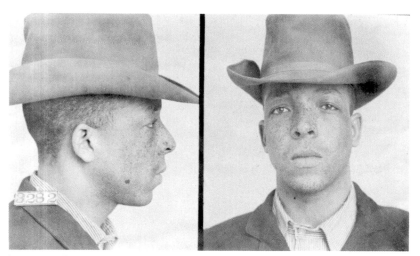

In 1902, Reeves went into the Indian Territory and captured his son, Bennie, who had shot his wife. Ben Reeves served ten years before being released for good behavior.

men and collected seven hundred dollars in fines; he always claimed that the largest number he brought in at one time was nineteen horse thieves, for which he was paid nine hundred dollars. On occasion he was also known to pack his bedroll and go out into the wilderness by himself, an image of the lone deputy that easily can be seen as inspiration for the Lone Ranger.

Among his most famous arrests was the nefarious Seminole To-Sa-Lo-Nah, also known as Greenleaf, who was wanted for the brutal murders of at least seven people, as well as for selling whiskey to the tribes. Four of his victims were Indians who had worked with deputies as posse men to try to capture him—he had shot the last one, in fact, twenty-four times. That made it very difficult to find an Indian tracker who would even speak his name. Greenleaf had successfully eluded capture for eighteen years when Reeves got the warrant for his arrest. Reeves used his own network of informants, men who trusted him to protect them, and one of them got word to him that Greenleaf had recently brought a wagonload of whiskey into the area. In the middle of the night, Reeves and his posse man crawled close enough to the house in which Greenleaf was staying to hear him whooping and shouting. When the house finally grew quiet, Reeves led his posse in an assault, jumping over a fence and getting the drop on the killer before he could go for his gun. After Reeves had put the cuffs on Greenleaf, a steady stream of people came to look at the vicious killer long believed to be uncatchable, now in chains.

Perhaps the Lone Ranger's most instantly identifiable feature was the black mask he wore to disguise his true identity. Although Reeves didn't wear a mask, like the fictional character he did sometimes use disguises to help him draw close to dangerous criminals. He was known to impersonate preachers, cowboys, hobos, farmers—whatever seemed suitable for the situation. Once, for example, he was tracking two brothers who had a five-thousand-dollar bounty on their heads. No one had been able to get near them. Knowing that the two men had remained in contact with their mother, Reeves supposedly shot two holes through an old hat, put it on along with ragged clothes and shoes with broken heels, hid his pistol and handcuffs under his clothes—then walked twenty miles to the mother's home. He arrived there filthy, sweating, and thirsty and pleaded with her for water and a square meal, complaining that he was on the run from a posse. The woman invited him in and permitted him to stay the night, telling him that her two boys were also on the run and suggesting they might work together. After dark the two fugitives snuck into the house. While they were sleeping, Reeves snapped his cuffs on both of them. When he marched them out in the morning, their mother is said to have walked with them for the first several miles, yelling and cursing at Reeves every single step of the way.

In another case, he learned that two wanted men were traveling on a certain road. Cutting across the brush to get ahead of them, he ran his wagon into a ditch. When the two men rode by, they saw a lone black man struggling to get his wagon back on the trail. They offered to help him, and when they placed their hands on the wagon, he revealed his identity and took them into custody.

Perhaps his best-known deception led to the capture of the killer Jim Webb in 1883. Webb was foreman of the Washington and McLish Ranch on the Chickasaw Nation. A black minister, Reverend William Steward, owned a piece of adjoining land. When Steward set a controlled fire to burn some brush on his property, it got out of control and burned off feed grass on Bill Washington's spread. Washington sent his foreman to see Steward and set things right, but their conversation grew heated and Webb killed him. Reeves was given the warrant for his arrest.

Reeves and his posse man, Floyd Wilson, rode up to the ranch pretending to be cowboys looking for work. As they approached, they saw Webb and one of his ranch hands, a man named Frank Smith, sitting on the veranda with their pistols ready in their laps. Reeves explained that they had been riding for a spell and were hoping to get some breakfast and feed for their horses. Webb told them to take the horses over to the stable, but as they did he kept a wary eye on them. As the horses watered, Bass took his Winchester from his saddle and stood it up against a wall, hoping to calm any suspicions Webb might hold. Then Reeves and Wilson sat down for breakfast. There was a mirror in the bunkhouse, and in the reflection Reeves saw Webb and Smith having a serious discussion, seemingly about them. Reeves told his man that when he gave the sign, he would grab Webb, and Wilson needed to take down Smith.

After the meal, the deputy and his posse man sat down with Webb and Smith, supposedly to have a friendly chat about possible employment. Something happened during the conversation to convince Reeves that Webb was on to him. He reacted just like the Lone Ranger would have done on the radio or in the early years of television: He grabbed Webb by the throat and started squeezing. His posse man was too stunned to move, and Smith raised his pistol. Before he could take aim, Reeves, still holding Webb tightly by the throat, drew his own six-gun and fired. Smith reeled backward, mortally wounded.

Wilson slipped the irons on Webb's wrists and they got him out of there quickly. Webb was delivered to the court to be tried for the murder of Reverend Steward. Somewhat surprisingly, he was released on seventeen thousand dollars' bail, truly a small fortune, supposedly put up by Bill Washington. As soon as Webb was released, he took off. The bail was forfeited.

He wasn't heard from for more than two years, when Reeves suddenly got word that he'd returned to the ranch. Reeves had no intention of letting Webb get away a second time.

Reeves and posse man John Cantrell headed back into the Territory, where they learned that Webb had recently been seen at Bywater's General Store. When they got to the store, Reeves sent Cantrell ahead to scout out the situation. Webb was there, sitting by a window—and he spotted the two men as they rode up. He jumped out a side window and made for his horse. Reeves cut off his escape. Webb turned and started running for the brush. He had his pistol and Winchester with him. As Reeves closed in on him, Webb spun around and pegged several shots at him. At least one of those shots took a button off Reeves's coat; another supposedly knocked his hat off his head. Reeves reined in his horse and jumped off. Taking his own Winchester out of its scabbard, he aimed and fired twice. Historians put the distance between them anywhere between two hundred and five hundred yards. Both of Reeves's shots found their mark, ripping into Webb's chest; he fell in his tracks.

Reeves, Cantrell, and Jim Bywater approached Webb carefully. Playing possum was a well-known trick, and Reeves wasn't about to fall for it. But when they came closer they saw the blood flowing from Webb's wounds. He was still alive, a revolver in his hand, but his injuries were bad. Reeves didn't take any chances; holding his gun on Webb, he ordered him to throw away his weapon. Webb tossed it into the bushes, then asked Reeves to come close. Bywater later reported that with his dying breath, Webb said to Reeves, "You are a brave man. I want you to accept my revolver and holster as a present. Take it, for with it I have killed eleven men, four of them in Indian Territory. I expected you would be number twelve, but you were too good for me."

No one was too surprised that Reeves was able to put two slugs into Webb at more than two hundred yards. Hitting a running target at several hundred feet wasn't extraordinary for him. Reeves's training growing up as a slave had enabled him to become, just like the fictional Lone Ranger, a crack shot. Historians tell several amazing stories about his proficiency with guns. He wore two Colt revolvers butt-forward for a quick draw, and he carried a Winchester in his saddle. Historian Art Burton, the author of the Reeves biography *Black Gun, Silver Star*, once interviewed an elderly man who many years earlier had worked for the legendary deputy James Bud Ledbetter. Ledbetter was renowned as a crack shot himself, one time killing five men in a gunfight without being so much as scratched. This elderly man had been riding with Ledbetter when they tracked down a wanted man. He had holed himself up well, and Ledbetter's posse couldn't get close; they'd spent the afternoon throwing lead at him but hadn't come close to hitting anything. Finally Ledbetter got angry because all they were doing was wasting his ammunition inventory, so he sent a man back to Muskogee to get Bass Reeves. The sun was just starting to set when Reeves arrived. Whether the desperado knew that Reeves was there or just grew tired of being shot at, he suddenly took off across a field. The posse opened up on him, but he was at least a quarter mile away, out of range of their pistols. Finally Ledbetter yelled above the din, "Get 'im, Bass!"

Bass responded very calmly and cooly, promising, "I will break his neck." He put his Winchester to his shoulder, took aim, and fired a single shot—right through the outlaw's throat. Then he slipped his rifle back into its scabbard, got on his horse, and rode away.

The Lone Ranger was a fictional character; Reeves was not. But some of the stories told about his shooting skills made him appear larger than life. Supposedly, for example, a desperado was hiding behind the thick trunk of a large tree. It seemed impossible to dislodge him. Somehow, Reeves fired a shot that ricocheted between branches to bring down the outlaw. On another occasion he purportedly rode over a rise and saw six wolves pulling down a steer. Shooting from a moving horse, he killed all six wolves with only eight shots—it took eight shots because two of his first shots were gut shots, so he had to shoot those wolves a second time!

Perhaps because he had spent so much time living and working with Indians, Bass Reeves also was considered the best manhunter among the marshals. When he got on a man's trail, he wouldn't quit until he brought him in. At one point, Reeves was tracking an outlaw named Bob Dozier, a successful rancher who had turned to crime; he was a cattle thief and a bank robber; he held up stagecoaches and bushwhacked travelers going through the Territory; he was a con man and a fence; and it was rumored that he tortured people for information before he killed them. He had successfully eluded deputies—until Reeves picked up his scent.

Because Dozier was known to keep moving, Reeves knew it would be easier to pursue him alone or, at times, with just one posse man. Reeves chased him for months without laying eyes on him. But he wouldn't give up. When Dozier found out that the great Bass Reeves was on his trail, he sent word that if Reeves didn't stop he would be obliged to kill him. Apparently Reeves sent his own return message to the outlaw: To make that play, Dozier would have to stop running, and Reeves made it clear he would welcome that confrontation.

Reeves and his posse man pursued Dozier into the Cherokee Hills, eventually picking up fresh tracks. The outlaw was riding with one other man, and they had only a few hours' lead. A fierce lightning storm erupted, washing out the tracks, and Reeves decided to bed down. As Reeves and his posse man rode into a ravine, Dozier opened up on him. A shot whizzed right by his head. The two lawmen made for cover, successfully putting timber between themselves and the ambush. Reeves finally found a safe place behind a tree and didn't move. Several quiet minutes passed; then Reeves spotted a shadow moving between trees, trying to circle around on him. He waited. The next time that man moved, Reeves stepped out from behind the tree and fired twice, bringing down that shadow.

However, he had been forced to reveal himself, and the second outlaw opened up on him. Reeves stood upright—then fell facedown in the brush. He lay there motionless, his eyes wide open, his Colt cocked and ready. After a few minutes, the shooter stepped out from behind a tree. He waited, watching and listening. Finally he took a couple of wary steps toward the prone figure, probably assuming Reeves was dead and his posse man had fled, knowing he was no match for an experienced hand.

As the gunman came closer, Reeves was probably smiling. When Dozier was only a few yards away, Reeves suddenly raised his Colt and shouted at him to throw away his gun. Dozier dived for the good earth but he wasn't quick enough. Reeves put his first shot through the outlaw's neck. They had finally reached the end of the trail.

One man did get away from Reeves, though: the legendary Indian Ned Christie. His place in history remains unsettled: To some he was a vicious outlaw; to others he was a warrior fighting the railroads for the rights of Indians. At one point Reeves believed he had trapped Ned Christie in his impregnable cabin, so he burned it down. Christie wasn't there. Later it was reported that Christie had killed Reeves, causing the *Eufaula Indian Journal* to report in 1891, "Deputy Marshall [*sic*] Bass Reeves lacks lots of being dead as was reported recently from Muskogee to the Dallas News. He turned up Saturday from west with two wagons of prisoners going to Ft. Smith. He had twelve prisoners in all; Eight for whisky vending, three for larceny and one for murder." Christie eventually was trapped in his "mountain fort" by a sixteen-man posse and died there.

It might be that the Lone Ranger's greatest attribute was his courage. As every red-blooded American boy knew, no matter what the odds, the Lone Ranger sat tall in the saddle. The same was true of Reeves: Historians wrote that he had no fear of anything that walked the face of the earth. In the Territory, outlaws were known to post notes on trees in an area known as "the dead line," warning deputies that if they crossed that line they would be killed. Several of those notes were addressed specifically to Reeves; at his retirement, in fact, Reeves claimed to have made a nice collection of them.

It was said that Reeves never blinked, even when he was looking danger in the eye. Among the many stories admirers told to illustrate his bravery was of the day the murderous Brunter brothers got the drop on him. One of the three brothers had his pistol aimed right at Reeves's chest and ordered him off his horse. "What are you doing here?" he asked Reeves.

"Why, I've come to arrest you," Reeves replied. He then asked the date, explaining that by law he had to write down the date of the arrest on the warrant. The brothers apparently found that amusing, considering that they were holding him at gunpoint. "Here, look at this," Reeves continued, handing over the warrant to the outlaw holding the gun. As the man glanced at it, his two brothers moved closer to look at it over his shoulders—and while their attention was diverted, Reeves grabbed the barrel of the gun and pushed it away, holding on to it while the man wasted three shots. At the same time, he drew his own gun with his other hand, shot a second brother, slammed the third brother over the head with his pistol, then stuck the barrel in the first outlaw's stomach.

His career wasn't without controversy. In 1886, he was arrested for the murder of his trail cook, William Leech, and eventually tried by Judge Parker. Although Parker is remembered in history as the Hanging Judge, he was in fact respected for running a strict but fair courtroom. While it's probable that no deputy kept Parker's courtroom more crowded than Reeves, and the two men were said to be on friendly terms, this was a fair trial. In the courtroom of Judge

Judge Parker's ornate courtroom in Fort Smith, Arkansas, about 1890. When Reeves was tried for the shooting of his trail cook several years earlier, Judge Parker had presided in a courtroom located in a converted military barracks.

Isaac Parker, the law was respected. Reeves testified that his rifle had gone off accidentally while he was cleaning it, striking Leech in the neck. Initially the wound was not considered serious and Reeves immediately tried to get medical help, but eventually the cook took a turn for the worse and died. However, nine people testified against Reeves—every one of them a fugitive he had captured and was bringing to Fort Smith. They testified that there was bad blood between the two men, and that when the cook fed boiling oil to Reeves's dog, the deputy had lost his temper and shot him.

The case against Reeves pretty much fell apart when another witness testified that all those men actually had been chained in the prisoners' tent at the time of the shooting and couldn't have seen it happen. After deliberating for a full day, the jury found Reeves not guilty.

Although racism really wasn't an issue during most of Reeves's career, it ironically became important at the end of it. Judge Parker died in 1896, and two years later Reeves was transferred to Muskogee, in the Northern District of the federal court. He worked there until 1907, when Oklahoma was admitted to the Union and immediately instituted a series of harsh Jim Crow laws. Although these laws made Indians "honorary whites," they were specifically designed to keep the races apart. That made it almost impossible for a black man

Judge Isaac Parker, shortly before his death in 1896.

After Judge Parker's death, Reeves transferred to Muskogee, in the Indian Territory, where this photo of federal marshals and local police officers was taken in about 1900.

such as Reeves to enforce the law on white people. Rather than retiring, the sixty-seven-year-old Bass Reeves joined the Muskogee police department and actually walked a beat—with the help of a cane—for two more years, until a lifetime of adventure caught up with him. He died in 1910, and as institutionalized racism became part of American culture, he was mostly lost to history. In fact, it isn't even known where he is buried.

As this country has begun recovering that history, the fact and legend of Bass Reeves has emerged. Did he serve as the model for the Lone Ranger? There is no specific evidence that he did, and the men credited with creating the character in 1933 never spoke about it. But the parallels between the real Bass Reeves and the fictional Lone Ranger are too strong to ignore. If the character was not based on Reeves, the coincidences would be almost as impossible to believe as the facts of Bass Reeves's extraordinary life.

GEORGE ARMSTRONG CUSTER

A General's Reckoning

n the hot sunny afternoon of June 25, 1876, Lieutenant Colonel George Armstrong Custer, his younger brother Tom Custer, and two other men brought their mounts to a halt atop the Crow's Nest, a bluff above the Little Bighorn River in the Montana Territory. Custer raised his binoculars and looked into the distance—and what he saw must have taken his breath away. Nestled in a valley almost fifteen miles distant was the largest Indian encampment he had ever seen. He knew immediately that he had found Sitting Bull and Crazy Horse. There was little visible activity in the village, leading Colonel Custer to believe he had caught them by surprise. That was an extraordinary bit of good luck. "We've caught them napping," he said. He immediately sent a note to Captain Frederick Benteen, an experienced officer commanding a nearby battalion. "Come on," the note read. "Big village. Be quick. Bring packs."

Custer knew he had come upon the main Cheyenne and Lakota Sioux camp. One of his scouts reportedly told him, "General, I have been with these Indians for thirty years, and this is the largest village I have ever heard of." Based on the best available intelligence, Custer assumed there would be no more than two thousand hostiles in the camp. His strategy was clear. As he had written just two years earlier in his well-received book, *My Life on the Plains*, "Indians contemplating a battle . . . are always anxious to have their women and children removed from all danger. . . . [T]heir necessary exposure in case of conflict, would operate as a powerful argument in favor of peace."

Although his force of seven hundred troopers was outnumbered, it appeared that Custer intended to apply the same strategy he had previously used with great success: He would capture the Indian women, children, and elderly and use them as hostages and human shields. If his troops could occupy the village before the Indians organized their resistance, the warriors would be forced to surrender or shoot their own people. Initially, Custer planned to wait until the following morning to launch his attack, but when he received a report that hostiles had been seen on his trail, he feared losing the advantage of surprise. He had no way of knowing that those warriors had come out of the village and were riding away when they were spotted.

Had Custer waited through that night, it is quite possible that his scouts would have discovered the truth: What he had seen through his binoculars was only one end of a massive encampment that stretched for several miles along the river. Although the actual number of warriors has never been determined, it was many thousands more than he had estimated, and they were well armed with modern weaponry.

Custer split his force into three battalions. Major Marcus Reno's second detachment was to lead the charge into the village from the south to create a diversion; then, while the hostiles rushed to meet this attack, Custer's men would come down into the valley from the hills and take hostages. The Indians would be forced to kill their own families or surrender.

At noon, Custer ordered the attack to begin. Reno's men crossed the Little Bighorn and charged—and were stunned to discover that the village was much larger than anyone had

Custer expected the Indians to flee Major Reno's diversionary attack. Instead, according to brave Flying Hawk, as seen in this illustration by Amos Bad Heart Buffalo, "The dust was thick and we could hardly see. We got right among the soldiers and killed a lot with our bows and arrows and tomahawks. Crazy Horse was ahead of all, and he killed a lot of them with his war club."

realized. Hundreds of armed warriors, rather than dispersing as Custer believed they would, instead began fighting back. Reno had led his men into a trap. His charge was halted almost a mile from the village, and the Indians counterattacked his exposed flank with a force more than five times his. Furthermore, unlike his troops, most of whom were armed with single-shot rifles, many of the Indians carried repeaters. Reno was forced to fall back into the woods, telling his men, "All those who wish to make their escape take your pistols and follow me." After holding there briefly, he led a chaotic retreat to the top of the bluff, losing about a third of his men, where he was reinforced by the three companies commanded by Captain Benteen. Their fortunate arrival may well have saved Reno's troops from annihilation, but the combined forces were pinned down for crucial minutes in that position and could not move to help Custer.

When Custer first came upon the camp, it is probable that he envisioned an illustrious future. He was already a well-known soldier and Indian fighter, having been the youngest

Two great warriors, Colonel Custer and Crazy Horse, meet in this allegorical drawing by Kills Two.

Although, according to the Cheyenne chief Two Moons, the battle at Little Bighorn
lasted only "as long as it takes for a hungry man to eat his dinner," it will forever be part of
American folklore. The chaos of those brief moments was depicted by Charles M. Russell in
his 1903 painting *The Custer Fight*.

brevet—or, temporarily appointed—brigadier general in the Union army at twenty-three years old. He had been present at Lee's surrender at Appomattox and had later toured the South with President Andrew Johnson. This final victory over Crazy Horse in the Great Sioux War would raise his status to that of an American hero. He was hard on the path to glory. Even the presidency was possible.

When Colonel Custer heard gunfire, indicating Reno's troops had engaged the Indians, he turned in his saddle to face his men. "Courage, boys!" he yelled. "We've got them. We'll finish them off and then go home to our station." He did not know that Reno's attack had failed.

Then he raised his hand in the air and began his charge into history.

Custer's men were massacred. After forcing Reno to retreat, the main contingent of Lakota and Cheyenne warriors had turned to meet Custer. They surrounded his force and tightened the ring. Every soldier was killed, 210 men, and many of their bodies mutilated. There was no one left alive to report exactly what had happened. While the native peoples told the story from their point of view, their many versions were confused and contradictory. Countless historians have investigated and written about it, but the actual details of the battle will never be fully known. "Custer's Last Stand," as this worst defeat in American military history quickly became known, has become part of American mythology. Custer himself has become a historical enigma, as often praised for his courage in giving up his life for his country as he is vilified for his impetuousness in leading his men to slaughter. His name has become synonymous with defeat, and his actions that day have been cited as the ultimate example of hubris; his ego and ambition have been blamed for the decisions that resulted in the tragic loss of so many lives. Although several books published in the aftermath of the battle portrayed him as heroic, President U. S. Grant purportedly told a reporter for the *New York Herald*, "I regard Custer's Massacre as a sacrifice of troops, brought on by Custer himself; that was wholly unnecessary—wholly unnecessary."

Was Custer at fault, as Grant believed, for splitting his forces or for engaging the enemy without sufficient intelligence? Or, as many other people believe, was he betrayed by Major Reno and Captain Benteen, who were known to dislike him and were later accused of cowardice?

There is no question that George Armstrong Custer's contributions to the victories in the Civil War and the Indian wars have been largely forgotten, and instead he is remembered almost exclusively for this devastating defeat. This is not the end that anyone would have expected.

George Custer was born in the small town of New Rumley, Ohio, in 1839. His father, a farmer and a blacksmith, belonged to the New Rumley Invincibles, the local militia, and often brought his son to their meetings. Dressed in a Daniel Boone outfit made for him by his mother, Autie (as he was called) loved the ceremony of those meetings, and by the time he was four he could execute the entire manual of arms—using a wooden stick. When war against Mexico was being debated in 1846, he stunned the corps of Invincibles by waving a small flag and declaring, "My voice for war!"

His passion for the military never wavered. Although, at that time, most of the cadets at the US Military Academy at West Point came from wealthy and well-connected families, Custer managed to convince a congressman to sponsor him for the Class of 1862. He managed to get into plenty of trouble at West Point. Each cadet was permitted 100 demerits every six months and, every six months, Cinnamon, as he was nicknamed because he would use sweet-smelling cinnamon oils on his unusually long blond hair, would manage to get close to that limit before the period ended and the clock started again. His infractions were always minor: He'd be late for supper, his long blond hair would be out of place, he'd swing his arms while marching, or he'd get into a snowball fight. His mischievous personality just couldn't conform to the strict code of conduct. In his career at the Point he compiled 726 total demerits, which still ranks as one of the worst conduct records in Academy history. He was quite popular with his classmates, though. Once, in Spanish class, he asked the instructor how to say "Class dismissed" in Spanish. When the instructor replied, everybody stood up and walked out—another incident that helped him set that record.

Unfortunately, he wasn't a good student, either. When the Civil War started in 1861, more than a third of his class dropped out to join the Confederacy. The rest of the class was graduated a year early to serve in the war—and academically he finished at the very bottom of the remaining thirty-four students. Ironically, he received his worst grades in Cavalry Tactics.

Few people would have predicted that a poor student who wouldn't follow orders would soon distinguish himself on the battlefield, but as it turned out, George Custer proved to be a natural leader, a man of great courage, who—unlike many fellow officers—always rode at the front of his force when his men charged into battle. Those other officers might have found him arrogant and vain, but no one questioned his bravery.

When he graduated, he was offered a cushy and safe assignment or the opportunity to go right into combat. He chose to go to war; when he was told they didn't have a mount for him, he managed to find his own horse. Second Lieutenant Custer joined the Second Cavalry in time to fight in the First Battle of Bull Run. He began distinguishing himself as a staff

Custer distinguished himself in battle during the Civil War, and he is shown in this 1864 engraving presenting captured battle flags to the US war department.

officer for General George McClellan during the Union army's first attempt to capture the Confederate capital, Richmond. At one point during their march south, McClellan's men were trying to find a safe place to cross the Chickahominy River, which was at flood tide. When Custer overheard General Joe Johnson complaining to his staff that he wished he knew how deep the river was, Custer, with typical bravado, spurred his horse into the middle of it, continuing even as the water rose up to his neck, then turned and announced, "This is how deep it is, General." McClellan then assigned Custer to lead four companies of the Fourth Michigan Infantry into battle. Custer's force captured fifty prisoners—and the first Rebel battle flag of the war. McClellan described Custer as "a reckless, gallant boy, undeterred by fatigue, unconscious of fear," and promoted him to the rank of captain.

Custer had learned the value of self-promotion and rarely hesitated to set himself apart from other officers. Following the example of his commander, General Alfred Pleasonton, he began wearing extravagant, customized uniforms. Cavalry captain James Kidd described him as "[a]n officer superbly mounted, who sat on his charger as if to the manor born." He wore

Known by his troops
for wearing flamboyant
uniforms, Custer posed
for this 1865 portrait in
the traditional Union
blues.

a black velvet jacket trimmed with gold lace and brass buttons, a wide-brimmed hat turned down on one side, a sword and belt, and gilt spurs on high-top boots. And around his neck was "a necktie of brilliant crimson tied in a graceful knot at the throat, the lower ends falling carelessly in front," which stood out brightly against his blond mustache and flowing blond hair.

Another officer wrote that Custer "is one of the funniest-looking beings you ever saw, and looks like a circus rider gone mad."

Custer contended that there was a good reason for his choice of uniform. "I want my men to recognize me on any part of the field," he wrote. And, given the smoke and confusion of close combat, that made a lot of sense. If initially turned off by his flamboyant style, his troops were won over by his aggressive tactics and his willingness to lead attacks. There are reports that he had as many as a dozen horses shot out from under him during the Civil War, proof that he was usually in the thick of the action. Eventually his men began wearing similar red kerchiefs as a matter of pride.

Throughout his career, however, Custer was criticized for his seemingly endless pursuit of attention and recognition. At times, he would allow reporters to go out with his men on patrols. Some people believed that need for recognition caused him to behave recklessly.

It was at Gettysburg that George Custer became nationally famous. Three days before the battle began, he was promoted to brigadier general of volunteers, a temporary rank, and given command of the newly formed Michigan Brigade. At twenty-three years old, he was the youngest general in the army, but almost immediately, he showed his grit. At Hunterstown, on the road to Gettysburg, he led a charge into the mouth of Jeb Stuart's troops. When his horse was shot and fell, he was nearly captured but was saved when a heroic private galloped forward and swooped him up, while at the same time shooting at least one Confederate soldier.

When Stuart attempted to flank the Union's lines and attack the rear, he found Custer waiting for him at a place called Two Taverns. Ordered to counterattack, Custer stood before his troops, drew his saber, shouted "Come on, you Wolverines!" and raced into the action. He was said to be a veritable demon in the heat of battle, striking ceaselessly with any weapon available to him—slashing with his sword, firing his pistol—constantly urging his men forward, always forward. Within minutes, his horse was shot, but he commandeered a bugler's horse and continued the fight. Seven hundred men clashed along a fence line, fighting for victory and their lives in close quarters. The sounds of battle were described as louder than a collision of giants; a relentless roar of men and horses, of carbines and pistols firing, of metal sabers clashing, and the cries of the wounded. And in the middle of it all was Custer. When he lost a second mount, he found another and never left the battlefield. His ability to stay in the middle of every fight without being wounded, even as one horse after the next was shot out from under him, became known far beyond his Wolverines as "Custer's Luck."

Finally Stuart withdrew; it was the first time in the war that his cavalry had been stopped. In his report, Custer wrote, "I challenge the annals of warfare to produce a more brilliant or successful charge of cavalry." There were 254 Union casualties—219 of them were Custer's men. Reporting Custer's actions at Gettysburg, the *New York Herald* called him "the boy General with his flowing yellow curls."

The public—and the newspapers—took notice. As Custer continued to distinguish himself throughout the remainder of the war, the media reported each success in increasingly larger headlines. His unusual manner of dress, his brilliant tactical maneuvers, his bravery, and the resulting victories made him great copy. Marching with General Philip Sheridan, Custer's Third Division contributed to the victory in the 1864 Valley Campaign. In the battle of Yellow Tavern he led a saber charge into Jeb Stuart's cannon, "advancing boldly," he reported, "and when within 200 yards of the battery, charged it with a yell which spread terror before them. Two pieces of cannon, two limbers . . . and a large number of prisoners were among the results of this charge." Although he did not report it, supposedly his troops moved so quickly that they captured Jeb Stuart's dinner.

Two weeks later, after the Wolverines had routed the Rebels at Haws Shop, an officer serving under Custer wrote in awe, "For all this Brigade has accomplished all praise is due to Gen. Custer. So brave a man I never saw and as competent as brave. Under him a man is ashamed to be cowardly. Under him our men can achieve wonders."

Custer's wedding in 1864 to Elizabeth Bacon, the daughter of a politically powerful judge, was a major social event attended by hundreds of prominent guests. Unlike most military wives, Libbie Custer became known for camping with her husband in the field whenever it was deemed safe, explaining years later, "It is infinitely worse to be left behind, a prey to all the horrors of imagining what may be happening to one we love."

Custer's lovely wife, Libbie, seen here with her husband (seated) and his brother Tom Custer (a two-time Medal of Honor recipient who also perished at Little Bighorn), often traveled with her husband on the frontier.

In the final battle of the Civil War, when Robert E. Lee began his retreat at Appomattox Station, Custer's division cut off his last route of escape, then captured and secured supplies that Lee's troops needed desperately. He received the first truce flag from a Confederate force. The newly appointed major general of temporary volunteers was in attendance at the Appomattox Court House when Lee offered his sword in surrender to Grant. In recognition of Custer's valor, his commander, General Sheridan, purchased the table on which the surrender document was signed and presented it as a gift to Libbie Custer.

George Custer emerged from the Civil War as a national hero, although at the conclusion of hostilities, his temporary promotion to general of the volunteers ended and he was returned to his permanent rank, once again becoming Captain Custer. Beginning with George Washington, America had rewarded victorious military leaders with political office. General U. S. Grant was already on his way to becoming president, and Custer certainly could have moved into business or politics and transformed his fame into a safe and financially secure life. Railroad and mining companies offered him jobs. He might have accepted the offer to become adjutant general of the army of Mexican president Benito Juárez, which would have put him right back in the middle of battle, this time fighting Emperor Maximilian. But the army refused to give him the year's leave he requested, meaning he would have had to resign his commission if he wanted to fight for Mexican freedom. He considered running for Congress from Michigan but decided against it, telling Libbie that the political world had surprised him. "I dare not write all that goes on underhand," he said.

When President Andrew Johnson toured the country, trying to build support for his Reconstruction policies, he brought George and Libbie Custer with him, knowing that even those who opposed him would turn out to cheer the Custers. Captain Custer's admittedly large ego was probably bursting from all the attention. He considered all the offers, but in the end, he was a soldier. He loved the challenges of leadership, he loved being with his men on a campaign, he loved the planning and the execution of strategy, but most of all he loved the taste of battle.

There was only one war left to fight. The Plains Indians were on the warpath.

Since the beginning of American westward expansion, the native tribes had been continuously pushed into smaller and smaller areas. Those tribes that had tried to fight back were eventually defeated, often at great cost. By the end of the Civil War, only a few tribes—the Sioux, Cheyennes, Arapahos, Kiowas, and Comanches—had the will and the resources to fight for their land and their traditions. The army was sent west to subdue those tribes and force them onto reservations.

This 1865 *Harper's Weekly* photograph
shows General Philip Sheridan (*second
from left*) with his generals—Wesley
Merritt, George Crook, James William
Forsyth, and George Armstrong
Custer—around a table examining a
document.

When Congress created four cavalry units to fight the Indians on the western frontier,
Custer used his political contacts to secure an appointment as lieutenant colonel of the
Seventh Cavalry. Obtaining this command had not been easy; while in Washington, he had
become involved in a complicated political situation. He had testified in a corruption hearing
against the secretary of war, angering President Grant. Generals Sherman and Sheridan had
interceded successfully on his behalf, but certainly there was additional pressure on him to
bring back some victories. As General William T. Sherman wrote, Custer "came to duty
immediately upon being appointed . . . and is ready and willing now to fight the Indians."

Custer probably discovered rather quickly that the tactics he had mastered against the
Confederacy had little value on the Great Plains. The Civil War had been fought in proper
military fashion by two great armies that stood face-to-face and battled until one side was
decimated. In that type of warfare, Custer's chosen strategy of attacking ferociously and
hitting the enemy before they were prepared for the fight often proved decisive. But the
Indians did not fight static battles. Frequently outnumbered and fighting a better-equipped
enemy, they had mastered the art of guerrilla warfare. Rather than fighting as one army with
a centralized command structure, they would travel and live in small groups. Rather than
trying to take and hold territory, raiding parties would attack isolated targets—wagon trains

or settlers, for example—then disappear. And rather than fighting a pitched battle when attacked, they would fade into the protective hills and forests.

Custer found himself chasing an elusive enemy. By the time he would be notified of an attack, homesteads would already have been burned to the ground, victims slaughtered, and the Indians long gone. Through the summer of 1867, Custer's Seventh Cavalry was reduced to providing limited security when possible, but mostly chasing ghosts. His biggest enemy turned out to be his own growing frustration and anger.

Any doubts his troops might have begun harboring about his leadership ability were reinforced one day when he spotted a herd of antelope far in the distance. He released the pack of dogs he brought along to track Indians to pursue the herd—and then suddenly took off after them. He rode so fast and so hard that he almost lost sight of his column. He was about to turn back when he saw the first buffalo he had ever laid eyes on and raced toward them. He brought his horse alongside one and ran gloriously at full speed next to this huge animal—and when he finally moved to shoot it with his pistol, the buffalo jostled him, causing him to shoot his own horse in the head. He was thrown into the dirt, but except for some bruises, he was uninjured. Only then did he realize that he was lost and alone on the vast prairie. As he would describe this incident, "How far I had traveled, or in what direction from the column, I was at a loss to know . . . I had lost all reckoning."

Once again, Custer was very lucky: Several hours later his men found him—before the Indians did.

The Indians were there; the Seventh Cavalry just couldn't find them. Instead they kept coming upon the ruins of their attacks. Although Custer had seen many men killed, wounded, and horribly disfigured during the war, this was the first time he had seen evidence of the Indians' brutality. "I discovered the bodies of the three station-keepers, so mangled and burned as to be barely recognizable as human beings. The Indians have evidently tortured them . . ." It was determined they had been killed by Sioux and Cheyennes.

Custer pushed his men hard, and they began to resent him for it. They also resented that Seventh Cavalry officers continued to eat well, while their rations included old bread and maggot-infested meat. In the heat of battle, Custer had been able to mold his troops, but in the summer heat of the plains, he was losing control. To maintain discipline he began tightening his rules. After gold was discovered in the region, thirty-five soldiers deserted and set out to seek their fortunes in the mines. In response, Custer issued a harsh and highly controversial order: Catch them and shoot them. He was reported to have said, loudly enough for all his men to hear, "Don't bring one back alive."

There were alternative punishments—military regulations also permitted him to whip or tattoo them—but he chose the harshest sentence. Three of those deserters were dealt with according to his orders; two of them died of their wounds. By the middle of the summer, his men were on the verge of mutiny. Frustrated, tired, and lonely, Custer made a rash and inexplicable decision: He took seventy-six men with him and rode to eastern Kansas to be with his wife. He deserted his command, and that mistake was compounded when, during the three-day ride, two of his men were picked off by a band of about twenty-five Indians—and still he kept going. Soon after reuniting with Libbie, he was arrested for being absent without leave and for ordering deserters shot without a trial. His court-martial lasted a month, and only a few officers—including his brother Tom—testified on his behalf. The court found him guilty as charged and suspended him from duty without pay for a year. His fall from the heights had been brutally quick; his once-promising career was shattered.

George Custer had been prepared to deal with pretty much anything—except failure. He had always been able to skirt the rules and get away with it, but not this time. He spent that year trying to rehabilitate his reputation, writing magazine articles detailing his Civil War exploits and justifying the actions for which he had been suspended.

Meanwhile, the Indians grew bolder. During the summer of 1868, for example, they killed 110 settlers, raped thirteen women, and stole more than a thousand head of cattle. General Sheridan was made commander of the Department of Missouri, a huge area encompassing parts of six future states and the Indian Territory. At his request, Custer's suspension was ended several months early and he was given orders to "march my command in search of the winter hiding places of the hostile Indians, and wherever found to administer such punishment for past deprecations as my force was able to." He was ordered to "destroy their villages and ponies, to kill or hang all warriors, and bring back the women and children."

Custer was extremely pleased to be recalled, and he had every intention of fulfilling those orders. He knew his career depended on it. On November 26, 1868, Colonel Custer's scouts located a large Cheyenne village near the Washita River in what is now Oklahoma. The Indians had camped there for the winter. Fearful that his presence would be discovered, Custer decided not to wait for his scouts to gather intelligence. Instead, he planned his attack. Had he waited, he would have learned that the people in this village had nothing to do with attacks on settlers: This was a peaceful camp located on reservation land, where they had settled after the government guaranteed their safety to the chief Black Kettle. A white flag actually was flying from a large teepee, further evidence that this tribe had given up the fight.

Custer also would have discovered this was simply the westernmost village of a huge

Indian camp stretching more than ten miles along the river. In addition to the estimated 250 people in this village, more than six thousand native people from many tribes had made camp there for the winter.

But even that knowledge might not have discouraged his attack. His determination was so strong that when an aide wondered aloud if there might be more Indians in the camp than was believed, Custer replied firmly, "All I'm afraid of is we won't find enough. There aren't enough Indians in the world to defeat the Seventh Cavalry."

Custer's reputation as an Indian fighter was established in his 1868 attack on a large Cheyenne village on the Washita River, where he first employed the tactics that would doom his troops on the Little Bighorn.

He divided his 720 men into four elements and, at dawn, attacked from four positions. The signal to attack was the unit band striking up the song "Garry Owens." The unprepared Cheyennes were unable to mount any kind of defense and instead dispersed into the surrounding hills and foliage. The chief, Black Kettle, and his wife were killed in the first moments of the fighting. While Custer later reported killing 103 Cheyennes, that figure is generally accepted to be greatly exaggerated, with the actual number being closer to fifty. But that number included many noncombatants—women and even children. The Seventh Cavalry also took fifty-three hostages, who were put on horses and dispersed among the troops. But in the midst of the battle, several warriors reached their horses and escaped. Major Joel Elliott, Custer's second in command, took seventeen men and raced downstream in pursuit.

As the battle raged, Custer must have been stunned when he looked up at the top of the rise and saw as many as a thousand warriors "armed and caparisoned in full war costume" looking down upon his force. "[T]his seemed inexplicable," he wrote later. "Who could these new parties be, and from whence came they?" It was only after the battle that he learned the true size of the camp. However, his desperate strategy had been successful—it would have been impossible for those warriors to attack without risking the lives of the hostages. Custer feigned an advance, and rather than engaging him, the Indians dispersed.

Fully aware that he was outnumbered, Custer waited for nightfall and then ordered his troops to burn the village to the ground, destroy the herd of horses, and withdraw—without waiting for Major Elliott and his men to return or sending out scouts to find him. Many of his men considered leaving troops behind on the battlefield an unpardonable sin, among them Elliott's close friend, H Company captain Frederick Benteen. Custer claimed that he had ordered the withdrawal to prevent additional casualties and that he was confident that Elliott would return on his own.

Elliott and all his men seemed to have disappeared. Two weeks after the battle, Custer returned to the river with a large force, and, as he described, "We suddenly came upon the stark, stiff, naked and horribly mutilated bodies of our dead comrades. . . . Undoubtedly numbered more than one hundred to one, Elliott dismounted his men, tied their horses together and prepared to sell their lives as dearly as possible. . . . The bodies of Elliott and his band . . . were found lying within a circle not exceeding twenty yards." Major Elliott's force had been wiped out, apparently in a single charge.

Although it would have been impossible for Custer to know it, as he bent over the bodies of his men, he was looking at his own future.

Despite this loss, the media celebrated the battle of Washita as the first major victory of this frustrating campaign, helping to at least partially restore Custer's tarnished reputation. He became known as a great Indian fighter. And his innovative strategy of taking hostages to prevent Indian counterattacks was replicated successfully by other commanders. At the battle of North Fork three years later, the 284 men of Colonel Ranald Mackenzie's Fourth Cavalry defeated 500 Comanche warriors by taking 130 women and children to shield their withdrawal and used those hostages to force the tribe to return to the reservation and release its white prisoners.

But there were rumblings of dissent. As the public learned the details of the attack on a peaceful tribe, some insisted that it was a massacre of innocents rather than a great victory. Then *The New York Times* published an anonymous letter accusing Custer of abandoning Elliott's men in the field. The irate Custer responded by meeting with his officers and demanding to know who had written it, threatening to horsewhip that person. However, when Captain Benteen stepped forward and admitted it was his work, Custer backed off, although clearly from that point forward there was bitterness between the two officers.

To protect himself from further criticism, Custer surrounded himself with family members, close friends, and proven supporters, including his brother Tom—a two-time Medal of Honor winner—his brother Boston, and his brother-in-law James Calhoun.

Soldiers are prone to dehumanize the enemy during wartime, but Custer's feelings about the Indians were ambivalent. On one hand, he wrote that hunting buffalo was as exciting as hunting Indians. On the other, he showed great sympathy for the tribes in his book, even suggesting that if he had been treated as unfairly as the government had dealt with the Indians, he might have rebelled, too. Earlier in his life he had learned sign language to teach deaf children and had also studied Spanish at West Point, which made him one of the few officers able to communicate with the Plains Indians in the sign-language Spanish that the tribes used. And finally, there are accounts that he had a long-term relationship with an Indian woman named Spring Grass, who had been taken as a hostage at the Washita River. She was "an exceedingly comely squaw," he wrote, "possessing a bright cheery face [and] a countenance beaming with intelligence." According to Captain Benteen, Custer shared his tent with her both in camp and during his campaigns, when she served as a translator. Spring Grass eventually bore two children, although rumors hinted strongly that their father was Tom Custer, because George Custer suffered from gonorrhea contracted during his time at West Point.

The army's inability to gain control over all the tribes eventually led to a change in strategy. Rather than capturing the Indians, the army would destroy their source of food—the Plains buffalo. The government planned to starve the Indians onto reservations. Unlike the Indians,

The ambitious George Custer clearly understood the value of publicity, often allowing reporters to ride with his troops. This portrait seems to illustrate the no-nonsense attitude that caused him to reject a cautious approach when his scouts discovered the encampment at Little Bighorn.

buffalo were a very easy target. It is estimated that more than four and a half million buffalo were killed by 1872.

Colonel Custer remained a valuable public-relations tool for the government during this period. When Grand Duke Alexis of Russia wanted to tour the West and see wild Indians, for example, Custer and Buffalo Bill Cody were assigned to make all the arrangements. To ensure the grand duke's safety, Custer supposedly recruited some reservation Indians to "attack" the train, with all the requisite whooping and hollering. Before this event began, these Indians were given a considerable amount of beer; so much beer, in fact, that those show Indians got carried away and seemed to actually be attacking the train. Alexis was so convinced the attack was real that he had to be restrained from shooting at them.

To an ambitious man like Custer, who lived for the battle—and for the acclaim that came with victory—these assignments must have been terribly boring. But Custer's Luck held once again—and he managed to turn a mundane task into career gold: The military was needed to protect the men who were building America's railroads as they expanded into Indian lands. In 1873, the Northern Pacific approached the Black Hills, the sacred lands promised to the Sioux forever in the Fort Laramie treaty of 1868. That expansion came to an unexpected halt when the company went bankrupt, taking with it numerous other businesses and precipitating the Panic of 1873, the worst economic crisis in the early history of America. Unemployment skyrocketed and the government became desperate to find new sources of revenue. For several years, there had been rumors of vast gold deposits in the Black Hills—exactly what was needed to restore the failing economy. On July 2, 1874, Custer led a thousand troops out of Fort Rice on the Missouri River into the Black Hills to protect the surveyors searching for gold.

Naturally, accompanying this expedition were eager young newspapermen from New York and Philadelphia anxious to report the news of a new American gold rush—and to bestow the proper credit on the stalwart Colonel Custer, who was leading the way into the future.

On July 27, the first strike was reported on French Creek. In what can accurately be described as a masterstroke of public relations, somehow George Custer, a military officer who had never touched a shovel, managed to receive at least partial credit for the gold strike. Within days, the *Bismarck Tribune* reported, "Gold in the Grass Roots and in Every Panful of Earth Below: Anybody Can Find It—No Former Experience Necessary."

For Custer, the timing seemed perfect: Within months, his colorful autobiography, *My Life on the Plains*, was published. This supposedly true tale of the adventures of a fighting man on the frontier sold well and was met with critical acclaim, going a long way toward restoring his image. Only those who were with him during those times knew the truth, and the increasingly bitter Benteen suggested the book might more accurately be titled *My Lie on the Plains*.

Within a year, more than fifteen thousand miners raced west to the Black Hills to find their fortunes. Initially, the government attempted to lease or even buy this land from the Sioux, but the tribe rejected every offer. There was no price for sacred land. Fighting for the last part of their traditional lands that they still held, bands of Sioux warriors began attacking prospectors. The government ordered the Sioux to return to their reservation within sixty days, warning that if they resisted, force would be brought against them. When the Indians refused, General Sheridan ordered three battalions—one of them Custer's Seventh Cavalry—to find and surround the Indian camps and round them up—or wipe them out.

For the Indian fighter George Custer, this was an opportunity to get back in the saddle and ride to what he must have believed would be the greatest victory of his career. He was so confident, that when he was offered additional troops and two Gatling guns—essentially machine guns and the most fearsome weapon on the Plains—he turned them down, believing those weapons weren't needed and would only slow down his advance. The possibility that his mostly inexperienced and undertrained troops might be outnumbered did not shake him; the Plains Indians had never defeated a force the size of his Seventh Cavalry.

Custer simply did not appreciate the determination of the tribes camped on the banks of the Little Bighorn River. This was not only a battle for their sacred land, but their last chance to protect their way of life. Freedom to roam the plains was being taken from them. They weren't fighting for something; they were fighting for everything. Sitting Bull was their great chief, which meant he was in charge of the civil affairs, including all negotiations with the United States government, but when the fighting began, Crazy Horse was in command. Crazy Horse was himself a great warrior, a veteran of many indigenous battles, and an excellent tactician. He is credited with devising some of the basic strategies of guerrilla warfare on which special operations are still based. And in his daring and bravery, he was at least the equal of Custer.

Both sides seemed to know this battle was coming. As Custer prepared to mount up and leave, Libbie had a nightmare that he would die in battle and be scalped, so she pleaded with him to cut his long golden hair. To please her, he did. And during a sacred ceremony, a Sun Dance, Sitting Bull too had a vision: He had seen soldiers and their horses falling upside down from the sky like grasshoppers into his camp. This, he told his people, meant there would be a great victory.

Historians also wonder about one additional premonition: The night before the battle, Custer supposedly ordered his men to finish their whiskey rations, perhaps trying to help his raw troops find their courage; or, as some have suggested, he knew what was waiting for him.

There is no question that when planning his attack, Custer drew on his success at the Washita River. He divided his forces into three components; he commanded the largest force, while Major Reno and Captain Benteen were in charge of smaller units. He might not have liked Benteen, but obviously he thought him a capable officer. Reno was ordered to charge into the village, presumably to create the diversion that would allow Custer to take hostages. Custer and Reno anticipated that the Indians would flee when attacked, as they had done previously; this was a grievous miscalculation. The warriors so outnumbered Reno's troops that rather than flee, they initiated their own counterattack, trapping Reno.

Custer had dressed in a white buckskin suit with a bright red tie around his neck for the battle. As Reno's troops swept down on the camp, Custer waved his gray hat at him in approval. But by the time Reno's advance had been stopped and his troops were in retreat, Custer was moving along the ridgeline to launch his own attack and was not aware of what was happening.

After Benteen received Custer's message, "Come quick," he moved forward with his supply train, but when he reached the battlefield, the besieged Reno ordered him to stay there

Custer often wore a fringed white buckskin jacket, like this one in the Smithsonian, reportedly so that his troops could easily identify him during a battle.

CUSTER'S LAST FIGHT.

The Original Painting has been Presented to the Seventh Regiment U.S. Cavalry

BY **ANHEUSER BUSCH BREWING ASSOCIATION,**

Although the massacre shocked the nation in the midst of its centennial celebration, by 1889, Custer's heroic last fight was being celebrated in one of the very first beer advertisements, a colored lithograph that hung in saloons throughout the country and helped create the enduring image of the brave soldiers. Many of the details are wrong. The original painting, donated to the Seventh Cavalry, was destroyed in a barracks fire.

and reinforce his troops. The appearance of these reinforcements forced the native warriors to cease their attack. But rather than trying to ascertain Custer's situation and perhaps provide the timely assistance that might have saved him, Reno and Benteen remained in their defensive position much too long. Late in the battle, an officer in Reno's command, Captain Weir, insisted that they find Custer. When Reno refused, Weir took the initiative and led his company toward Custer's position. Far away in the swirling dust he saw riders and got ready to attack—and then he realized that all those riders were Indians and they were riding in a circle, shooting at the ground. Reno and Benteen had followed Weir, but when they discovered it was too late, they retreated to their defensive position and fought it out for the rest of the day.

It will never be known whether Custer fully understood Reno's predicament. But at some point, he must have realized that his only hope of victory lay in taking sufficient hostages to force the warriors to lay down their weapons. When it became apparent that Sioux warriors blocked his path, it was no longer a matter of victory—he was fighting for survival. He retreated up the slope, trying to reach high ground. There was no cover for his troops, so he ordered them to kill their horses to provide some defense. But it was hopeless. His soldiers were rapidly overwhelmed by a massive force attacking with guns, arrows, clubs, and lances. Custer was shot in his breast, and then in his temple, the second shot killing him.

In about twenty minutes, all 225 of Custer's men were dead. Sitting Bull supposedly once told an interviewer that Custer laughed in the last moment of his life, although that's doubtful, because evidence indicates that the Indians were not even aware that Custer was among the dead. In addition to George Custer, his brothers Tom and Boston and his nephew Henry Reed died on what has become known as Last Stand Hill. An Associated Press reporter sent to cover Custer's victory was the first AP reporter to die in combat. His notes were found on his body, concluding, "I go with Custer and will be at the death."

The nation, celebrating its centennial, was stunned and shaken by the unexpected news of Custer's Last Stand. It was said that America's heart was broken. The day after the battle, the Indians packed up their camp and began moving. But this great victory soon proved to be the last major battle of the Indian wars: The defeat caused the army to increase its efforts to subdue the tribes, and within five years, almost all Sioux and Cheyennes would be settled on reservations.

The nation replayed the battle of Little Bighorn for many years, trying to understand how one of its most brilliant leaders had been so brutally slaughtered. Benteen was criticized for reinforcing Reno rather than Custer, and people wondered if the animosity between the two men had played any role in his decision. But, in fact, he had little choice: Reno was his commanding officer and had ordered him to stay. Reno himself was accused of both cowardice

Painted only six years after the battle, this lithograph already demonstrates the esteem with which the heroic Custer, standing taller than all his men, a pistol in one hand and a sword in the other, was being portrayed.

and drunkenness at Little Bighorn. He demanded a court of inquiry be convened; while it did not sustain the charges, it also offered no rebuttals to the claims made against him. But as William Taylor, a soldier who served at Little Bighorn under Reno, later wrote bitterly, "Reno proved incompetent and Benteen showed his indifference—I will not use the uglier words that have often been in my mind. Both failed Custer and he had to fight it out alone."

Did General Custer's hubris cause him to underestimate his enemy and lead his men into a massacre? Although no one ever questioned George Custer's bravery, military historians have been critical of Custer's tactical decisions, from his initial refusal to accept additional men and weapons to his choice to split up his already outnumbered force and attack without sufficient intelligence.

Years earlier, Custer had written, "My every thought was ambitious. I desired to link my name with acts and men, and in such a manner as to be a mark of honor, not only to the present but to future generations." Although he achieved his aim to be remembered in history, it is not as he had hoped, because the name George Armstrong Custer will always be associated with one of the most devastating defeats in American history.

THE REALITY OF AN "INDIAN SUMMER"

Few things are as welcome as an Indian summer, that sudden and unexpected change in the fall weather after the first frost that brings a brief return to the balmy temperatures of summer. But originally, rather than being welcomed, the possibility of an Indian summer was absolutely

Unlike the mood depicted in this pastoral watercolor of Indians camping outside Fort Laramie in about 1860, the early settlers lived in terror of Indian raids.

MASSACRE OF SETTLERS.

When the early settlers tried to bring European values to the Native Americans, the Indians resisted. The first recorded Indian attack took place in March 1622, when Powhatans killed 347 men, women, and children in Jamestown in their houses and fields.

terrifying. In the early days of the West, the fear of Indian raids forced settlers to live together in walled forts from spring through the early fall. At the first frost, the Indians would pack up, leave their villages, and move to their winter camping grounds. When they were gone, the settlers would return to their homesteads and make preparations for the winter. For those settlers, after spending months in crowded, confined surroundings, it was like being released from prison. They actually looked forward to the cold of winter.

But as sometimes happened, the weather would turn once again, bringing back the warm sun to melt the snows—and with it would come the Indians. "Indian summer" meant Indian attack. As Henry Howe wrote, "The melting of the snow saddened every countenance and the general warmth of the sun filled every heart with horror. The apprehension of another visit from the Indians, and being driven back to the detested fort, was painful in the highest degree."

But as the country grew and the Indians were forced onto reservations, these fears diminished, and over time the term evolved to refer solely to the delightful change in the weather, as it does today.

Buffalo Bill and Annie Oakley

The Radical Opportunists

The Deadwood stage was bouncing over rough terrain, trying to make time. Inside the coach, five very important men were holding on to the straps for dear life. Up on the box, the driver and shotgun were nervously craning their necks, scanning the horizon for any sign of trouble. They'd heard tell that Indians had been seen in these parts and feared an attack. The driver whipped his team, trying to coax a little more speed out of them—and then they heard the first terrible cry.

Indians were closing in fast from both sides, screaming their blood-curdling war whoops, firing their weapons, and waving their war lances as they raced in for the kill. The driver whipped his team again. The guard turned in his seat and counted six pursuers. He let loose with his first volley, knocking one of the attackers right out of his saddle. The coach was bouncing crazily over the hard ground. "Hold tight," the driver shouted to his passengers, "and keep your heads down!"

The Indians were shooting back; the driver hunched low in his seat. The guard had reloaded and fired again. A second attacker went sprawling. For a few seconds, the Indians seemed to be closing the gap, but by then the stage was up to full speed, spewing clouds of dust. The driver whipped his horses again and again. With one last *Hey-yaa!* from the driver, the stage pulled away. The Indians pulled up short. One of them angrily stabbed his long lance into the ground, and then they turned and trotted back from where they had come, leaving the banners on the lance ruffling in the wind.

After a few seconds of silence, all twenty thousand people in the audience began cheering. The driver, Buffalo Bill, spun the stagecoach around, creating a dust devil, and brought it to a stop directly in front of the grandstand. He hopped down and opened the door, and the king of Denmark, the king of Belgium, the king of Greece, and the king of Saxony—all in London to celebrate Queen Victoria's jubilee—climbed out to the loud hurrahs of the audience and waved, and then a mighty roar erupted as the future king, Edward, Prince of Wales, emerged. When the cheering stopped, he said to Bill Cody, in a voice loud enough for all to hear, "Colonel, you never held four kings like these before, have you?"

For more than three decades, Buffalo Bill's Wild West shows thrilled America and Europe, as seen in this 1907 reenactment of a battle from the Indian wars.

Buffalo Bill responded, just as loudly, "I've held four kings, but four kings and the Prince of Wales makes a royal flush such as no man has ever held before!" And with a great wave of his hat, Bill Cody ended the show.

Some courageous men explored and settled the West, and other brave settlers fought the Native American warriors for the right to live there, but William "Buffalo Bill" Cody, with important assistance from Annie Oakley, Sitting Bull, and Geronimo, successfully merchandised it. For three decades, Buffalo Bill Cody's *Wild West* brought the spirit and the adventure of life on the frontier to audiences around the world, successfully creating the romantic, rip-roaring image of the Old West that persists to this day. Presidents, kings, Queen Victoria, and Pope Leo XIII were all captivated by the action-packed performance.

In addition to the Indian attack on the Deadwood stage—and Cody actually had purchased the old Deadwood stage for this scene—the show included, among many other en-

The attempted robbery of the original Deadwood stage was a highlight of the show, and Cody would invite local dignitaries to participate as passengers.

tertainments, pioneers defending their homestead against an Indian attack; a stage or train robbery; Indians attacking a wagon train; races between Pony Express riders and between an Indian on foot and a pony; buffalo hunting; displays of roping and riding, bulldogging and sharpshooting; and even a sad reenactment of General Custer's Last Stand. Buffalo Bill and his cast of hundreds of "authentic Red Indians" brought the Old West to life for tens of thousands of people and, in so doing, made himself the most famous American in the whole world.

While most people loved the show, few of them ever wondered how accurate it was—or whether Buffalo Bill and Annie Oakley had ever played a real role in the Old West. Were those two legendary figures true survivors of a time gone by, or were they simply entertainers earning a fine living from the exploitation of a myth? Ironically, Buffalo Bill Cody is probably remembered more for the amazing shows he created than for his very real accomplishments riding the ranges of the West.

After a parade down Fifth Avenue, the *Wild West Show* settled into Madison Square
Garden for the winter of 1886. As more than five thousand spectators—including General
Sherman—watched on opening night, "One big bull elk forgot his cue, [and] sauntered
slowly down the arena, inspecting the pretty girls in the boxes with critical stares and gazing
at the rest of the spectators in a tired way."

William Cody was born in rural Iowa in 1846 to educated parents. When he was seven years old, Isaac and Mary Ann Cody sold their farm and moved to Fort Leavenworth, Kansas, arriving in the middle of the raging debate over slavery. In that part of the state, Isaac Cody's antislavery sentiments were not popular, and eventually he was stabbed while giving an impassioned speech. He died a few years later while trying to bring antislavery settlers from Ohio into the state, leaving his family close to ruin. To support them, young Bill Cody took an assortment of jobs, including "boy extra" on wagon trains, teamster, bull whacker on cattle drives, and, finally, army scout. How he developed his renowned tracking and shooting skills isn't known.

As he wrote in his autobiography, *Buffalo Bill's Own Story*, his first encounter with Indians occurred while he was scouting for the army. Soldiers were trying to quash a threatened Mormon rebellion in Salt Lake City. "Presently the moon rose," he wrote, "dead ahead of me; and painted boldly across its face was the figure of an Indian. He wore this war-bonnet of the Sioux, at his shoulder was a rifle pointed at someone in the river-bottom 30 feet below; in another second he would drop one of my friends. I raised my old muzzle-loader and fired. The figure collapsed, tumbled down the bank and landed with a splash in the water. . . . So began my career as an Indian fighter."

Almost as if in preparation for the spectacular shows he would eventually produce, Cody had a range of real-life experiences in most of the situations his performers would later replicate. When out trapping with a friend, he had slipped and broken his leg; his friend left to get help to bring him home, and Cody was discovered by a band of Indians, who spared his life only because he was just a "papoose," as he heard them describe him, and because he had previously met their leader, Chief Rain-in-the-Face. On another hunt, he ran across a band of murderous outlaws and was forced to shoot one of them to make his escape.

Bill Cody was only thirteen years old when he headed west to mine for gold but instead signed on with the Pony Express. After building and tending stations, he became one of the youngest riders on that trail—or, as he later would portray it, a lone figure dashing across the stormy prairies carrying the mail! In his autobiography, he claimed to have made the longest Pony Express journey ever, 322 miles round-trip. He also recalled, "Being jumped by a band of Sioux Indians . . . but it fortunately happened I was mounted on the fleetest horse belonging to the Express company. . . . Being cut off from retreat back to Horse Shoe, I put spurs to my horse, and lying flat on his back, kept straight for Sweetwater."

It was while working as a rider that he began to gain fame as an Indian fighter. At one point, the Indians had become so troublesome that all service had to stop, so Cody joined Wild Bill Hickok and twenty or more other men to look for a horse herd that had been stolen. They found the Indians, who had "never before been followed into their own country by white men," camped by a river. Led by Hickok, they attacked, capturing not just their own horses but more than a hundred Indian ponies.

How many of these tales told by Cody in his bestselling autobiography are accurate will never be known, because so much is impossible to verify. But when it was originally published in 1879, his biographers believed that most of it was true, and none of the people he depicted ever contradicted his version of events.

At the beginning of the Civil War, he rode with Chandler's Jayhawkers, an abolitionist militia that he joined happily to "retaliate upon the Missourians for the brutal manner in which they had treated and robbed my family." He awoke one day and found himself enlisted in the Seventh Kansas Cavalry, although he claimed no memory of exactly how that happened. His most notable service was acting as a courier for Hickok, who was operating as a spy within the Confederate army, gathering important intelligence that affected the battles in Missouri.

After the war, Bill Cody continued scouting for the army, serving in '67 as a guide for Brevet Major General George Custer, and later fighting the Plains tribes himself in many death-defying encounters. During this tour of duty, he took part in sixteen battles, including the 1869 fight against the Cheyennes at Summit Springs, Colorado. He fancied himself an expert Indian fighter, and in his autobiography he sometimes described braves he had killed as "good Indians." The irony of that statement would be evident several years later. As his fame spread on the Plains, the army assigned him to work with Custer, guiding wealthy dignitaries on western hunting expeditions, mostly Europeans such as Grand Duke Alexis of Russia, who wanted the excitement of seeing a real wild Indian. For his service, in 1872 he became one of only four civilian scouts ever awarded the Medal of Honor, which, although not yet the rarely awarded medal it would become, was even then held in great esteem and given only to those who served with honor and valor.

In the late 1860s, he took up a challenge from a renowned scout and buffalo hunter named Billy Comstock to see which of them could kill the most buffalo in eight hours. This was another area of his expertise: In addition to scouting, he earned his living supplying buffalo to feed the crews building the Kansas Pacific Railway—a lot of buffalo. He once claimed he'd killed 4,280 head in seventeen months. The wager with Comstock was five hundred dollars. More than a hundred spectators turned out to see the contest. Using Lucretia, as he affectionately named his breech-loading Springfield rifle, he killed 69 to Comstock's 46 and, in addition to winning the bet, became known from that day forward as the one and only Buffalo Bill.

By the time he had acquired that nickname, a young woman named Phoebe Ann Cates was already astounding people with her uncanny marksmanship. Born in a rural Ohio cabin in 1860, she often said, "I was eight years old when I made my first shot," describing shooting a squirrel in the head to preserve its meat for the stew pot. At the time, ladies of any age were not known for their marksmanship; in fact, most of them didn't even shoot guns. Although "Annie" apparently could perform all the standard "womanly" tasks, such as cooking, sewing, and embroidering, she also could outshoot pretty much any man. As a teenager, she supported her family by selling game she had hunted and trapped to local hotels and restaurants, and she claimed she had earned enough to pay off the mortgage on the family farm.

While she was still a very young woman, one of her regular customers, enterprising Cincinnati hotel owner Jack Frost, arranged a one-hundred-dollar betting match between Frank E. Butler, the star and owner of the Baughman & Butler traveling marksmen show, and five-foot-tall Annie Cates. Through twenty-four rounds of live-bird trapshooting, they matched each other shot for shot, but after he missed his twenty-fifth shot, she successfully hit the bird and won the match. Rather than being upset about losing to a young girl, Frank Butler

Annie Oakley at work in 1892

fell in love with her. Within a year, she had become the star of Butler's show and, at some point soon after, also became his wife. Their marriage lasted fifty years. It's generally accepted that she adopted the name Oakley from the Cincinnati neighborhood in which they briefly lived.

Frank Butler understood the appeal of a small, lovely, and very feminine woman who could outshoot any he-man who challenged her, and he essentially retired to manage her career. Billing her as "Little Sure Shot," he promoted her as the sharpest shooter in the world, "the peerless wing and rifle shot"—and routinely risked his life to prove it: Holding a lit cigarette between his lips, he would let her shoot it out of his mouth. Using a rifle, a shotgun, and a handgun, she could extinguish a candle at thirty paces, split a playing card facing her sideways from ninety feet away, hit dimes tossed into the air, and riddle dropped playing cards with numerous shots before they hit the ground.

For several years, they toured the new vaudeville circuit in an act that included their dog, who sat patiently and still and allowed Annie to shoot an apple off his head. In 1885, she accepted an offer to join the new *Buffalo Bill's Wild West* extravaganza, and within a year had become the second most popular performer in the show, second only to Buffalo Bill himself.

Although popular fiction plots of the day often turned on fortuitous and unexpected meetings, such was exactly the case when Bill Cody met Edward Judson in 1869. Cody had been ordered to scout for an expedition hunting a band of Sioux that had attacked Union Pacific workers near O'Fallon's Station in Nebraska and was told Judson would be riding along. Judson turned out to be an extraordinarily eccentric character, at the time becoming quite famous under the pseudonym Ned Buntline. Buntline was a writer, journalist, and publicist, a man known for delivering passionate temperance lectures—after which he would often go out and celebrate by getting drunk. It was Buntline who introduced Bill Cody to the art of selling the West and introduced Buffalo Bill to the world. Buntline understood that Americans were thrilled by the hair-raising stories of cowboys and Indians in the Old West and set out to profit from it. After meeting Cody and hearing his stories, Buntline wrote an adventure serial for Street and Smith's *New York Weekly* entitled "Buffalo Bill, the King of the Border Men." The popularity of that story convinced Buntline to write and publish the first of dozens of dime novels featuring Cody's exploits: *Buffalo Bill, The Scouts of the Plains; or, Red Deviltry as It Is*. These action-packed adventure stories of a heroic Buffalo Bill defending his life and his honor against the most evil villains of the West became tremendously popular, turning Cody into a national hero. Taking advantage of this fame, Buntline convinced Cody to star in a rousing play he had written and was producing entitled *The Scouts of the Plains*. "There's money in it," Cody reported being told by Buntline, "and you will prove a big card, as your character is a novelty on stage."

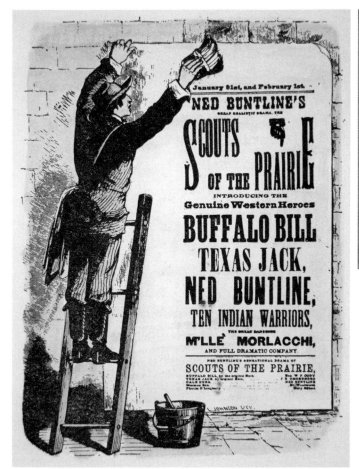

Ned Buntline's 1872 show set the stage for the creation of the western myth. Although the Chicago *Times* called it a "combination of incongruous drama, execrable acting, renowned performers, mixed audience, intolerable stench, scalping, blood and thunder," audiences loved it.

Cody decided, "A fortune is what we're after, and we'll at least give the wheel a turn or two to see what luck we have." Starring Cody, Texas Jack Omohundro, a young Italian actress playing an Indian maiden, and eventually Wild Bill Hickok, the play toured eastern cities for years. As Cody described it, "[T]here were between forty and fifty 'supers' dressed as Indians. . . . We blazed away at each other with blank cartridges . . . We would kill them all off in one act, but they would come up again ready for business in the next."

What the play lacked in dramatic conventions, it made up for in exuberance. "An extraordinary production," wrote the *Boston Journal*, "with more wild Indians, scalping knives

Buffalo Bill was already America's first matinee idol when he added to his legend by killing Cheyenne chief Yellow Hair and claiming, "The first scalp for Custer!"

and gun powder to the square inch than any drama ever before heard of." The *Norfolk Journal* reported that "one of the largest audiences ever assembled within [Opera House] walls" saw "the crowning piece of the night . . . which excited juveniles to the wildest demonstrations of delight . . . whenever Texas Jack and Buffalo Bill appeared on stage the audience cheered . . ."

A different type of entertainment apparently was taking place backstage as men accustomed to a rougher type of living adjusted to show business. There were stories of all-night card games, brawls, wrecked furniture, and the occasional arrest. But for Cody, the lines between reality and theater truly became blurred when the army called him into service to scout for the Fifth Cavalry in the Sioux Wars after his friend, Colonel George Custer, was killed and his troops massacred at Little Bighorn.

A legendary story Bill Cody told in his memoirs perfectly illustrated how he straddled the line between real life and entertainment: By mid-July 1876, the Fifth Cavalry had been chasing the Cheyennes for more than a week, intent on avenging Custer's death. When Cody awoke on the morning of July 17, he sensed there would be a fight that day. So he dressed for the battle carefully, putting on the scouting costume he wore in Buntline's show: a red silk shirt with billowing sleeves and decorative silver buttons, flared black pants with gold cross braiding embroidered on the thighs and held in place by a broad leather belt with a large rectangular metal buckle, a well-worn leather vest, comfortable boots, and a sombrero-like brown hat with the brim pushed up in front.

At daybreak, the Fifth Cavalry finally spotted the Cheyennes, who were getting ready to attack two couriers. Cody led fifteen men to cut them off. Then the Indian chief, who later was identified as Yellow Hair, "sang out to me, in his own tongue, 'I know you Pa-he-haska; if you want to fight, come ahead and fight me.'" They raced toward each other; the chief's shot missed, but Cody's shot struck the Indian's horse and it went down. An instant later, Cody's horse stepped in a gopher hole and stumbled. Cody fell off but scrambled to his feet; he was about twenty paces from the chief. They fired again: "My usual luck did not desert me on this occasion, for his bullet missed me, while mine struck him in the breast." Cody was on top of him in an instant: "Jerking his war bonnet off, I scientifically scalped him in about five seconds. . . . I swung the Indian chieftain's top-knot and bonnet in the air and shouted—'The first scalp for Custer!'"

How much of what he wrote was accurate and how much was entertainment has been debated almost since that time, although there is no doubt that Chief Yellow Hair was killed in that battle. What also became clear is that Buffalo Bill Cody had successfully made the transition from performance to performer. And when the two overlapped, it was even better.

Naturally, when Cody returned to the stage at the end of that campaign, this scene was incorporated into a show entitled *Buffalo Bill's First Scalp for Custer*. That show, as Cody admitted, "[a]fforded us ample opportunity to give a noisy, rattling, gunpowder entertainment, and to present a succession of scenes in the late Indian war."

For Cody, this brought a whole new meaning to the western concept of being "on a stage." After becoming comfortable in front of audiences, Cody struck off on his own, organizing "dramatic combinations," as he referred to them, while also appearing on the vaudeville circuit to spread the legend of Buffalo Bill. These shows often introduced genuine frontier characters such as Wild Bill Hickok to the stage, as well as real Indians in their actual war bonnets, fancy shooting and roping, and even some horse tricks. There was no shortage anywhere in the country of people wanting to experience even a small taste of Old West authenticity, and his stage shows proved very successful.

In 1883, Buffalo Bill decided to create a new type of entertainment, a Wild West show that would be bigger and more action-packed than anything anyone had previously done. As he later remembered, "I conceived the idea of organizing a large company of Indians, cowboys, Mexican vaqueros, famous riders and expert lasso throwers, with accessories of stage coach, emigrant wagons, bucking horses and a herd of buffalos, with which to give a realistic entertainment of wild life on the plains." It would be more like a circus than a play, performed outdoors with many individual scenes and exhibitions rather than following a single story line. It was to be a highly stylized dramatization of the settling of the West.

The first such extravaganza was presented as part of a Fourth of July celebration in North Platte, Nebraska, entitled *Wild West, Rocky Mountain and Prairie Exhibition*. The success of that event led him to create *Buffalo Bill's Wild West*. The three-hour-long show thrilled audiences, and Cody proved to be quite a creative showman. He tried for three years to hire his former adversary, the great Sioux chief Sitting Bull. Initially the government refused to allow it, insisting that the Sioux stay on the Pine Ridge reservation rather than "visiting places where they would naturally come in contact with evil associates and degrading immoralities." Finally, the secretary of the interior approved the request in 1885. Less than a decade after defeating Custer at Little Bighorn, Sitting Bull would endure being taunted and booed by the same audiences that also paid him well to sign photographs of himself afterward.

That was the same year that Annie Oakley joined the troupe, performing tricks such as sighting a target in a mirror and shooting over her shoulder. Although by this time there were other female sharpshooters, Annie's conservative and feminine style set her apart. Women loved watching her best men in contests—and do so in a very ladylike fashion.

Chief Sitting Bull toured with the *Wild West Show* for four months in 1875. During that time, he befriended Annie Oakley, calling her Watanya Cicilia, which translated to Little Sure Shot.

While giving an exhibition a year earlier, she had met Sitting Bull, who noted that she was about the same age his own daughter would have been if she had survived the Indian wars and gave her the name Watanya Cicilia, which in Lakota means Little Sure Shot. During the time they spent together traveling with Buffalo Bill's show, they became close, and he adopted her into the Hunkpapa Lakota tribe, an honor that she took seriously.

In 1886, the show set down for the entire summer on New York's Staten Island, drawing almost 336,000 spectators to that season's production, "The Drama of Civilization." Many patrons traveled by ferry from Manhattan, passing the newly installed Statue of Liberty, then taking a four-mile ride on the new rail line. When the weather turned cold, the show moved inside, to Madison Square Garden. Bringing the Wild West to sophisticated New York caused a sensation, resulting in a great deal of national publicity for Annie Oakley. Her ability to drill bullet holes in falling cards was the inspiration for a common slang term for a free or complimentary ticket to an event—an "Annie Oakley"—because holes had already been punched in it.

That same season, Buffalo Bill added to his cast fifteen-year-old sharpshooter Lillian Smith, "the Champion Girl Shot," who quickly developed a rivalry with Annie Oakley.

The popularity of the show led Mark Twain to encourage Cody to take it to Europe, to bring the epic story of the settlement of the West to the celebration of Queen Victoria's fiftieth year on the throne: "It is often said on the other side of the water that none of the exhibitions which we send to England are purely and distinctly American. If you will take the Wild West show over there you can remove that reproach." Cody packed 300 performers, including 97 Indians, 18 buffalo, 181 horses, 10 elk, 4 donkeys, 5 Texas longhorns, 2 deer, 10 mules, and the Deadwood stage on several ships and sailed to England. The troupe toured for six months, often drawing crowds of more than thirty thousand people. This glamorized version of the American West became the accepted European version of life on the frontier. Although the image of the cowboy became symbolic of the brave-if-not-so-sophisticated nation, Cody's Indians also created a fervor, and Europeans rushed to touch them when a rumor spread in France that brief contact with an Indian assured fertility.

The show gave two command performances for Queen Victoria, one of them causing a sensation. As Cody wrote, "When the standard bearer passed the royal box with Old Glory her Majesty arose, bowed deeply and impressively to the banner, and the entire court party came up standing . . . and all, saluted." This marked the first time in history that a British monarch had saluted the American flag.

As soon as the show returned from its triumphant tour, Annie Oakley resigned. Various reasons were given but they all centered on the same issue: She just didn't like Lillian Smith. She resumed touring as a solo act, briefly joined a competing Wild West show, and even appeared onstage in a trifle called *Deadwood Dick*. Smith eventually fell in love with a cowboy and left the show as well, darkening her skin and touring in *Mexican Joe's Wild West* show as Princess Winona, the Indian Girl Shot. Her departure allowed Annie Oakley to rejoin Cody's show in time for another long tour of Europe.

The show became part of the Paris Exposition, staged to commemorate the one hundredth anniversary of the French Revolution. Oakley became the sensation of Europe: She reportedly took part in the lighting ceremony of the newly built Eiffel Tower; the president of France offered her a commission in the French army; the king of Senegal wanted to buy her so she might kill the tigers then terrorizing his country; and she nearly created a scandal when she ignored protocol and shook hands with the Princess of Wales.

When *Buffalo Bill's Wild West* set up in Italy, Cody and Sitting Bull visited Rome on a tour personally conducted by Pope Leo XIII. To promote the show, an Indian village was built

Buffalo Bill's shows were wildly successful throughout Europe, creating the romanticized impression of the American West that has become accepted as reality.

inside the Colosseum, and a mock shoot-out between cowboys and Indians was staged in St. Peter's Square—followed by a sharpshooting demonstration from Annie Oakley. And the show's concessionaires introduced another American creation to Italian audiences—popcorn!

While the show was wowing Europe, at home the United States Census Bureau officially declared the frontier settled. The dream of a nation stretching from ocean to ocean had come true. The Indian wars were over and most tribes were settled on reservations; the majority of the land had been explored and opened for settlement; the great buffalo herds were mostly gone; railroads crisscrossed the continent; and people were even talking to one another on the telephone. When Cody had first opened his show, it reflected current events, but within a decade, it was presenting a sometimes nostalgic look at a rapidly vanishing era of our history. The reality had been transformed into myth. And crowds loved it. In 1890, the show drew six million people and reported a million-dollar profit. Buffalo Bill Cody and Annie Oakley had become among the best-known Americans in the world. Bill Cody was consulted by presidents on just about all matters concerning the West, and among his friends were the most celebrated writers, painters, and inventors of the time.

Producing a show of that size was an enormous undertaking and required ingenuity to set up and move quickly from place to place at minimal cost. In 1899, for example, the show gave 341 performances in 200 days across 11,000 miles. To accomplish that, the troupe had to carry its own bleacher seating and canopies, electrical generators, and kitchens, and under the direction of James Bailey of the Barnum & Bailey Circus, they revolutionized methods of rapidly and safely loading and unloading railway flatcars.

Among the people who delighted in the performance was the inventor of the electric light, Thomas Edison, who in fact did light the show brightly, enabling it to become one of the first entertainments to be staged in the relative coolness of the night. Oakley and Edison had met in Paris at the 1889 exposition, where he was demonstrating his phonograph. In 1894, he invited her to the Black Maria, which is what he called his photo studio, where he used his kinetograph, the earliest movie camera, to capture the smoke as she fired her guns—as well as visually recording glass balls shattering when she hit them. The "moving pictures" he shot eventually were shown in Kinetoscope parlors and cost five cents to view, causing these halls to become known as *nickelodeons*—and turning Annie Oakley into one of the world's first "movie" stars. After proving he could capture rising smoke on film, Edison also brought Buffalo Bill and several Indians to his West Orange, New Jersey, studio and recorded them.

The success of the *Wild West Show* found Cody in the odd position of being the employer and, at times, the guardian of the same Indians whose tribes he had been at war with only years earlier. It is possible he had even fought some of these specific individuals in battle. But Buffalo Bill proved to be an enlightened employer, paying his cast equal wages and treating all of them—including Indians, black cowboys, and women—with great respect. Indians, in particular, earned a much better wage than would have been possible on a reservation and were able to make their case for fair treatment in show programs and when speaking to newspapers. Cody's abolitionist upbringing transformed easily into common decency, and he was said to be respected by all the people he dealt with. He was known to be an advocate for women's suffrage and at every opportunity fought for fair treatment of Native Americans.

Annie Oakley and Frank Butler had left the show at the beginning of the new century, and Oakley once again took to the stage, starring as *The Western Girl*, a play written for her that involved her using a pistol, rifle, and rope to vanquish the bad guys. A story published in William Randolph Hearst's newspapers in 1904 accused her of being addicted to cocaine and claimed she had been arrested. Outraged by that attack, she sued fifty-six newspapers for libel—winning fifty-five of those cases and restoring her reputation.

The Butlers never quite mastered the art of settling down: building then selling houses in several places, preferring to stay at resorts or in a New York City apartment. Annie Oakley was quoted as admitting, "I went all to pieces under the care of a home." She retired from touring in 1913.

Toward the end of his life, Cody explained, "[T]he west of the old times, with its strong characters, its stern battles and its tremendous stretches of loneliness, can never be blotted from my mind."

By then, *Buffalo Bill's Wild West* had lost its luster. Through the years, several others had attempted to launch competitive Wild West shows, although none of them had been able to survive more than a few seasons. But in 1903, *The Great Train Robbery*, the first Western motion picture, had been released. It was a huge success and further established the Western as a popular cultural form—and cut deeply into the audiences for live shows.

Buffalo Bill had earned a fortune bringing the Wild West to the East Coast and Europe. He'd invested those profits in everything from Arizona mines to filmmaking, publishing, and even a crazy idea about selling fresh spring water all over the country, but in the end, he had little money to show for it. In '08, he'd sold a substantial interest in the show to *Pawnee Bill's Wild West and Great Far East Show* but continued starring in it. In 1910, he began a three-year farewell tour, and the show finally closed forever in 1913.

Buffalo Bill immediately secured backing to produce a five-reel Western picture, *The Indian Wars*. He toured with other shows for another two years, until his health failed. When his death was reported, quite prematurely, he remarked, "I have yet a great life work to complete before I pass over the river. I have been supervising the taking of motion pictures. These start with the opening of the west . . ."

In 1915, Frank and Annie Butler drove their car to visit him while he was appearing in a show entitled *Sells Floto Circus & Buffalo Bill Himself*. That was the last time they were together. When he died at home in 1917, the nation mourned. As the respected western historian and writer William Lightfoot Visscher wrote, "Prominent men and women from many states and civilized nations journeyed to Denver to attend his funeral. Cities did him honor and legislatures adjourned for the obsequies . . ."

From Pine Ridge, the Oglala Sioux sent a telegram, part of which read, "Know that the Oglalas found in Buffalo Bill a warm and lasting friend; that our hearts are heavy from the burden of his passing . . ." It was signed *Chief Jack Red Cloud*.

And Annie Oakley said simply, "He was the kindest hearted, broadest minded, simpliest [*sic*] most loyal man I ever knew. He was in very fact the personification of those sturdy and lovable qualities that really made the West . . ."

Annie Oakley continued to give occasional performances for charity and was especially active raising money to aid the war effort throughout World War I. A strong supporter of women's suffrage, she offered to raise an entire regiment of women capable of fighting in that war. She was sixty-six years old when she died in November 1926, and only three weeks later, Frank Butler, her husband of fifty years, also died.

But both Buffalo Bill and Annie Oakley have lived on in the legends they helped create.

Annie Oakley would be remembered in numerous movies, beginning with the 1935 film *Annie Oakley*, and most successfully in Irving Berlin's Broadway musical and subsequent hit film *Annie Get Your Gun*; while the story of Buffalo Bill has been told in numerous entertainment formats, and he has been played by numerous actors, from Roy Rogers to Paul Newman.

Buffalo Bill and Annie Oakley created the passion for western entertainment that remains so firmly embedded in American culture. Annie Oakley, for all her talent with a gun, never set foot in the Old West. William Cody, on the other hand, played an important role not only in settling the West but also in creating the myths that would end up at least partially obscuring what really happened in this exciting but dangerous time. It was his vision that laid the foundation for all the wonderful storytellers who would follow him, who would turn the hardest days in the Old West into one of the world's most popular entertainment subjects.

While honoring Bill Cody, the state legislature of California properly noted, "[I]n his death that romantic and stirring chapter in our national history that began with Daniel Boone is forever closed."

THE AMERICAN INDIAN: WITH NO RESERVATIONS

Lonesome Dove author Larry McMurtry wrote, "Most of the traditions which we associate with the American West were invented by pulp writers, poster artists, impresarios and advertising men." And without question, at the heart of that invention is the American Indian.

The Indians played an essential role in the actual settling of the West and then played an even larger role in all the glorified stories told about it. The actual relationship between the white settlers and the several hundred different tribes that had lived on the land for thousands of years is extraordinarily complex, but in the legends it generally has been described as an almost continuous battle between mostly innocent settlers wanting to live in peace and the warlike Indians who slaughtered them.

Actually, the many millions of Indians living on the North American continent when Europeans arrived generally left the newcomers alone. In fact, an early problem faced by settlers was that too many of them wanted to leave the settlements and live among the tribes. Ben Franklin said, "No European who has tasted Savage life can afterwards bear to live in our societies."

Most of the tribes didn't care very much about the settlers; they were too busy fighting other tribes. In some ways, theirs was a relatively sophisticated society: Hundreds of years before the American Constitution was written, the Iroquois Great Law of Peace apparently included the freedoms of speech and religion, a separation of powers in government, and the right of women to participate in government. Prior to the American Revolution, the relationship between the largest tribes and the British was good; the Indians even adopted some elements of the British lifestyle and

This 1776 illustration depicts a British Loyalist and American colonist fighting over a banner, while a Native American watches what he believed to be a battle over Indian lands. The Indians sided with the British, anticipating that a British victory would end westward expansion.

farming techniques. And when that war erupted, they fought alongside the British to maintain that relationship.

Following the Revolution, the question that was to shape this new nation—Who owned the land on which the Indians lived?—was strongly debated. George Washington's secretary of war, Henry Knox, believed that "the Indians being the prior occupants, possess the right of the soil."

Responding to President Monroe's attempts to buy their land, a Choctaw chief laid out the Indians' desire: "We wish to remain here, where we have grown up as the herbs of the woods; and do not wish to be transplanted into another soil."

The Indian wars that would spring up like brush fires across the continent for most of the nineteenth century began in the Southeast after the British surrender at Yorktown. But by 1830, all the tribes east of the Mississippi had been pacified, and those tribes were "removed" into the Indian Territory. Andrew Jackson had promised the Indians that the land would be theirs "as long as grass will grow green and the river waters will flow." In actuality, within a decade, more than four million white settlers had crossed the Appalachians into the vast Mississippi valley.

The government negotiated several treaties with the Indians, then proceeded to break those pacts when the land became valuable. The terrifying—then, years later, thrilling—fighting began with the discovery of gold in the Dakotas in 1849 and the decision to build a transcontinental railroad. Great Plains tribes such as the Lakota Sioux, Navajos, Cheyennes,

Comanches, Apaches, Kiowas, and Arapahos lived and hunted on those lands and fought to protect their way of life. But mostly they fought soldiers, not settlers. Although attacks on wagon trains were common in dime novels, Wild West shows, and movies, they were uncommon in real life. It's estimated that fewer than four hundred settlers were killed in Indian attacks, and the settlers probably killed an equal number of Indians. Settlers were much more likely to hire Indians as guides or trade with them than fight them.

As the tribes settled on reservations, government Indian agents and traders arrived, both to provide assistance and to exploit them whenever it was possible.

The Dawes Act of 1887 and ensuing legislation allowed the federal government to sell lands to white settlers that had already been granted by treaty to the tribes. This 1911 poster offers settlers "fine lands in the West" for easy payments.

But the fighting between the army and the Plains Indians was brutal. General Sherman gave his troops orders to kill all Indians—and even their dogs—and burn their villages to the ground. When that failed, the cavalry killed the buffalo to starve the Indians into submission. In 1890, the Census Bureau estimated that in the forty different Indian wars, nineteen thousand white men, women, and children had been killed, along with at least thirty thousand Indians. But the real number of Indian dead is likely in the hundreds of thousands, as countless more tens of thousands died of disease and other factors during long forced marches to designated lands.

Although it is understood that the victors get to write the history, in recent years, Americans have reassessed the country's victory in the Indian wars. Many people have gained a greater understanding of the Indian point of view, perhaps best explained by Chief Black Hawk, who said, upon his surrender in 1832, "We told them to leave us alone, and keep away from us; they followed on, and beset our paths, and they coiled themselves among us, like the snake. They poisoned us by their touch."

JESSE JAMES

 BLOODY POLITICS

On December 7, 1869, "a mist like pall" hung over the small town of Gallatin, Missouri. "The city," reported the *Booneville Weekly Adventures*, "was veiled from sight by the dense fog that prevailed, and an unusual stillness and quiet pervaded every quarter of the little city." Out of that fog and into legend rode the outlaw brothers Jesse and Frank James.

They dismounted and hitched their horses at the water trough in front of the Daviess County Savings Association. At twenty-six, Frank was four years older than Jesse; both brothers had ridden hard through the Civil War and its aftermath. And they hadn't forgotten for a bit what they'd seen and who had done them wrong. They intended to steal the money in this bank, no question about that, but that was not their main reason for being there. They had come to avenge the killing of a friend.

The owner of the bank, former Union captain John W. Sheets, was sitting at his desk in conversation with lawyer William McDonald when the James brothers walked through the door. As Sheets got up to greet these customers, McDonald started to leave. The two men cornered Sheets and pulled their six-shooters. They told him why he was about to die: He had caused the death of their former commander and good friend, "Bloody Bill" Anderson, and they were bound by oath to avenge it. The James brothers then shot him twice, once in the head and once in the heart. When the lawyer McDonald started running, they winged him in his arm, but he got away. Then they grabbed several hundred dollars from the safe and till and took off. A posse pursued them out of town and shots were exchanged. One of the James brothers fell from his horse, which galloped away, but the other brother grabbed his arm and swung him up onto *his* horse, and they outraced their pursuers. As the *Kansas City Daily Journal* reported, "There is a boldness and recklessness about this robbery and murder that is almost beyond belief."

It turned out that Jesse and Frank James had made a mistake—they had killed the wrong man. Although Sheets had been on the team that tracked down and ambushed the murderous Anderson, in fact, it was Major Samuel Cox who deserved credit for bringing an end to Bloody

Bill's reign of terror. Not that the James brothers cared particularly; killing came pretty easily to them. And the result of this bank robbery was far greater than they could have imagined: It made Jesse James famous.

Although bank robberies weren't uncommon, this was such a cold-blooded killing that Missouri governor Thomas T. Crittenden offered the largest reward in state history, ten thousand dollars, for the capture of the outlaws. Among those who read the breathless newspaper account was the founder and editor of the *Kansas City Times*, John Newman Edwards.

In Jesse James, John Edwards found the man he had been looking for. During the war, the James brothers had served with Bloody Bill, who commanded one of the Confederacy's most successful—and vicious—guerrilla units. As an element of Quantrill's Raiders, they had participated in the Centralia massacre, in which more than a hundred Union troops had been slaughtered. After the war, Jesse and Frank James essentially refused to surrender, instead hitting the outlaw trail.

Brothers Frank and Jesse James in about 1870, just after they had become infamous bank robbers

The former colonel John Edwards also had been a proud Confederate. He had served as adjutant to General Joseph Shelby, commanding a division and organizing an extremely successful intelligence operation. Rather than surrender at the conclusion of the war, Edwards fled to Mexico with Shelby and about a thousand men and remained there for several years. When amnesty was granted to most Confederate soldiers, he returned and founded the *Kansas City Times*, a highly political newspaper that championed former Rebel leaders. In its pages, he railed against the corruption, oppression, and criminality of the Republican government, urging ex-Confederates to fight for political power.

Edwards's objective was to restore a sense of pride in the defeated Rebels, and Jesse James proved the perfect symbol for him. As he once wrote of James, "We called him outlaw, and he was—but fate made him so. When the war closed Jesse James had no home . . . hunted, shot, driven away . . . a price upon his head—what else could a man do . . . except what he did? When he was hunted he turned savagely about and hunted his hunters," adding at another time, "They are outlaws through no fault or crime other than participating in a civil war that was not successful. [They are] now so wantonly and unjustly hunted and denounced by all who have partisan passions to gratify."

According to Edwards's newspaper, and the other journals that joined him, rather than a bank robber, train robber, thug, and killer, Jesse James was a political symbol: He was the courageous representative of the defiant South; a man so noble in defeat that he might have "sat with Arthur at the Round Table"; a man of the Confederacy who struck back against the excesses of the carpetbaggers by robbing their banks and their trains—but was careful not to

The journalist John Edwards, whose purple prose transformed the bank robber Jesse James into a Southern hero

trouble innocent people. It worked: The general public had no love for either the banks or the railroads, which were controlled by fat cats in the North and the East who cared not at all for the troubles of the poor workingman. All Jesse James was doing was fighting back for all the people who had no fight left in them. He became the nation's most revered outlaw.

Jesse James readily accepted the mythical role that Edwards had created for him, regularly writing letters to the paper claiming to be innocent of the crimes he was accused of committing, describing his latest exploits, and even leaving press releases at the scenes of his crimes. His tawdry life has been romanticized in literature, theater, and music, and it is accurate to claim that Jesse James wrote the first chapter in the colorful history of American outlaws.

But the question remains: How accurate—if at all—was Edwards's portrayal? Was there, in reality, any political motivation behind James's life of crime, or was he simply a bad guy who served a symbolic purpose? Was he a hero of the downtrodden South, or was he the same person once described by Robert Pinkerton as "the worst man, without any exception, in America. He is utterly devoid of fear and has no more compunction about cold blooded murder than he has about eating his breakfast"?

He certainly was a son of the Old South. Jesse Woodson James was born in Clay County, Missouri, an area known as "Little Dixie," in 1847. His father, Robert James, was a farmer and Baptist minister who was prosperous enough to own six slaves. But the lure of gold drew

Jesse James's father, Baptist minister Robert S. James, was a founder of William Jewell College in Liberty, Missouri, while his mother, Zerelda, was a strong woman who eventually sold pebbles from her son's grave site as souvenirs.

him to California, where he died. It appears that the James boys got their character from their mother, Zerelda James, who hardly fit the definition of a genteel Southern belle. She was a big woman, strong both physically and in temperament. After her husband's death, she married twice more, the second time to Dr. Reuben Samuel, with whom she had four children and owned seven slaves. Zerelda was a practical woman; after Jesse was killed, for example, she profited by selling pebbles off his grave as souvenirs—being careful to replenish those stones each morning so as not to disappoint her customers.

She also was a staunch supporter of the Confederacy. Missouri was a border state, and in the years before war erupted, it was bitterly divided between abolitionists and the proslavery faction—which included Zerelda James and her family. As part of the Missouri Compromise, Missouri had been admitted to the Union as a slave state in 1820, while Maine was admitted as a free state. In 1854, the Kansas-Nebraska Act opened up those two Indian territories to settlers, ruling that the people who lived there would vote on whether these territories would permit slavery. In Kansas, each side set up a state government—and then organized militias to protect its supporters and enforce its orders. In a prelude to the Civil War, the free-state Kansas Jayhawkers and the mostly proslavery Missouri bushwhackers fought a vicious war. Although these two groups supposedly were fighting for their political beliefs, many of the men on both sides were just bandits who used these ideals as an excuse for arson, looting, beatings, and even wholesale murder.

When the Civil War began in April 1861, Missouri officially remained in the Union and declared itself neutral but actually sent troops and supplies to both sides. With Zerelda's encouragement—and wearing the clothes she'd sewn for him—eighteen-year-old Frank James set off to join the Rebels. After he was captured and sent home by Union troops, the local militia forced him to sign an oath swearing loyalty to the Republic. Instead of honoring that oath, he hooked up with Quantrill's Raiders, an especially violent group of bushwhackers. Utilizing guerrilla tactics tailored to each situation, small bands of William Quantrill's men attacked Jayhawkers, Union troops, and pro-Union civilians, in an attempt to drive them out of the territory. They were known to use disguises—including dressing in Union uniforms to infiltrate their ranks—and to organize well-planned attacks and stage ambushes. And, like regular military units, on occasion they did not hesitate to attack towns and kill civilians.

Frank James was an intelligent young man who loved Shakespeare and had once dreamed of going to college and becoming a teacher; instead, he earned a reputation as a fearsome guerrilla fighter. Between raids, he would return to the family farm and regale his relatives with tales of his attacks on Yankees. Jesse certainly listened in awe to his older brother's

The young guns: portraits of twenty-one-year-old Frank and sixteen-year-old Jesse taken during the Civil War

stories—and although he had hoped to follow his father into the ministry, he instead began dreaming of joining his brother in the fight to preserve their way of life.

Attempting to stop these hit-and-run raids, Union troops arrested anyone who had aided or abetted the Raiders, especially the female relatives of known guerrilla fighters. They were held in a three-story house in Kansas City. Four of these women were killed and others were badly injured when the building collapsed in August 1863. Quantrill retaliated by bringing all of his small bands together—an estimated four hundred men—and attacking the town of Lawrence, Kansas. Frank James joined this massacre, which resulted in at least a quarter of the town being burned to the ground and the cold-blooded murders of 150 men and boys. Irate Union troops set out to find and punish the killers.

Jesse James was plowing the family's fields when a Union patrol arrived and demanded to know where his brother was hiding. Sixteen-year-old Jesse refused to answer—and was beaten and horsewhipped. His stepfather Reuben Samuel was tortured, suspended from a tree, then dropped several times until he gave up the information. He barely survived. Apparently the bluecoats found Frank James's band, but he managed to escape. When he rejoined the militia, his younger brother was riding with him.

After the Lawrence massacre, Quantrill's Raiders split into three large bands, and Frank and Jesse James rode with Bloody Bill Anderson's eighty-man army. The savage lessons they learned fighting with Anderson would be put to use after the war ended.

Anderson had joined Quantrill after Union militiamen had hanged his father and uncle. His three sisters were among the Kansas City hostages; in the collapse, one of them died and the other two suffered injuries that would plague them for the rest of their lives. Whatever humanity Anderson had at that point disappeared, and as he once said, "I ask no quarter and give none." He was known to torture captives, scalping them and cutting off their ears. Anderson and his teenage lieutenant, Archie Clement, who became known to authorities as "Bill Anderson's scalper and head devil," served as young Jesse James's mentors. "Little Arch," as the latter was known, was only a bit over five feet tall and was full-up angry at the world.

Jesse James was with them when they rode into the town of Centralia, Missouri, in

Bloody Bill Anderson became a guerrilla in 1862 after Jayhawkers hanged his father and his uncle, stole all their possessions, and burned their home to the ground.

September 1864, a few weeks after six of Anderson's men had been killed and scalped by federal troops. Bloody Bill's men stopped a train and captured twenty-two of General Sherman's soldiers on their way home on furlough. They were stripped, lined up, and shot numerous times; then their bodies were mutilated. A witness described the event as "a carnival of blood." About one hundred fifty Union soldiers were sent to track Anderson down; instead, his men ambushed the patrol and killed every member of it, even the wounded. Jesse James received credit for killing the patrol's commander, Major A. V. E. Johnson. Then, in a truly mad frenzy, the Raiders disemboweled, scalped, crushed, and decapitated the bodies of their victims.

At sixteen, Jesse James was probably the youngest participant in these atrocities. A month after the Centralia massacre, three hundred men of the Missouri state militia, led by Major Samuel P. Cox, found Anderson's camp near Orrick, Missouri. In the ensuing gun battle, Anderson was shot twice in the back of his head. Among his possessions was a rope in which he had tied a knot for each man he killed personally; Cox's men counted fifty-four knots. After Anderson's body was photographed as evidence of his death, his head was severed and mounted on top of a telegraph pole.

The James brothers managed to get away, eventually rejoining Quantrill in an ill-fated attempt to ride to Washington and kill President Lincoln. Several weeks after General Lee's surrender at Appomattox, a militia force surprised Quantrill's men near Taylorsville, Kentucky; Quantrill was shot and died a month later of his wounds. There are conflicting reports about exactly what happened next. According to T. J. Stiles, author of the acclaimed biography *Jesse James: Last Rebel of the Civil War,* James was captured by Union forces and held prisoner in a hotel that had been used as a hospital, where he was forced to surrender. But according to Judge Thomas Shouse, who had been friends with both James brothers, Jesse told him that he had been shot in his right lung by a "mini-ball" fired by drunken Union soldiers as he rode into Lexington, Missouri, carrying a white flag of surrender, prepared to sign the Union's loyalty oath. He claimed that was the seventh time he had been wounded. His horse was killed, and as he later wrote, "I ran through the woods pursued by two men on horseback. . . . I was near a creek. I lay in the water all night, it seemed that my body was on fire." A farmer plowing nearby helped him, and eventually he made it back to his family, who by then were living in Rulo, Nebraska. For eight weeks he hovered between life and death, at one point telling his mother, "I don't want to die in a northern state." Among the women who nursed him back to health was his lovely cousin Zerelda "Zee" Mimms, whom he would later marry.

He later claimed that while he was recovering, five militiamen came to his house, prepared to kill him. It was fight or die, he later wrote: "Surrender had played out for me." He struggled to get out of bed, fired once through the front door, then flung it open, and with a pistol in each hand, commenced firing, bringing down four of them. He knew then that he would never be allowed to live peacefully.

At the end of the war, Frank James surrendered in Kentucky, then violated postwar regulations by sneaking home. On his dangerous journey, he got into a gunfight with four Union soldiers; he killed two of them and wounded a third, and a bullet nipped him in the left hip. He made it home, but he couldn't stay there. For men like the James brothers, returning to any kind of normal civilian life proved impossible. The war had transformed them into different people; after what they had seen, after what they had done, after all the destruction the war caused, there was nothing for them to go back to. And, in addition, as Jesse had learned, Union militiamen weren't about to forgive them, no matter what Lincoln and Grant had promised.

In addition to Frank and Jesse James, among the people permanently scarred by the war were Cole and James Younger. They were farm boys from Kansas, two of the fourteen children of Henry Washington Younger. Although a slave owner, Henry was a Union sympathizer, as was his whole family. But when Jayhawkers began raiding the family farm, stealing livestock

The outlaw Cole Younger in 1903; after serving twenty-five years in prison, he published his autobiography and partnered with Frank James to create a Wild West show.

and destroying property, Cole Younger turned against them and eventually joined Quantrill's Raiders. Any ambivalence he might have felt disappeared when Union militiamen killed his father. Cole rode into Lawrence, Kansas, with Quantrill and Frank James, and when they rode out a day later, all of them would be bonded forever.

Cole's little brother James also joined Quantrill and stayed with the Raiders when Cole joined the regular Confederate army and, as a captain, led troops into Louisiana and California. When the Younger brothers finally made it home after the war, the family farm was a ruin.

Several of the former guerrillas stayed loosely together during Reconstruction under the leadership of Little Arch Clement, who is generally believed to have turned them into outlaws. On the cold morning of February 13, 1866, they began to show the world the valuable lessons they had learned, when about thirteen of them rode into Liberty, Missouri, dressed in the long blue coats of the Union soldiers. There were only a few people on the street, and no one suspected that this was the beginning of a bank robbery—because never before in peacetime had a bank robbery taken place in the light of day.

There is no record of exactly whose idea it was to hold up the Clay County Savings Bank in broad daylight, but several important facts linked the plan directly to the James brothers: The bank was owned by a man named Greenup Bird, who years earlier had been especially harsh on Reuben Samuel in negotiations over a debt. Also, disguising themselves as Union soldiers was an old Raiders trick. And, finally, the bank was filled with Yankee dollars.

Using the same raiding tactics they had perfected during the war, the men dismounted and took their assigned positions, creating a series of perimeters around the bank. Jesse wasn't among them, because he was still recovering from his chest wound and unable to ride, although it is believed that he helped plan the job. Frank James and Cole Younger entered the bank and pulled their pistols. The only other person in the bank was Bird's son. He and his father put all the bank's money into a large grain sack. The robbers escaped with $58,072.64, the modern-day equivalent of almost a million dollars.

No one had been hurt during the robbery, but the gang made its escape a-whoopin' and a-hollerin' out of town—and wildly firing guns in the air. As the men raced down the main street, two other young men watched them—and for no reason anyone could ever figure, Arch Clement took aim and shot one of them dead. As was later remarked, Arch just liked killing. A few days after the robbery, the victim's family reportedly received a letter signed by a man no one had ever heard of at the time named Jesse James, who apologized for the murder and stated that the gang had not intended to kill anyone.

The take was so large that if money had been the motivation, most members of that crew could have quit robbing right then and lived comfortably for the rest of their lives. Some of them did, in fact, but not the James boys, nor the Youngers. For them, this was just the beginning of a crime spree that would last almost two decades and grow to include dozens of bank, train, and stagecoach robberies.

The first robbery in which Jesse was believed to be an active participant took place at the end of October, when bandits stole $2,011.50 from the Alexander Mitchell and Company bank in Lexington, Missouri. The robbers followed a pattern that was to become familiar: One man would ask a clerk to change a large bill, and then at least one other "customer" would pull his gun and announce the holdup. Six weeks after this job, the state militia caught up with Arch Clement, drinking in a Lexington saloon. Clement got on his horse and tried to ride his way out of it, but he was shot in the chest. A second shot knocked him off his horse. As he lay dying in the dirt, trying to cock his revolver with his teeth, he said, "I've done what I've always said I would do . . . die before I'd surrender."

In the months following Clement's death, several members of his gang either were caught and hanged or just had enough and rode off, leaving the core crew that gained renown as the James-Younger Gang. Due primarily to the eventual notoriety of Jesse James, it became the best-known gang in the Old West, though there are historians who doubt it deserves that recognition.

As bank robbing became a more popular crime, it became more and more difficult to pin any holdup on a specific gang, and even when the gang could be identified, it was almost impossible to know who exactly was riding with it at that point. The better known the James-Younger Gang became, for example, the more robberies were attributed to it, as if there were some status attached to being held up by Jesse James and Cole Younger. The next job attributed to them—that they may or may not have pulled off—was the Hughes and Wasson Bank in Richmond, Missouri; fourteen robbers stole about thirty-five hundred dollars—and killed three men who got in their way. Four former bushwhackers were eventually caught and lynched for this robbery.

But there is no doubt that Jesse James and Cole Younger led eight men into Russellville, Kentucky, on May 20, 1868, and rode out with exactly $9,035.92. As the gang made its escape, shooting into the air to discourage gawkers, one member shot at the metal fish weather vane atop the courthouse, sending it spinning. Almost a century later, that historic weather vane, with a bullet hole through it, could still be seen on the roof of the new courthouse, where it had been placed to honor the town's history. One man was eventually convicted for that robbery, for which he served three years in prison.

As the robberies continued, the fame—and fear—spread. On June 3, 1871, a gang of men rode into Corydon, Iowa, intending to rob the county treasurer of tax receipts. As usual, they began by asking to change a large bill. But before they pulled their guns, they were informed that the safe was time locked. The kindly clerk suggested they could get change at the Ocobock Brothers Bank, which was opening that very day. They thanked the man and helped celebrate the new bank's opening by stealing about six thousand dollars. Following this robbery, authorities hired the famed Pinkerton detective agency, renowned as the best modern crime solvers in the world, to finally bring this gang to justice.

The banks began falling like targets in a shooting gallery, and the gang began expanding its efforts. In 1872, the men stole the cash box from the Kansas City Exposition. Although most reports claim they got almost ten thousand dollars, the treasurer later claimed it was only $998. Shots were fired while they were making their getaway, and a young girl was slightly wounded. Soon afterward, an anonymous letter published in the *Kansas City Weekly Times* admitted, "It is true I shot a little girl, though it was not intentional; and if the parents will give me their address through the columns of [this newspaper] I will send them money to pay her doctor's bill."

In July 1873, the gang pulled off its first train robbery outside Adair, Iowa. The men removed a track rail, believing that this would force the Chicago, Rock Island & Pacific conductor to stop the train. Unfortunately, the train derailed, killing the engineer and injuring many passengers. The gang boarded the train dressed in the white sheets of Ku Klux Klan members and stole $2,337. During the holdup, Jesse supposedly told the passengers that the gang was stealing from the rich to help the poor. The railroad immediately offered a $5,500 reward for the conviction of these robbers. Six months later, the gang robbed its first stagecoach, this time wearing Union army blue coats and getting away with anywhere between one thousand and eight thousand dollars—but returning a purse untouched to a man who claimed to have fought for the Confederacy.

At the end of January 1874, the gang stopped an Iron Mountain Railway express near Gads Hill, Missouri. For the first time, the men robbed train passengers—asking each person to hold out his hands for inspection, permitting workingmen with calluses to keep their money. They took $10,000 from the safe and $3,400 from passengers. As they were making their escape, one of the robbers, later identified by his handwriting as Jesse James, left a note reading, "The most daring robbery on record! The southbound train on the Iron Mountain Railroad was stopped here this evening by five heavily armed men and robbed of _____ dollars. . . . The robbers were all large men, none of them under six feet tall. They were masked . . ."

The fame of the James-Younger Gang resulted in individual *cartes-de-visite*, collectible business-card-size portraits, of the best-known members. This 1876 composite includes the eight most infamous outlaws and their final victim.

A magazine illustration showing Frank and Jesse James holding up the Chicago & Alton Railroad in 1879—escaping with six thousand dollars

The gang followed no discernible pattern and stayed on the move. Its reputation continued to grow throughout the country, but especially throughout the former Confederacy, where sympathizers helped the men evade the law. At times they lived a reasonably normal life, at least for robbers and killers. Within months of each other early in 1874, for example, both Jesse and Frank married and set up households.

Their fame was such that almost every crime in the region initially was attributed to them. Jesse's audacious scheme of leaving notes at robberies helped the newspapers create his populist image. Some Southern newspapers began to portray him in almost heroic terms, repeating the completely untrue claim that he robbed from the rich and gave to the poor. In actuality, the gang robbed from pretty much everybody, and kept all of it.

In March 1874, Pinkerton operative Joseph Whicher arrived in Clay County, intending to go out to the James farm disguised as a fugitive from justice and confront Jesse and Frank.

One day later, his body was discovered with three bullet holes in it. By the time the body was found, the pigs had gotten to it. At just about the same time, three Pinkertons went to St. Clair County, Missouri, to deal with the Youngers. In a shoot-out, John Younger and two of the Pinks were killed.

For reasons obvious and personal, the founder of Pinkerton's, Allan Pinkerton, responded harshly to the murder of his three men. On the night of January 25, 1875, as Reuben and Zerelda Samuel and their nine-year-old son, Archie, slept, Pinks silently surrounded the farmhouse. One of them hurled an incendiary device through the window. Reuben found a shovel and pushed it into the fireplace—and seconds later it exploded. Zerelda's arm was so badly ripped apart that it had to be amputated; shrapnel tore into Archie Samuel's body and killed him. Eight Pinks were indicted for murder, although none was ever tried for the crime. The Pinkertons, facing the unenviable task of pursuing popular criminals living in an environment supportive of them and hostile to the detectives, dropped the case. The gang had defeated the best law-enforcement agency in the country.

John Edwards used his editorial pages to raise both fury at the carpetbaggers and sympathy for the people who fought them, causing the Missouri legislature to propose a bill granting amnesty to the James-Younger Gang. But when Daniel Askew, a local farmer who was believed to have helped the Pinkertons plan their raid, was murdered on April 12, that offer was rescinded.

After the disastrous attempt to rob the Northfield, Minnesota, bank, this posse pursued the three Younger brothers for almost three weeks before capturing them in a swamp.

It's doubtful Jesse would have accepted it, anyway. The killing of his half brother and maiming of his mother pushed Jesse James far beyond any possibility of redemption. His only purpose in life was to punish the North. To build support, Jesse routinely wrote letters to newspapers, claiming as he did in the *Nashville Banner*, "[F]or 10 years the radical papers in Mo. and other states have charged nearly every daring robbery in America to the James and Youngers. It is enough persecution for the northern papers to persecute us without the papers in the south persecuting us, the land we fought for four years to save from northern tyranny . . ." In a postscript to this letter, the obviously proud James asks that a copy of it be sent to his mother in Clay County.

Perhaps believing the tales that made it appear invincible, the gang made the fatal decision to move north for its next caper, far from the friendly surroundings that provided cover for it. The men chose the First National Bank of Northfield, Minnesota, supposedly because of its connection to two Union generals, Benjamin Butler and Adelbert Ames. Ames was believed to have recently made a fifty-thousand-dollar deposit. They planned the job for weeks but failed to take into account the very different environment in Minnesota. Northfield was a small town of hardworking, tough people and farmers who dressed plainly, and the only weapons they carried were long guns. Many of the residents had seen action with the First Minnesota during the war. From the moment the robbers rode into town, dressed in linen dusters and carrying pistols, they attracted suspicion. Three members of the gang went into the bank, while five men waited outside, several of whom began riding up and down Division Street, firing their weapons into the air, attempting to scare people off the streets.

The First National Bank of Northfield, Minnesota, was the last robbery of the infamous James-Younger Gang. Every gang member was wounded, two of them were killed, and the three Younger brothers were captured—for bags of nickels.

These people didn't scare easily. Instead, one man peered into the bank through a window and began shouting, "They're robbing the bank, boys! Go get your guns!"

The robbery went wrong from the beginning. When a cashier refused to open the safe, he was killed. Rather than the fifty thousand, the gang found only bags of nickels worth about twenty-three dollars. Townspeople reached for their guns and started firing while the robbers were still inside the bank. The *Sunday Times* of Chicago praised them: "The robbers did not get into the vault, nor did they find the cashier's drawer, except the nickel drawer, and the handful of nickels taken from it was thrown to the floor. The citizens of Northfield behaved like old veterans, as many of them are." The proprietor of the local hardware store initially believed the robbery was a promotional stunt for a local theater company, but when he realized it was for real, he picked up a single-shot Remington and took aim. Other people threw rocks at them, or fired bird shot from shotguns. Soon deadly fire was coming from every direction as the gang tried to make its escape. Two members of the gang were killed, and every other member was wounded as they made their getaway. Frank James was shot in his right leg; Jesse was hit in his thigh. In addition to the cashier, one local citizen was killed in the gunfight. The men split up when they got out of town in an attempt to evade the posses they knew would be coming for them. Supposedly they burned fourteen mills in the county to create a distraction. While the James brothers successfully evaded the estimated thousand men searching for them, somehow making it safely into the Dakotas, two weeks after the raid, all three Younger brothers were captured in a swamp. Cole Younger had been shot eleven times but survived. Rather than face execution, they pleaded guilty and were sentenced to life imprisonment. Bob Younger died in prison of tuberculosis in 1889, but Cole and Jim were paroled after serving twenty-five years. That Northfield raid marked the bloody end of the legendary James-Younger Gang.

For the next three years, Frank and Jesse lay low. They supposedly spent almost two years hiding out in Mexico until some of the heat was off, then returned. "Those years," Frank James said, "of quiet, upright life, were the happiest I have spent since my boyhood. My old life grew more detestable the further I got away from it." Jesse and Zee lived under the name Howard, and until the day Jesse died, his two surviving children did not know their real last name or their father's identity. Although Frank had decided he was done with the criminal life and wanted to live peacefully, Jesse clearly harbored other ideas.

The times had changed. The hatreds instilled by the war were calming. People had moved on, and the support that Jesse had once enjoyed was gone. Even the newspaperman Edwards would no longer publish his letters. But James had become addicted to danger and fame, and apparently also to laudanum, an opiate that dulled the senses and was often used as a painkiller.

Supposedly, while visiting the boomtown of Las Vegas to see if his family might settle there, Jesse encountered Billy the Kid and unsuccessfully attempted to persuade him to ride to Tennessee with him. When his brother Frank refused to return to a life of crime, Jesse recruited a new band of outlaws. Among them was his first cousin Wood Hite, who had also ridden with Bloody Bill during the war, and an alcoholic gunfighter, a horse thief, a slow-witted farmer, and the younger brother of an old friend. Jesse James was now the sole leader of this motley gang, in charge of making all the plans.

They struck first in October 1879, rolling a boulder across railroad tracks and stopping a Chicago & Alton Railroad express at Glendale, Missouri. They got away clean with six thousand dollars. Jesse James was back in business.

A month later, a Kansas City newspaper reported that a former member of the James-Younger Gang had killed Jesse. The story got a lot of coverage, but it was quickly proven false, although no one figured out why the claim had been made. Meanwhile, Jesse had used his share of the loot to buy a racehorse. The horse won enough races to show some early promise, but when Jesse took him to Atlanta and bet heavily on him, he lost, forcing Jesse to sell him to have enough money to get home.

That Jesse's new gang lacked the loyalty of his first gang, loyalty that had been forged in common experience, became obvious when Jesse got into an argument with one of his new members and shot him dead. The gang also lacked the ambition of the early days, settling for robbing a tourist stagecoach of two thousand dollars, then missing a coal-mine payroll and instead getting away with a paltry thirteen. In March 1881, they robbed a courier carrying the payroll for workers digging a canal at Muscle Shoals, Alabama. They took the five-thousand-dollar payroll but let the paymaster keep the fifty dollars in his own wallet.

By that point, disintegrating loyalties had put everyone at risk, including Frank James, who was afraid his new identity and location would be exposed. For reasons that have never been determined, although he simply might have needed money, Frank James decided to rejoin the outfit. Where once Frank had been in command and Jesse dutifully followed his older brother's orders, now Jesse was clearly the leader and decision maker. Under his leadership, the James brothers returned to their old ways, jumping aboard and stopping a Chicago, Rock Island & Pacific Railroad train at Winston, Missouri, on July 15, 1881. During the robbery, Jesse decided that the conductor was the man who had assisted the Pinkertons when they had bombed his parents' home, and he apparently shot him in the back without warning. When a passenger came to the conductor's assistance, he was also shot and killed, and it is generally believed that Frank James pulled the trigger. The gang netted only $650.

Public opinion had turned completely against the James brothers. Even residents of their hometown, who had once celebrated them, admitted that they needed to be stopped. It was commonly accepted that their continued presence in the area gave the whole of Missouri a poor reputation, limiting immigration and economic expansion. In Governor Crittenden's 1881 inaugural address, he stated that capturing the James brothers was his top priority and that he was not going to allow political considerations to get in the way, proclaiming, "Missouri cannot be the home and abiding place of lawlessness of any character." Laws passed when the James-Younger Gang enjoyed popular support prevented the governor from offering a sizeable reward, but after the murders in Winston, he convinced the railroad to put up a reward of ten thousand dollars each (the equivalent of about a quarter million dollars today) for the capture of Frank and Jesse James.

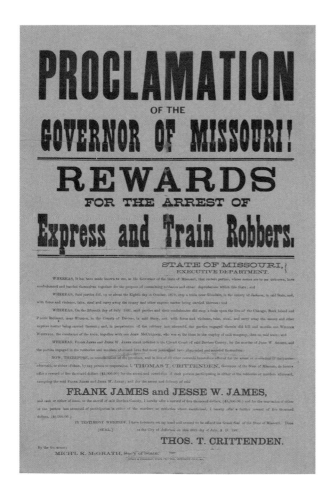

Missouri governor Crittenden offered five thousand dollars for the arrest and conviction of the men who had robbed two trains—but offered double that reward each for Frank and Jesse James.

In early September 1881, the James Gang, now including newcomer Charley Ford, flagged down a St. Louis, Alton & Chicago Railroad train as it slowed to go through an area known as the Blue Cut in Glendale, Missouri. Although five of the robbers were masked, Jesse James was not and actually told passengers who was holding them up. The train's safe was almost empty, so the gang relieved the passengers of their money, watches, and jewelry, fleeing with about a thousand dollars. As it turned out, this was Jesse James's last robbery.

That ten-thousand-dollar reward stirred up a lot of interest. Jesse was no longer that larger-than-life character whose name alone evoked terror. Realizing that there were now few people he could trust, Jesse settled with his family in St. Joseph, Missouri, living there under the name of Thomas Howard.

To keep his gang close, Jesse let Charley and his younger brother Bob Ford stay with him. The rest of his gang was scattered nearby: His cousin Wood Hite was staying with another gang member, Dick Liddil, at the home of Charley Ford's sister Martha Bolton. Apparently Martha was a lovely woman, as both Hite and Liddil were said to be smitten with her. There were even some reports that Jesse also had cast his eyes in her direction. But something happened in that house in early December. There already was some bad blood between Hite and Liddil about the split on the Blue Cut job, but the tension erupted one morning and they

Robert Ford was twenty years old when he shot unarmed Jesse James in the back of the head. He later reenacted the deed onstage in the play *How I Killed Jesse James*—but most people condemned his cowardly action and the play failed.

In death, Jesse James's celebrity grew. Only Buffalo Bill appeared as a hero in more dime novels, in addition to numerous "true accounts" and even touring stage shows.

took to shooting at each other. Both men were wounded, but probably not seriously. Then Martha and Bob Ford came upon the scene, and the twenty-one-year-old Bob Ford shot Hite once in the head, settling the dispute. Jesse James's cousin was buried in a shallow grave on the property. Liddil and Ford knew they had a serious problem: No one wanted to hazard a guess at what actions Jesse might take when he learned his cousin had been killed.

Charley and Bob Ford were looking for a way out of this mess, and in January they found it. They met secretly with Governor Crittenden and the Clay County sheriff and were not at all surprised to discover they shared some goals, the foremost of which was to rid Missouri, and perhaps the world, of Jesse James. In addition to the ten-thousand-dollar reward, the Ford brothers wanted a blanket pardon for all their crimes, including the murder they were about to commit, as well as a pardon for Liddil. The governor apparently was amenable, although the extent of that amenability would later be debated. Several days later, Liddil surrendered to the sheriff, although no announcement was made to the press so as not to alert Jesse.

Sometime in March 1882, Jesse began planning his next stickup, finally deciding to rob the bank in Platte City, Missouri. To pull it off, though, he told Charley Ford, he needed some other people. Ford suggested his brother Bob. Preparations were stepped up in late March. The robbery was planned for the first week in April.

At breakfast on the morning of April 3, Jesse was surprised to find an article in the local newspaper reporting that Liddil had surrendered. Word had leaked out. Oddly, he didn't ask the Ford brothers if they knew anything about this, a natural question, and the fact that he didn't ask made them very nervous. Instead, he cursed Liddil as a traitor and declared that he deserved to hang. After breakfast, Jesse had some chores to do. It was a warm day, so he took off his coat. Jesse always wore his guns, but he also wore a coat so no one would wonder why a peaceful man named Tom Howard was carrying two six-shooters. When he took off his coat, he also took off his gun belt and laid his guns on the bed. This was very unusual for him, as he was never to be found without his guns at arms' length. It was the opportunity the Fords had been waiting for. As they were talking, Jesse suddenly noticed that a picture hanging on the wall was askew and did something completely out of character. He stood on a chair, turned his back to the Fords, and started straightening the picture, or dusting it.

Bob Ford shot him dead. Both Ford brothers had pulled their weapons; there were reports that Charley fired too and missed. But Bob Ford's one shot hit Jesse James under his right ear, and he fell. He was thirty-four years old when he died.

Bob Ford sent wires to the governor and the sheriff, claiming the reward, then both brothers surrendered to the local marshal. As word spread that Thomas Howard was actually

The assassination of Jesse James made national headlines. The popular *Police Gazette* immediately published this fanciful illustration (*above left*). The photo of the outlaw in death became a national sensation, and crowds flocked to see the house in St. Joseph where he was murdered.

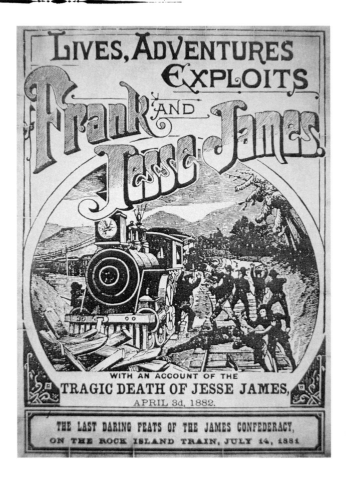

This softcover edition from Chicago's Stein Publishing House was typical of the numerous books rushed into print after James's murder.

the feared killer Jesse James, the people of St. Joseph rushed to the house to catch a glimpse of his body, stunned to discover that the most wanted man in the country had been living comfortably among them.

The Fords were arrested. Two weeks later, within hours, both men were indicted for the murder of Jesse James, pleaded guilty, were sentenced to hang, were pardoned by Governor Crittenden, and walked out of the prison free men. Rather than the ten-thousand-dollar reward, they ended up with about six hundred, as the governor divided the money among many deserving parties—himself included. And, rather than being acclaimed for finally bringing Jesse James to eternal justice, the Fords were scorned as cowards for shooting him in the back.

Within a month of Jesse's death, the newspaperman John Edwards began corresponding with the governor to arrange Frank James's surrender. For the next three years, Frank fought charges accusing him of committing numerous crimes in several states. He was tried on only two of the murder-robberies and was acquitted. Many respectable men testified to his good character. In February 1885, he was cleared of all charges. For him, the Civil War and all the battles that followed finally were over.

Charley and Bob Ford toured in a theater production entitled *The Brother's Vow; or, the Bandit's Revenge*, in which they reenacted the murder of Jesse James. Initially it was quite successful, but over time audiences lost interest, and it closed, leaving them almost broke. In 1884, Charley Ford, addicted to morphine and suffering from tuberculosis, and distraught at being considered a coward, committed suicide. Bob Ford held several jobs, earning some money posing for photographs with rubes in dime museums, billed as "the man who killed Jesse James." By 1892, he was running a tent saloon in Creede, Colorado. A man named Ed O'Kelley shot and killed him there after an argument.

Frank James held several jobs, even touring with Cole Younger for a bit in a theatrical production called *The Great Cole Younger and Frank James Historical Wild West Show*. Frank James died of a heart attack in 1915.

The legend of Jesse James has been told in almost every American cultural medium—but two often-asked questions have never been satisfactorily answered. One: Was Jesse James a hero of the Old South, fighting against the evils of Reconstruction and the carpetbaggers' intent to profit from the destruction of war, or was he an outlaw who took advantage of the political situation? When he raged, "Just let a party of men commit a bold robbery, and the cry is hang them, but [President] Grant and his party can steal millions, and it is all right," was he simply an actor playing a role created for him by John Edwards, or did he really mean it? The answer, most probably, is a bit of both. He started out with a set of skills perfected in the war; then he clearly embraced and enjoyed playing the noble character fighting for Southern dignity, and perhaps at times he truly meant it. But even after that was no longer relevant, he continued robbing and killing. He knew no other way.

The second and equally intriguing question is, Why would he take off his guns and turn his back on two men he did not know especially well and probably didn't trust? He never went anywhere without his guns. Historians have offered a variety of explanations, describing the act as everything from foolhardy to courageous. Bob Ford once said he thought it was a trick: that Jesse wanted to make it appear that he trusted them so that he might later take action against them. Others have suggested that perhaps Jesse was tired and careless and willing to let fate play its hand. As he himself once wrote, "Justice is slow but sure, and there is a just God that will bring all to justice."

DOC HOLLIDAY

Desperate Measures

lthough it reads like an advertisement for a movie, this is a true story: The gunslinger Doc Holliday spent most of his life preparing to die, until he finally found a reason to live—and it almost killed him.

Without a doubt, John Henry Holliday was the meanest, toughest, and probably the most violent dentist in American history; although, truth be told, he definitely could fill a cavity. His close friend Wyatt Earp described him as "a philosopher whom life had made a caustic wit . . . the most skillful gambler, and the nerviest, fastest, deadliest man with a six gun I ever saw."

Unlike the other famous gunslingers of the Old West, John Holliday was a wealthy, well-educated man. His father, Henry Holliday, was a soldier, druggist, and planter who had fought the Indians in 1838, the Mexicans in 1846, and the Union army in 1861, rising to the rank of major before being forced by illness to resign his commission. His mother, Alice, was a classic Southern belle. His cousin, Mattie Holliday, who lived to be one hundred, served as the model for the character Melanie in Margaret Mitchell's *Gone With the Wind*. John Henry was born in Griffin, Georgia, in 1852, but a decade later, the family, fleeing General Sherman's March to the Sea, moved to Valdosta, Georgia, where Henry Holliday eventually was elected mayor. When John Henry was fifteen years old, his mother died of tuberculosis, the same disease that would later kill his adopted brother and shape the course of his own life.

Nothing about his childhood suggested that he would one day wind up in the most famous gunfight in American history, the showdown at the O.K. Corral. John Henry received a classical education, studying grammar, mathematics, French, Latin, and ancient Greek. When it came time for him to pick a career, dentistry seemed an appropriate path to follow; his cousin had founded Philadelphia's Pennsylvania College of Dental Surgery. He graduated from there in 1872, after writing a thesis on diseases of the teeth, and joined a practice in Atlanta. Under normal circumstances, he would have gone on to have a fine life: He would have married a genteel woman and started a family; at night, he would sit by the parlor fire in his comfortable Georgia home; and he would die in old age, surrounded by loved ones.

Instead, he started coughing.

In 1873, when he was only twenty-two years old, John Holliday was diagnosed with tuberculosis, at that time a fatal disease. The cause wasn't known, and there was no cure. He consulted the best doctors in Atlanta, and their opinion was unanimous: The only treatment was to move to a drier climate, which was believed to prolong life. As it turned out, he might well have had another reason to leave Georgia: It's possible that he had shot his first victim.

According to the story, written years later by lawman-turned-journalist Bat Masterson, John Henry and some friends came upon a group of black teenagers enjoying a popular swimming hole on the Withlacoochee River. Supposedly the two groups got into an argument, and Holliday produced a double-barreled shotgun. He shot and killed two of them and wounded several others, although his family insisted the story wasn't true and he had simply fired over their heads to scare them away.

Legends are born of reality, which is exaggerated and embellished until it shines brightly. Although the actual facts of that day are hazy, the meaning is clear: Even at a young age, there was a dark and dangerous side to John Henry Holliday.

Whatever the reason, Holliday moved to Dallas and opened a dental practice. His skills were obvious: At the Dallas County Fair, he won several awards, including "best set of teeth in gold." Dallas was a booming cow town, the railroad making it a hub for shipping grain, cotton, and buffalo hides. It might have been a smart place for a skilled dentist to set up shop, but not too many people there were willing to risk their lives visiting a dentist infected with consumption. As he soon discovered, though, there was another trade at which he excelled: John Holliday was a gambling man. As Masterson wrote, "Gambling was not only the principal and best-paying industry of the town at the time, but it was also reckoned among its most respectable."

The cards loved him. He possessed two traits that were essential for any gambler: intelligence and a poker face. If there was a single benefit to living with a death sentence, this was it: Nothing seemed to really make a difference to him. Win or lose, he was going to be dead in a few years. That knowledge made it easy for him to hide his emotions and draw the next card—or, when necessary, draw his gun.

When money and alcohol are put on the same table, tempers can get mighty thin. The first time a gambling man backed down in the Old West, he might just as well keep moving, because people would learn about it and wouldn't hesitate to take advantage. In 1875, Holliday was arrested after trading wild shots with saloon keeper Charles Austin. He was acquitted but, supposedly, a few days later, got into another gunfight and this time killed "a prominent citizen." There is at least some evidence that this incident was just a story Holliday concocted to impress people. Apparently it worked, because by the time he settled in Jacksboro, Texas, in 1876, he was said to be carrying two guns and a knife and had become known as "the Deadly Dentist"! Allegedly he had to hightail it out of Jacksboro after killing a black soldier from nearby Fort Richardson—with the army, the Texas Rangers, the US marshal, the local sheriff, and a posse of citizens in hot pursuit, trying to collect the reward placed on his head. There actually may be some truth to that one, as there is a record of a Private Jacob Smith being shot around that time by an "unknown assailant."

Gamblers are always chasing the next big pot, and Holliday moved often, usually carrying with him some tale of violence for which there was little evidence. Supposedly, for example, while dealing faro in Denver under the alias Tom Mackey in 1875, he slashed the throat of a bully named Buddy Ryan. He also is credited with three killings in Cheyenne. It is possible; Masterson was blunt in his assessment, pointing out, "Holliday had a mean disposition and an ungovernable temper, and under the influence of liquor was a most dangerous man." True or not, these stories served a purpose: Holliday had figured out pretty quickly that a reputation for being good with a gun would often make people hesitate before drawing on you.

While on the trail, John Henry hadn't forgotten his dental training, and when he found himself staying in one place for more than a short spell, he'd hang out his shingle, which gave him the nickname by which he would eventually gain renown, "Doc" Holliday.

A gambler's place of work is the saloon, and nobody ever claimed that Doc Holliday didn't enjoy a drink or two or several more. Why not—one thing he knew for sure was that it wasn't the whiskey that was going to kill him. He was what we'd now call a functioning alcoholic, with a hair-trigger temper. In a barroom fight in Breckenridge, Texas, he beat a gambler named Henry Kahn with his walking stick. Kahn returned later that day and shot Holliday. His wounds were so serious that the *Dallas Weekly Herald* quite prematurely reported his death. Upon his recovery, he settled in the rowdy town of Fort Griffin, where only a few years earlier a band of Kiowas had attacked a wagon train and killed seven men. But for Doc Holliday, that's where the tall tales ended and his life as an American western legend took root.

While working as a card dealer at the pugilist John Shanssey's saloon in 1877, he met a truly formidable woman named Mary Katherine Horony, a curvaceous twenty-six-year-old dance-hall girl and sometime prostitute better known as "Big Nose Kate," who would be his primary female companion for the rest of his life. The Hungarian-born, well-bred, and well-educated Kate was a fine match for him: She didn't seem to give two hoots about very much, either, especially what people thought of her. She was tough, stubborn, and hot tempered

This portrait of thirty-one-year-old Doc Holliday was taken only months after the shoot-out at the O.K. Corral.

and often told people that she belonged to no man, nor to any madam—she worked as a prostitute because she liked both the benefits and the freedom. And, ironically, she had already been married once—to a dentist, who had died.

Soon after Holliday and Kate got together, she had an opportunity to show how much she cared for him: She got to break him out of prison. In one version of the story, Doc had been playing poker with a gambler named Ed Bailey, who insisted on sifting through the discards in violation of the rules of Western Poker. Doc finally had had enough and claimed the pot. Bailey pulled his revolver, but before he could fire, Holliday whipped out his knife and gutted him. In another version, Doc was actually arrested for "illegal gambling." Whatever the reason for his arrest, he was put under guard in a locked hotel room because the town didn't have a jail. In the first version, a lynch mob was forming, and Kate was forced to take action to save his life. In both stories, she set fire to an old shed behind the hotel. When the fire threatened to engulf the town, everyone rushed to fight it. With their attention diverted, Kate broke Doc out of the hotel. Some say she pulled two six-shooters on the jailer and forced him to open the door. Guns or no, she got him out, and they took off for Dodge City.

John Shanssey also introduced Doc Holliday to deputy US marshal Wyatt Earp. Shanssey and Earp had met several years earlier, when the future lawman had refereed one of the future saloon man's bouts. This time, Earp had come to "the Flats," as the town near Fort Griffin was called, hunting a train robber named "Dirty Dave" Rudabaugh. Perhaps at Shanssey's request, Doc told Earp what he knew: While playing cards with Rudabaugh a few days earlier, he'd heard the man say something about going back to Dodge City. Earp sent that information by telegraph to Dodge City's assistant deputy, Bat Masterson, who eventually made the arrest. But that encounter marked the beginning of the most important relationship of Doc Holliday's life.

Wyatt Earp was himself an ornery character. He'd been a boxer and a gambler; he'd worked on the railroads, as a constable, and as a horse thief. There were a lot of men like him in the Old West, people who just flowed with the opportunities life presented to them. For the previous few years, he'd been working mostly as a strongman, keeping the peace in brothels. He'd moved to Wichita in '74 to keep the peace in his brother Virgil's house of ill repute, while also working as a part-time peace officer for the city. When Earp first crossed paths with Doc Holliday in '77, he had recently been named Dodge City's chief deputy marshal.

Presumably, Earp welcomed the Doc and Kate, who found lodging at Deacon Cox's boardinghouse when they arrived in Dodge. If it wasn't the roughest town in the West, it definitely was high on the list. As a letter that appeared in the *Washington Evening Star* complained, "Dodge City is a wicked little town. Its character is so clearly and egregiously bad that one might conclude . . . that it was marked for special Providential punishment."

The night on which Holliday and Earp forged the friendship that would last for the rest of their lives began when as many as fifty cowboys just off the trail came galloping down Front Street, raising a holy ruckus. After shooting out most of the shop windows, they ended up at the Long Branch Saloon, where Doc was in the back room, quietly tending to his nightly business. There is no record of how the cards were treating him that night. Soon Deputy Earp walked through the swinging doors, not having the slightest idea what was waiting inside for him. The cowboys were led by Tobe Driskill and Ed Morrison, a man who had been humiliated by Wyatt in Wichita several years earlier and had been itching to get even. Earp

In 1883, the Dodge City Peace Commission ended the Dodge City War without a shot being fired.

pushed open the door and found fifty pistols and rifles pointed at him. As Wyatt Earp told the story years later, Morrison warned him, "Pray and jerk your gun. Your time has come, Earp!"

Before anyone could make a move, Holliday got up from his table quickly and quietly, pulled his own gun, and aimed it squarely at the back of Morrison's head. "No, friend," he said. "You draw or throw your hands up. Any of you bastards pulls a gun and your leader loses what's left of his brains." Fifty guns hit the floor. Earp punctuated the stand-down by slamming Morrison over his head with his Colt before taking him and Driskill to jail. As he later wrote, "The only way anyone could have appreciated the feeling I had for Doc after the

Driskill-Morrison business would have been to have stood in my boots at the time Doc came through the Long Branch doorway."

Word spreads lickety-split when one man stands up to a saloon full of armed cowhands. Doc Holliday earned himself a reputation that night. People might have wondered if he had been drunk or crazy, but after that, no one ever doubted his courage.

Not surprisingly, Doc and Kate had a tumultuous relationship, breaking up and getting back together several times. Neither one of them liked to stay still for too long. When she took off on him in '78, Doc decided to join the Earp brothers, Wyatt, Morgan, and Virgil, in Tombstone, Arizona. Tombstone was one of the West's last mining boomtowns, built on a mesa above the Tough Nut Silver Mine. By the time Doc Holliday rode into Tombstone in 1880, the town already had an estimated 110 saloons, 14 gambling halls, a plentiful number of brothels, and 1 bowling alley.

Supposedly he'd left several bodies along the trail between Dodge and Tombstone. In Las Vegas, then part of the New Mexico Territory, for example, he got into a shoot-out with an old army scout named Mike Gordon. When Gordon's former girlfriend, one of the saloon girls, refused to leave town with him, he'd started shooting up the place. As Holliday tried to get out of there, Gordon pegged a shot at him. Doc put two shots into his chest. Likely it was considered self-defense, as the coroner's jury ruled that Gordon's fatal wounds "had been inflicted by some person unknown to that jury."

Doc almost settled another score before heading for Tombstone, trading shots with bartender Charlie White in Vegas's Plaza Hotel saloon. This feud had started in Dodge. According to the future governor of New Mexico, Miguel Antonio Otero, who was a witness to this duel, "The two men faced each other and began shooting. They shoot and shoot with no one scoring a hit. Finally, Charlie White is down!" A scalp wound had stunned him senseless, but he recovered and left town.

A bad situation was already brewing in Tombstone when Holliday rode into town. Until the Earps arrived there, Tombstone had pretty much been run by a loosely knit gang known as the Cowboys. Mostly ranchers and cowboys who had been living there before the big mining companies came in and staked their claims, the Cowboys consisted of men like the Clantons, the McLaury brothers, Curly Bill Brocius, and Johnny Ringo, all of them known to be handy with a six-shooter. As long as they limited their activities to running across the border into Sonora and rustling Mexican cattle, nobody paid them too much mind, but after the Mexican government had gotten involved, making that too risky, the gang began stealing US cavalry beef. The Earps had been brought in to tame the town and had done a pretty good job of it. As the *Tombstone Daily Epitaph* reported, "Since the retirement of Ben Sippy as marshal and the appointment of V.W. Earp to fill the vacancy the town has been noted for its quietness and good order. The fractious and much dreaded cowboys when they came to town were upon their good behavior and no unseemly brawls were indulged in, and it was hoped by our citizens that no more such deeds would occur as led to the killing of Marshal White one year ago."

Hostility simmered between the lawmen and the Cowboys. The county sheriff, John Behan, stood between them, although he tended to lean toward the gang. Doc made his presence known soon after arriving, getting into a drunken brawl with another gambler in the

Tombstone, Arizona, in 1881 had a population of 4,000, 600 dwellings—and 2 churches. The large building in the foreground (*opposite*) is the Tough Nut mine hoisting works.

Oriental Saloon. Milt Joyce, the saloon's owner, had disarmed Doc, and when he refused to return his gun, Holliday got himself another weapon and walked in shooting. Joyce raised his gun to shoot back, and Holliday shot the weapon out of his hand, then shot the bartender in the toe. When Doc's attention was diverted, Joyce picked up his gun and whomped Holliday over the head with it, knocking him out cold. Holliday was arrested. He was found guilty of assault and battery and fined $20, plus $11.25 in court costs.

By this time, Doc's consumption had taken hold and was beginning to affect him. He'd lost considerable weight and ended most nights drunk. He was on a sure path to a sorry end. It turned out, though, that the Cowboys thought they might help that along just a bit. On

the Ides of March (March 15) 1881, four masked bandits held up the Kinnear & Company stagecoach. The driver and one passenger were killed during the robbery. The Cowboys claimed Doc Holliday had been one of the bandits, and as evidence, they offered an affidavit that had been signed by a very drunk Big Nose Kate during one of their fights. On July 5, Doc Holliday was arrested and charged with murder and stage robbery; Wyatt Earp and a local saloon keeper put up his five-thousand-dollar bail, then set out to prove his innocence. When Kate sobered up, she insisted that Sheriff Behan and Milt Joyce had supplied the drink as well as the pen and paper and that she hadn't known what she was signing. Other people testified that they had been with Holliday at the time of the robbery. After hearing all the evidence, the district attorney called the charges "ridiculous," and Holliday was released from bond. It didn't take Doc long to find out that Cowboy Ike Clanton was behind the ruse. He knew that one day soon, they would be settling up.

Ike Clanton knew that the real killers were some of the boys he was riding with. Wyatt Earp was especially interested in putting the cuffs on them; the election for sheriff was coming up, and he intended to replace the slippery Behan in that job, which paid a handsome sum. The story is that Wyatt made a deal with Clanton: If Clanton told him where the robbers were hiding out, Wyatt would let him keep the whole $3,600 reward, content in the knowledge that capturing those killers would just about guarantee his election. Ike Clanton agreed and provided the information, but before Earp could act, three of those men were caught rustling cattle and killed. That set Ike on edge; he began getting paranoid that Earp might reveal his double-dealing, which for him would be a death sentence.

In July, several Mexican smugglers were attacked and killed in Skeleton Canyon, and the silver they were carrying was stolen. The perpetrators were never identified, but Mexicans living near the border felt sure this was the work of the Cowboys.

A month later, the head of the Cowboys and Ike's father, Newman Haynes Clanton, better known as Old Man Clanton, and six of his men were driving a herd to market in Tombstone through Guadalupe Canyon, the main smuggling route over the border. After making camp, they were ambushed; five men died, including Old Man Clanton. Although the evidence pointed to Mexicans seeking retribution for the Skeleton Canyon attack, the Cowboys believed the Earps and Doc Holliday were somehow involved. It was not an unreasonable assumption: Wyatt Earp and Doc Holliday eventually showed up in town wounded, Doc using a cane.

By the fall, the relationship between the law and the Cowboys was about as dangerous as tinder in a drought, just waiting for a spark. The Cowboys were openly threatening to "clean out the Earps," along with Holliday, if they didn't clear out of town. Ironically, in his friendship with the Earps—especially with Wyatt and Morgan—Doc Holliday had finally found the thing worth living for, and for which he was willing to put his life on the line.

The gunfight at the O.K. Corral took place on October 26, 1881. It took about thirty seconds to write a chapter in American history that will never be forgotten. As the *Epitaph* reported the next day, "Stormy as were the early days of Tombstone nothing ever occurred equal to the event of yesterday."

The stage had been set the night before outside the Alhambra Saloon, when Ike Clanton and Doc Holliday, both having far exceeded their alcohol limit, staggered around threatening to kill each other. Clanton supposedly promised that he was going to kill an Earp, and allegedly Doc responded by claiming to have killed Old Man Clanton and to be looking forward to adding Ike to his count. Virgil Earp had broken up the fight.

The thirty-second-long gunfight at the O.K. Corral has been the subject of numerous books, pieces of art, television shows, and Hollywood films in which Doc Holliday was played by Walter Huston, Stacy Keach, Victor Mature, Kirk Douglas, Jason Robards, Val Kilmer, and Dennis Quaid.

Meanwhile, Clanton had met up with Wyatt and supposedly told him flat out, "Your consumptive friend . . . he's a dead man tomorrow."

To which Earp responded, "Don't you tangle with Doc Holliday. He'll kill you before you've begun."

The morning of the twenty-sixth was gray and windy. Ike Clanton showed up early at Fly's Boardinghouse, demanding to see Holliday. Doc wasn't there, but later, when Big Nose Kate told him about Clanton's visit, he responded, "If God will let me live long enough, he will see me."

About one o'clock in the afternoon, tired of his threats, Virgil and Morgan Earp went looking for Ike Clanton. They found him walking on Fourth Street, carrying a Winchester rifle with a revolver on his hip. Virgil Earp approached him cautiously, then banged him on his head, taking both his weapons. He hauled him off to Judge Albert O. Wallace's courtroom. Wyatt found Clanton there and warned him: "You damn dirty cow thief. You have been threatening our lives, and I know it. I think I would be justified in shooting you down any place I would meet you. But if you are anxious to make a fight, I will go anywhere on earth to make a fight with you."

"Fight is my racket, and all I want is four feet of ground," Clanton supposedly replied. But he backed down from a fight right there, making it clear he didn't like the odds. Instead he was fined $27.50 and released.

As Wyatt Earp was leaving the courtroom, he bumped right into one of the Cowboys, Tom McLaury, at the front door. Earp apologized, but when McLaury bad-mouthed him, Earp smashed him in the head with his pistol.

With trouble brewing, marshal Virgil Earp swore in Morgan Earp and Doc Holliday, giving them the legal authority granted to all US deputy marshals: They could shoot to kill.

Almost two hours later, a local man named R. F. Coleman saw Ike and Billy Clanton and Frank and Tom McLaury in Dunbar's corral. At some point, they were joined by another one of the Cowboys, Billy Claibourne. The speculation is that they were planning to ambush Doc Holliday, who normally passed that way each morning. Coleman claimed that he found Sheriff Behan, warning him that those boys were looking for trouble and that it was his duty to disarm them.

Everybody in town knew what was coming: a showdown. Apparently several members of Tombstone's Citizens Committee volunteered to walk with the Earps. Wyatt turned them down, explaining that it was his responsibility to enforce the law and that's what he intended to do. But he did allow Doc Holliday to join him. The long trail Doc had been traveling for so many years had led him to this point. There is some evidence that at first Wyatt told Holliday that this wasn't his affair. But the result of that conversation was that Virgil Earp gave Holliday a ten-gauge shotgun, the type of double-barreled gun carried by coachmen, which he secreted under his greatcoat. In return, Doc handed Virgil his cane. Virgil planned to carry it as a way of making clear to the Cowboys that he wasn't armed and, if possible, of preventing bloodshed.

The four lawmen started walking shoulder-to-shoulder down the center of Fremont Street. Officially, they intended to enforce the law prohibiting people from carrying guns within Tombstone, but in fact they were going to get this thing settled. The Earps were dressed all in black; Doc Holliday was wearing gray. Sheriff Behan tried to derail them, apparently telling them that the Cowboys weren't armed. In response, Wyatt suggested that Behan go with him to talk to the boys. Supposedly Behan laughed and told him, "Hell, this is your fight, not mine."

Doc Holliday and the Earp brothers confronted the Clantons and McLaurys in a narrow fifteen-foot-wide space behind the O.K. Corral, between Fly's Photograph Gallery and Jersey's Livery Stable. For some reason, Claibourne had left the gang. The men faced one another for a few long seconds, then Virgil Earp shouted, "Give up your arms or throw up your arms!"

Another second passed; then it started. Billy Clanton and Frank McLaury went for their guns. Virgil warned them, "Hold on, I don't want that." But it was too late.

As eyewitness R. F. Coleman described it to a reporter the next day,

> There was some reply made by Frank McLaury, when firing became general, over thirty shots being fired. Tom McLaury fell first, but raised and fired again before he died. Bill Clanton fell next, and raised to fire again when Mr. Fly took his revolver from him. Frank McLaury ran a few rods and fell. Morgan Earp was shot through and fell. Doc Holliday was hit in the left hip but kept on firing. Virgil Earp was hit in the third or fourth fire, in the leg which staggered him but he kept up his effective work. Wyatt Earp stood up and fired in rapid succession, as cool as a cucumber, and was not hit.
>
> Doc Holliday was as calm as though at target practice and fired rapidly.

Thirty shots were fired in thirty seconds; then it was over. Tom McLaury, Frank McLaury, and Billy Clanton were dead. Doc Holliday was credited by the *Tombstone Nugget* with killing both McLaurys—he blew Tom McLaury away with both barrels at close range—and possibly wounding Billy Clanton. Ike Clanton, who took off running when the shooting started, survived. Morgan Earp was seriously wounded, but he would survive. And, as the *Epitaph* concluded, "Doc Holliday was hit upon the scabbard of his pistol, the leather breaking the force of the ball so that no material damage was done other than to make him limp a little in his walk."

When the smoke cleared, the mine whistles started whining. The miners rose to the surface, armed themselves, and raced into town to preserve law and order. Armed guards surrounded the jail and would remain there throughout the night. Sheriff Behan approached Wyatt Earp and told him boldly, "I'll have to arrest you."

Earp shook his head. "I won't be arrested today," he said. "I am right here and am not going away. You have deceived me. You told me these men were disarmed; I went to disarm them."

REMAINS OF McLAURY-EARP

Tom and Frank McLaury and Billy Clanton were buried in the same grave. The *Tombstone Epitaph* reported, "The funeral . . . procession headed by the Tombstone band, moved down Allen street and thence to the cemetery. The sidewalks were densely packed for three or four blocks. It was a most impressive and saddening sight and such a one as it is to be hoped may never occur again in this community."

Big Nose Kate said later that Doc Holliday returned to their room, sat on the bed, and wept. "That was awful," he said. "Awful."

Three days later, Ike Clanton filed charges, and Wyatt and Doc were arrested. An inquest into the shootings lasting almost a month concluded, "The defendants were fully justified in committing these homicides, that it was a necessary act done in the discharge of official duty."

The gunfight turned out to be only the beginning of the bloodletting. Two months later, marshal Virgil Earp was ambushed by three men with shotguns on his way to the Crystal Palace. He was hit twice and suffered permanent injury. The Cowboys believed to be responsible were arrested, but other members of the gang swore that these men were with them at the time of the attack, and they were acquitted.

In March of the following year, Morgan Earp was shot and killed while playing pool at Hatch's Saloon and Billiard Parlor. When Doc learned that the cowards had shot Morgan in the back, he apparently went ripping through the town, kicking open locked doors, hunting the killers. But they'd gotten away. Morgan was laid to rest wearing one of Doc's finest blue suits. The Doc and the Earps now understood that they could not depend on the law to protect them. That was the beginning of what has become known as "the Vendetta Ride."

Tombstone had become much too dangerous for the Earp family. All the women and children were packed up and, along with Morgan Earp's body, put on a train for California. Doc, Wyatt, and several others rode along to protect them. As the train pulled into Tucson, a lookout spotted Ike Clanton and Frank Stilwell, believed to be lying in wait to finish the job on Virgil. Stilwell had been bragging that he had fired the fatal shot into Morgan Earp's back, so no one was much surprised the next morning when Stilwell's thoroughly ventilated body was found lying in the dirt near the tracks. As the newspapers reported, he was buried the next day "unfollowed by a single mourner." Doc and Wyatt were named as his killers but suffered no repercussions for that act.

The bodies continued to pile up. Deputy Wyatt Earp's posse heard that some of the Cowboys were in the Dragoon Mountains; they found one of the gang, Florentino Cruz, and dispensed western justice upon him. Two days later, nine Cowboys led by Curly Bill Brocius ambushed the posse. Doc was quoted as telling a newspaperman, ". . . eight rustlers rose up from behind the bank and poured from thirty-five to forty shots at us. Our escape was miraculous. The shots cut our clothes and saddles and killed one horse, but did not hit us. I think we would have been killed if God Almighty wasn't on our side. Wyatt Earp turned loose with a shotgun and killed Curley Bill." After that, it turned out to be open season on the Cowboys: Johnny Barnes, who was also involved in the attack on Virgil, suffered wounds that eventually would kill him. A couple of months later, the body of Johnny Ringo—with a bullet hole in his right temple and his gun dangling from one finger—was found propped up in the trunk of a large tree in West Turkey Creek Canyon, Arizona Territory. Local authorities speculated that it might have been suicide, but there were serious hints that it was the work of Wyatt Earp. Within a year after the murder of Morgan Earp, at least five more Cowboys were killed by people unknown. The gang was decimated.

Doc Holliday was arrested in Denver, although once again, no charges stuck. Reporting his arrest, the *Denver Republican* wrote, "Holliday has a big reputation as a fighter, and has probably put more rustlers and cowboys under the sod than any other one man in the west. He had been the terror of the lawless element in Arizona, and with the Earps was the only man brave enough to face the bloodthirsty crowd which has made the name of Arizona a stench in the nostrils of decent men."

In 1883, Holliday settled in the mining town of Leadville, Colorado, the highest city above sea level in the country and a questionable place for a man with tuberculosis. The British writer Oscar Wilde had visited it a year earlier on his national lecture tour and remarked that it was there that he saw the only rational method of art criticism he'd ever encountered, on a notice hung in a saloon. It read, "Please do not shoot the pianist. He is doing his best." Although some believed Doc Holliday was completely broke and given to borrowing money, he worked as a faro dealer at the Board of Trade Saloon, drawing players from all around who wanted to say that they'd sat at the table with the great Doc Holliday.

Holliday spent a good deal of his time fighting reality with alcohol and the opiate laudanum. In 1884, he was involved in one of the last gunfights of his storied career, when a kid named Johnny Allen challenged him. Apparently Holliday ignored him as long as he could, but when Allen drew on him in Hyman's Saloon, Doc fired twice, hitting the kid in the arm. The bartender jumped on him to prevent him from shooting again. That was the seventeenth and final arrest of his life. A jury found him not guilty of attempted murder.

In the winter of '86, Doc Holliday and Wyatt Earp met for the last time, in the lobby of Denver's Windsor Hotel. Wyatt's wife, Josephine, wrote that the two men sat together and laughed and cried, and that she had rarely seen a man as happy as Doc Holliday was that day. She described him as frail, unsteady on his feet with a persistent cough.

Holliday eventually made it to the sulfurous Yampah Hot Springs near Glenwood Springs, Colorado, a place that supposedly had healing powers. But the tuberculosis had him wrapped. He spent the last two months of his life in bed, delirious at least some of the time. Doc had always told people that he intended to die with his boots on, the western way of saying he was going to

Doc Holliday's grave in Glenwood Springs, Colorado, has
become a popular tourist destination. To his own surprise, and
perhaps disappointment, he died in bed, with his boots off.

die fighting, but in fact his boots were off as he lay in bed. On November 8, 1887, he supposedly awoke and asked in a clear voice for a glass of whiskey. Like so much else in his life, some reports say the nurse gave it to him; other reports claim she refused. But it is generally believed that he sighed, looked down at his bare feet, and commented, "Damn, this is funny," and died.

After years of gunfights in which he was responsible for piling up a slew of bodies, Doc Holliday died with his boots off—but his reputation as a man who had found a friendship worth living and fighting for was intact. A few days after he was buried, the Leadville *Carbonate Chronicle* printed his obituary, which read in part, "There is scarcely one in the country who had acquired a greater notoriety than Doc Holliday, who enjoyed the reputation of being one of the most fearless men on the frontier, and whose devotion to his friends in the climax of the fiercest ordeal was inextinguishable. It was this, more than any other faculty that secured for him the reverence of a large circle who were prepared on the shortest notice to rally to his relief."

SHOOTING DOWN A LEGEND

Among the most common icons of the American West is the quick-drawing, sharpshooting sheriff, facing down an outlaw at high noon on a dusty street as the anxious folks take cover. Indeed, most western tales seem to end with guns blazing, and when the smoke clears, only the good guys are left standing.

It is generally believed that six-shooters tamed the West, that a man couldn't safely walk the streets without his Colt resting easily on his hip, and that the background music in most western towns was church bells and gunshots. The heroes were the men who shot quickest and straightest.

Contrary to the legend, not every man in the West carried a six-gun or was quick to draw. Gunfights were rare and mostly avoided if possible. As Doc Holliday learned, a big reputation was often more valuable than a gunslinger's skill, because it prevented people from drawing on you—or, just as likely, shooting you in the back. In fact, in most towns, once they had been settled for a few years, it actually was illegal to carry a gun. In most places, people were much more likely to be carrying a shotgun or a rifle than a pistol, because they were much more likely to need a gun for hunting than for protection. The heyday of the gunfighter (or the pistolero, as he was often called) began after the Civil War, when many

thousands of men came home with weapons and experience in using them. There actually were very few real showdowns, where two men faced each other a few feet apart and drew; they were so rare, in fact, that killing Davis Tutt on a street in Springfield, Missouri, made Wild Bill Hickok a national celebrity. And even in those few real duels, it rarely mattered who fired the quickest, but rather, whose aim was true. Most times, shooters would just keep firing until—or if—someone got hit. Weapons and bullets at the time were notoriously unreliable. As Buffalo Bill Cody once admitted, "We did the best we could, with the tools we had."

So, while quick draws were impressive in the movies, in real life, they rarely made any difference in the outcome. In fact, as Wyatt Earp once explained, "The most important lesson I learned . . . was that the winner of a gunplay usually was the one who took his time."

The notion of a fair fight was also mostly a Hollywood creation. Because it was a matter of survival rather than honor, in many shootings, the winner was simply the guy who got the drop on his opponent. Some

Charles Marion Russell, "the Cowboy Artist," tells an Old West story in his oil painting *Death of a Gambler:* Cards, alcohol, and guns all come together in a saloon and lead to an inevitable result.

men carried a pistol on their hip, knowing it would attract attention—but when necessary, they'd pull their serious weapon, often a small derringer, from under a coat or shirtsleeve and fire before their startled opponent could respond. It has been estimated that as many three out of four people who died from gunshots were killed by concealed second weapons. When gunfights did take place, they generally happened on the spur of the moment, sometimes breaking out when people were liquored up and angry, and the shooters, rather than standing at a distance from each other, were only a few feet apart.

Most guns used the "cap and ball" system, exploding black powder-propelled "bullets" little bigger than a marble that were accurate only to about fifty feet. Bat Masterson was quoted as advising, "If you want to hit a man in his chest, aim for his groin." If more than one person was involved, the situation quickly became chaotic: After the first few shots, the black smoke would have obscured everybody's vision for several seconds, making it even more difficult to fire rapidly and hit a target with the next shots.

The truth is that guns and rifles were common and absolutely necessary in the West, but they were used more for hunting and protection than for two-gun shoot-outs.

BILLY THE KID

Escape Artist

t about nine o'clock on the warm moonlit night of July 14, 1881, the sheriff of Lincoln County, New Mexico, Pat Garrett, rode out to old Fort Sumner with deputies John W. Poe and Kip McKinney. The famous fort had been abandoned by the army after the Civil War, and cattle baron Lucien Maxwell had transformed it into a beautiful hacienda. His family now lived in the officers' quarters, while Mexicans occupied many of the outer buildings. Lucien himself had died, and his son Pete was now running the compound. Garrett had received some reliable information that the outlaw Billy the Kid had holed up there with his girlfriend. He and his deputies would need to be quiet and careful: Billy the Kid was a cold-blooded killer. Garrett knew that better than most: He had captured the Kid just six months earlier, only to have the outlaw escape the noose by killing two of his deputies—while still wearing chains.

The weather was pleasant as the three lawmen unsaddled their horses outside the compound and entered the peach orchard on foot. They saw people sitting around evening campfires in the yard, conversing mostly in Spanish. Somebody was strumming a guitar. Garrett and his men stayed silently in the shadows, watching, without knowing exactly what they were looking for. The sheriff intended to have a private conversation with Pete Maxwell, who was a law-abiding citizen. As they lingered, a man stood up, hopped over a low fence, and walked directly toward Maxwell's house. In the firelight, they saw that he was wearing a broad-brimmed sombrero and a dark vest and pants; he was not wearing boots. They couldn't see his face and didn't pay him much attention.

To avoid being noticed, just in case the Kid was there, Garrett and his men backed up and took a safer path to the house. Around midnight, the sheriff placed Poe and McKinney on the porch, about twenty feet from the open door, and eased himself into Maxwell's dark bedroom. Garrett sat down at the head of the bed and shook Maxwell awake. Speaking in a whisper, he asked him if he knew the whereabouts of the Kid. Maxwell was not pleased to have been woken, but he told Garrett that the outlaw had indeed been there for a spell. Whether he was still there, he did not know.

As they conversed, they heard a man's voice outside demanding, "*¿Quien es?*" ("Who are you?") A split second later, a thin figure appeared in the doorway. Looking back outside, the man asked again, "*¿Quien es?*" Even in the dim light, Garrett could see that the man was holding a revolver in his right hand and a butcher knife in his left.

The man moved cautiously into the bedroom. Garrett guessed he was Pete Maxwell's brother-in-law, who had probably seen two men on the porch and wanted to know what was going on. The sheriff also knew he had a big advantage: The thin man didn't know he was there, and it would take a few seconds for his eyes to adjust to the dark. The man walked toward the bed, leaned down, and asked Maxwell in a soft voice, "*¿Quienes so esos hombres afuera, Pedro?*" ("Who are those men outside, Peter?")

It's impossible to know what Maxwell was thinking at that moment, but just above a whisper, he said to Garrett, "That's him."

The thin man stood up and started backing out of the room. He raised his gun and pointed it into the darkness. As Garrett later remembered, "Quickly as possible I drew my revolver and fired, threw my body aside and fired again." Garrett and Maxwell heard the man fall to the floor. Not knowing how badly he was hit, they scrambled out of the room. The Mexicans had heard the shots and were running toward Maxwell's place. Safely outside, Garrett waited to see if anyone else came out. No one did. "I think I got him," Garrett said finally.

They waited a bit longer, then Pete Maxwell put a lit candle in the window. In the flickering light, they saw the lifeless body of Billy the Kid sprawled on the floor. Garrett had shot him dead just above his heart. As Garrett concluded, "[T]he Kid was with his many victims." The legendary outlaw was twenty-one years old when he was killed that night.

If he actually *was* killed that night.

No one disagrees that Billy the Kid was one of the most ruthless outlaws to roam the Old West. As the *Spartanburg Herald* reported, "He was the perfect example of the real bad man, and his memory is respected accordingly by the few surviving friends and foes of his time, who knew the counterfeit bad man from the genuine." But since that night, when sheriff Pat Garrett fired two shots into the darkness, people have wondered who actually died on Pete Maxwell's floor.

Few names are better known in American folklore than Billy the Kid. Although his life as an outlaw lasted only four or five years, he accomplished enough during that brief span to ensure that he would be remembered forever. The only authentic photograph of the Kid, a two-by-three-inch ferrotype, was sold at auction in 2011 for $2.3 million, at that time making it the fourth most valuable photograph in the world. It was a tribute to his notoriety.

Perhaps surprising for someone so well known, there are very few verifiable facts about his life. It's generally believed that his name was William Henry McCarty Jr.—or, as he called himself, William H. Bonney—and that he was born about 1859, probably in New York City. He was the son of Irish immigrants who came to America to escape the Potato Famine. His father was long gone by the time his mother and stepfather opened a boardinghouse in Silver City, New Mexico. His mother, Catherine, tried to raise him right: He could read well and write in a legible hand; he was known to be polite and well mannered. But the New Mexico Territory was a hard place to grow up; gunplay was common, and the murder rate was high. The people who stayed at the family boardinghouse were on the move: miners, gamblers, merchants, women of pleasure, teamsters, and toughs. From these people, the impressionable boy learned the skills of survival. His proudest possession was a deck of Mexican cards; by the time he was eight, he could deal monte, and within a few years, he was said to be as skillful with cards as any of the gamblers in the local saloons.

Whatever chance Billy Bonney might have had for a decent life ended when he was fourteen years old and his mother died of tuberculosis. He stayed in Silver City for a short time after that, cleaning and washing dishes for neighbors who owned a hotel. His life was pretty much a scuffle; he didn't appear to have any particular destination. Although he didn't show much promise, he also didn't appear to be a bad sort. He fell in with the Mexican community and fully embraced its vibrant culture. Like most young men, he loved to dance and party. On occasion, he displayed a temper. The Mexicans called him El Chivato, "the Rascal." He committed the sort of minor offenses that have long been associated with teenagers: Once he was caught stealing cheese; another time, he was arrested for holding shirts a friend of his known as "Sombrero Jack" had stolen from the Chinese laundry run by Charley Sun and Sam Chung. Sheriff Harvey Whitehill put him in jail for that, figuring he'd give him a good scare, but instead he shimmied up and out of the jailhouse chimney and took off for a sorry future.

He kicked around the area, finding work as a ranch hand and shepherd until he fell in with John R. Mackie, a small-time criminal whose gang consisted mostly of teenage boys. Mackie might have recognized the possibilities in the young man: Billy Bonney had a slight build and a winning way about him. People took to him easily; his smallish stature was nonthreatening, and his easy smile was reassuring. But when it was necessary, he was quick on the draw and known to be an accurate shot. The gang stole horses and cattle from the government in Arizona and sold it to the government in New Mexico; then they would steal stock in New Mexico and take it to Arizona. However, on the night of August 17, 1877, seventeen-year-old Billy Bonney's life of crime took a more dangerous turn.

He was playing cards in George Atkin's cantina in Camp Grant, Arizona, with a blacksmith named Frank Cahill. Cahill's big mouth, which had earned him the nickname Windy, was working hard that night, throwing a string of insults at Bonney. Cahill was a small man with blacksmith's muscles and a mean temper. In some stories, the fight started because of a gambling disagreement; in others, as the result of drink; and in still others, Cahill called Billy a pimp, and Bonney responded by calling him a son of a bitch. Whatever the cause, suddenly Windy Cahill grabbed Bonney and threw him hard to the floor. The Kid got up, and Cahill pushed him down again. Billy got up once more, and Cahill shoved him a third time, but this time Cahill jumped on top of him and pinned his shoulders to the floor. Then he started punching him, again and again. The Kid had no chance of winning this fistfight, but somehow he managed to pull out the peacemaker he carried, a Colt .45, and fired one shot into Cahill's chest. Cahill slumped over and died the next day. Billy was locked up in the camp's guardhouse.

William Henry Bonney likely earned his nickname Billy the Kid after this shooting. It obviously was based on his youthful appearance. Fully grown, Billy Bonney stood five-foot-seven and weighed no more than 135 pounds; he was described by newsmen as "slender and slight, a hard rider and active as a cat." Other reports described him as "quite a handsome looking fellow, the only imperfection being two prominent front teeth slightly protruding like a squirrel's teeth." Although the shooting of Cahill appeared to be a case of self-defense, the Kid didn't wait around for the law's decision. Instead, he slipped out of the guardhouse and took off for New Mexico. That turned out to be the right move. After hearing the evidence, a coroner's jury ruled that because Cahill wasn't armed, the shooting was "criminal and unjustifiable." Billy the Kid was wanted for murder.

He stopped running when he reached Lincoln County and hired on with merchants and cattle ranchers Major Lawrence G. Murphy and James J. Dolan. Lincoln County consisted of thirty thousand square acres of some of the best cattle-grazing land in the country. Murphy and Dolan ran a large mercantile business, known as "the House" in honor of the mansion that served as their office. They were in fierce competition with newcomers Alexander McSween and John Tunstall, who were backed by the legendary cattle baron John Chisum. Their rivalry involved much more than money: The Irishmen Murphy and Dolan did not take kindly to the Englishman Tunstall trying to cut into their business. The fight between these two factions was known as the Lincoln County War, and Billy the Kid found himself right in the middle of it.

Initially he joined a gang of mostly teenage cattle rustlers run by gunman Jesse Evans; they called themselves "the Boys." It was a rough group, known to have committed several murders. The Boys had been hired by the House to steal cattle from Chisum's Jinglebob Ranch, which would then be sold to Mexicans and Indians. At first, McSween and Tunstall tried to fight back legally, but when the law failed them, they hired their own guns.

Somehow John Tunstall recruited Billy onto his side; one story claims that Billy was caught stealing a horse or cattle belonging to Tunstall and was arrested. Rather than put him in prison, Tunstall offered him a choice. If he agreed to testify against other members of the Boys, Tunstall would give him a job. It was a chance to make an honest living. Tunstall wasn't much more than a kid himself, being about twenty-four, and most reports indicate that he and Billy took a strong liking to each other. Apparently Tunstall once said, "That's the finest

When William Bonney reached Lincoln County, he hired on as a hand with merchants and cattlemen James Dolan and Major Lawrence Murphy, who ran their operation out of this mansion, known as the House.

Eventually Billy went to work for John Tunstall, whose efforts to compete with the House led to the Lincoln County War. When Tunstall was murdered, the Kid declared his own personal war on the House.

lad I ever met. He's a revelation to me everyday and would do anything to please me. I'm going to make a man out of that boy yet."

He never got the chance to do that. On February 18, 1878, Tunstall and several hands—Billy might have been among them—were driving nine horses to Lincoln on the Rio Feliz when they were cut off by a posse that had been deputized by Lincoln sheriff William Brady and included several members of the Boys. These killers now had the law backing their moves. At first, the Boys claimed the horses had been stolen, but clearly that was only a ruse. Three of them managed to isolate Tunstall in the brush, and when the shooting stopped, Tunstall's body was found lying in the dirt next to his buckboard, one shot in his breast and a second shot in the back of his head.

When Billy the Kid learned of the murder, he said, "He was the only man that ever treated me kindly, like I was born free and white," and then vowed, "I'll get every son of a bitch who helped kill John if it's the last thing I ever do."

Lincoln County justice of the peace "Squire" John Wilson swore in a posse of special constables, headed by ranch owner—and Tunstall's foreman—Dick Brewer, to arrest Tunstall's killers. Billy the Kid joined this group, "the Regulators," as they became known, when they set off to dispense justice. It was a very strange situation, two legally deputized posses hunting each other. The Regulators struck first, arresting two of the House's men and then killing them, allegedly as they tried to escape. The escalating war reached a new level about a month later, when Billy the Kid and five other Regulators ambushed and killed Sheriff Brady and his deputy as they walked down the street in Lincoln. Billy was slightly wounded in the gunfight. Although Brady was known to be sympathetic to the House, killing a lawman was serious business, even in a lawless environment, and people turned away from the Regulators, believing them to be no different than Murphy and Dolan's men.

Over the next months, both sides lost men. Dick Brewer was killed during a shoot-out at Blazer's Saw Mill, in which House man Buckshot Roberts also died. Frank McNab, who replaced Brewer as captain of the Regulators, was killed a month later; in return, Manuel Segovia, who was believed to have murdered McNab, was tracked down and killed, again allegedly trying to escape. The US cavalry joined the fight on the side of the House, giving

REWARD

($5,000.00)

Reward for the capture, dead or alive,
of one Wm. Wright, better known as

"BILLY THE KID"

Age, 18. Height, 5 feet, 3 inches.
Weight, 125 lbs. Light hair, blue
eyes and even features. He is
the leader of the worst band of
desperadoes the Territory has
ever had to deal with. The above
reward will be paid for his capture
or positive proof of his death.
                    JIM DALTON, Sheriff.

DEAD OR ALIVE!
"BILLY THE KID"

Although there is a lively market in Billy the Kid Wanted posters, most of them were created to take advantage of his fame after his death. The facts here are accurate, but the only verified "poster" was a reward notice published in the *Las Vegas Gazette*.

This 1880 illustration from the *Police Gazette* portrays Billy the Kid killing a man in a saloon, probably referring to the shooting of Joe Grant. The *Police Gazette* was known for its illustrations and photographs of popular criminals and scantily clad women.

their gunmen both legal cover and added firepower. Although nobody knows if Billy the Kid actually did any of the killing, it was agreed that he never held back.

The Lincoln County War came to a head at the five-day-long battle of Lincoln. On July 15, about forty of Dolan's men laid siege to McSween's house, where he was holed up with at least fifteen men. Supposedly, during a lull in the fighting, a House man called out to Billy to surrender, claiming he had a warrant for his arrest for the murder of Sheriff Brady and his deputy. Billy was said to reply, "We too have warrants for you and all your gang which we will serve on you hot from the muzzle of our guns!"

For three days, the town was a battlefield; then a column from Fort Stanton under the command of Colonel Nathan Dudley joined the fight on the side of the Dolans. Two days later, McSween's house went up in flames. McSween stepped out into his yard and was shot nine times. Several Regulators were killed attempting to escape the fire. But Billy Bonney was among the Regulators who slipped out the back and made it across the river.

News of the Lincoln County War was reported throughout the nation, and Billy the Kid—the murderous teenager—quickly caught the fancy of the public. In those stories, he was given credit for even more killings than he was known to be responsible for, ensuring his reputation while selling newspapers and novels.

McSween's death marked the end of the war. In total, twenty-two men had died. At the time, President Rutherford B. Hayes appointed Civil War general Lew Wallace governor of the New Mexico Territory. Determined to end the bitterness, Wallace offered amnesty to everyone who had fought in the war—except those indicted for murder. Because there was a warrant out for Billy the Kid for the murder of Sheriff Brady, he did not qualify for forgiveness. But Billy, being a bright sort, had a plan. He had witnessed James Dolan and two other men murder a Las Vegas lawyer, Huston Chapman. The Kid was hoping to arrange a deal; he wrote a letter to the new governor, stating that he would agree to testify against those three men in exchange for the same amnesty granted other Regulators. "I was present when Mr. Chapman was murdered," he wrote. "I know who did it. . . . If it is in your power to annully [*sic*] those indictments I hope you will do so as to give me a chance to explain. . . . I have no wish to fight any more indeed I have not raised an arm since your proclamation."

Meeting face-to-face with a feared killer was not out of the question for Governor Wallace. In addition to fighting in the war and trying to bring peace to a violent region, he was writing a novel that would become part of American literary history, *Ben-Hur*. On March 17, 1879, Wallace and Billy the Kid met in the home of a man named John Wilson. Billy carried his pistol in one hand and his Winchester in the other. Wallace agreed to Bonney's terms, but only if Bonney would submit to a token arrest and stay in jail until his testimony was completed. Billy was leery, supposedly telling Wallace, "There's no justice for me in the courts of this country. I've gone too far," but agreed to think it over. It was said that Wallace promised that if Bonney gave himself up, the governor would set him "scot free with a pardon in your pocket for all your misdeeds," but Bonney insisted that rather than his being "captured," he wanted it reported that he had surrendered. Two days after the meeting, he accepted the deal and surrendered to authorities.

He was held in a makeshift cell in the back of a store. His testimony helped to convict Dolan, but the local district attorney reneged on the deal; rather than letting him go, he

Lincoln, March 15. 1879.

W. H. Bonney.

Come to the house of old Squire Wilson (not the lawyer) at nine (9) o'clock next Monday night alone. I don't mean his office, but his residence. Follow along the foot of the mountain south of the town, come in on that side, and knock at the east door. I have authority to exempt you from prosecution, if you will testify to what you say you know.

The object of the meeting at Squire Wilson's is to arrange the matter in a way to make your life safe. To do that the utmost secrecy is to be used. So come alone. Don't tell anybody — not a living soul — where you are coming or the object. If you could trust Jesse Evans, you can trust me.

Lew. Wallace.

Billy the Kid's unusual correspondence with Governor Lew Wallace led to the wanted fugitive actually meeting face-to-face with the future author of the classic *Ben-Hur*. Billy believed they had worked out a deal that would result in his pardon, but when he was betrayed he escaped from prison and shot his way into legend.

Santa Fe Jail New Mex
March 2d 1881

Gov. Lew Wallace
        Dear Sir

    I wish you would come down to
the jail and see me. it will be to
your interest to come and see me, I have
some letters. which date back two
years, and there are Parties who
are very anxious to get them
.but I shall not dispose of them
untill I see you. that is if you
will come imediatly

        Yours Respect—
        Wm H Bonney

    "Billy the Kit"

Pat Garrett became famous for supposedly killing Billy the Kid. But his account has long been disputed. Inconsistencies in his story led to him becoming a controversial figure. Although he did not receive the reward money, citizens who felt threatened by the Kid collected the equivalent of twenty thousand dollars for him.

decided to bring him to trial for Sheriff Brady's killing. After three months sitting in his cell and with his own trial for murder now scheduled, Billy did what came naturally—he slipped out. He probably could have found safety and a long life across the border in Mexico, but he'd grown sweet on Pete Maxwell's younger sister, Paulita, so instead he rode for Fort Sumner, where he believed he could live among his Mexican friends.

Among the people he surely got to know around Fort Sumner at that time was a former buffalo hunter and cowpuncher by the name of Pat Garrett, who had part ownership of Beaver Smith's Saloon. Depending on which story you choose to believe, Pat Garrett and Billy the Kid either barely knew each other or had become such close friends and gambling buddies that they were called Big Casino and Little Casino.

It is possible that Billy the Kid might have settled down with Pete Maxwell's comely sister, but the sad truth is that he was in too deep. Although Bonney was a wanted man, it wasn't a big secret that he had been seen around Fort Sumner. In January 1880, Billy met a man named Joe Grant in a local saloon. They got to drinking, and Grant confided in him that he aimed to become famous by killing the outlaw Billy the Kid as soon as he could find him. Grant wasn't the first man to make that boast, but he made the mistake of picking the wrong man to make it to. Billy asked to see his six-shooter, then managed to either empty the shells or set it on an empty cylinder. He handed it back and then admitted that, in fact, he was the very man that Grant was seeking. In some tellings, he then got up and walked out of the saloon. Grant fired at him; his gun clicked on the empty chamber. Billy dispatched him with a single shot. "It was a game for two," he later explained, "and I got there first."

To survive, Billy organized his own gang, which became known as "the Rustlers," or Billy the Kid's Gang. There was no lack of young men willing to ride with the famous outlaw, among them Tom O'Folliard, Charlie Bowdre, Tom Pickett, and Dirty Dave Rudabaugh. As their name suggests, they rustled cattle and stole horses, just as Billy had done years earlier.

The presence of a famous outlaw who had escaped justice riding the range with impunity finally got the attention of Governor Wallace. In November, he appointed Pat Garrett sheriff of Lincoln County. He might have received that badge because he promised to bring law and order to the county, but many people believed it was because he had been friends with Billy Bonney and knew where he was most likely to be found.

In late November, the gang stole sixteen horses from Padre Polaco and headed out to White Oaks to sell them. On the way they stopped at "Whisky Jim" Greathouse's ranch and way station and sold him four. Billy the Kid also intended to meet with his lawyer in White Oaks to see if there was any way of making a deal with the government. White Oaks deputy Will Hudgens raised a posse and tracked the fugitives to the Greathouse Ranch. Hudgens sent a note inside, informing the outlaws that they were surrounded and demanding their surrender. Jim Greathouse personally delivered their refusal. Apparently stalling until it got dark enough for them to make their escape, the gang agreed to allow the blacksmith Jimmy Carlyle, who was trusted by both sides, to come inside and discuss the terms of surrender. Greathouse agreed to stay with the posse as a voluntary hostage to ensure Carlyle's safety.

The Rustlers passed the day drinking. When Carlyle failed to return, the posse threatened to shoot Greathouse. As it grew dark, a member of the posse accidentally fired his weapon. Hearing that shot, Carlyle believed that the posse had shot Greathouse and that therefore his own life was suddenly in great jeopardy. He made a run for it, leaping out of a window into the snow. Billy the Kid later wrote to Governor Wallace to explain what happened that day: "In a short time a shot was fired on the outside and Carlyle thinking Greathouse was killed, jumped through the window, breaking the sash as he went and was killed by his own party they thinking it was me trying to make my escape." Members of the posse swore that the

Sheriff Pat Garrett's posse pursued Billy the Kid for four days before trapping him in Stinking Springs. This 1880 photograph shows the posse arriving in Santa Fe with its captives.

shots came from inside and specifically blamed the Kid. It made no difference to Carlyle how it happened: Somebody shot him dead.

The posse opened up on the house, firing as many as seventy shots without nicking anyone. When night fell, the posse gave up and rode back to White Oaks, allowing the gang to make tracks. Three days later, the Greathouse Ranch burned to the ground. The arsonists were never found.

The killing of Jim Carlyle outraged the public. The *Las Vegas Gazette* railed in an editorial, "the gang is under the leadership of Billy the Kid, a desperate cuss, who is eligible for the post of captain of any crowd, no matter how mean or lawless. . . . Are the people of San Miguel

County to stand this any longer?" This editorial might well have been the first time the entire nickname "Billy the Kid" was used; until this point he was generally known as simply "the Kid."

In response, Governor Wallace posted a notice in that paper, announcing, "I will pay $500 reward to any person or persons who will capture William Bonny [*sic*], alias The Kid, and deliver him to any sheriff of New Mexico."

Sheriff Garrett knew his success in his job would be measured by his ability to bring Billy the Kid to justice. He organized a posse and quickly picked up Bonney's trail. On December 18, he learned that the gang was coming into Fort Sumner, and he beat them there and lay in wait for them. Around midnight, the posse heard horses coming into town. Tom O'Folliard was riding point. The posse opened fire, hitting O'Folliard, who screamed, "Don't shoot, I'm killed!" and died minutes later. The gunfire alerted the rest of the gang to the ambush and allowed them to make a getaway.

But the posse stayed on their trail, catching up with them four days later in Stinking Springs. They quietly surrounded the Kid and his men, who were asleep in an abandoned stone building. Just after sunrise, Charlie Bowdre went outside to feed the horses. The posse evidently mistook him for the Kid and shot him down. Then the posse shot a horse, which fell and blocked the only exit, trapping the gang inside without food or water and little ammo. The standoff lasted almost two days, during which Garrett's men cooked their meals over an open fire and screamed invitations to the gang to join them. At one point, the Kid challenged Garrett to "[c]ome up like a man and give us a fair fight." When Garrett responded that he didn't aim to do that, Billy chided him: "That's what I thought of you, you old long legged son of a bitch."

Finally, realizing that it was out of options, the gang surrendered. The men were taken to Las Vegas, where a large crowd gathered to see them. As Billy the Kid told a reporter from the *Gazette*, "If it hadn't been for that dead horse in the doorway I wouldn't be here today. I would have ridden out on my bay mare and taken my chances. . . . We could have stayed in that house but they . . . would have starved us out. I thought it was better to come out and get a good square meal."

Billy the Kid was locked up in the prison in Santa Fe to await trial. During that time, he wrote several letters to Governor Wallace, pleading for the governor to intercede. "I expect you have forgotten what you promised me, this month two years ago, but I have not and I think you ought to have come and seen me. . . . I have done everything that I promised you I would and you have done nothing that you promised me." The governor did not respond.

While pleading for a pardon, Billy and his men planned an escape and began to dig their way out of the prison. When this tunnel was discovered, the Kid was put in solitary confinement, chained to the floor of his cell.

In April, he was taken to Mesilla, a town to the south of Santa Fe, and tried for the murders of Buckshot Roberts and Sheriff William Brady. He was acquitted of the Roberts killing on a technicality, his attorney arguing successfully that Roberts was not shot on federal property, and therefore the federal court had no jurisdiction. However, Billy was not as fortunate in his second trial. After hearing one day of testimony, Judge Warren Bristol pronounced him guilty, then sentenced him to "hang, until you are dead, dead, dead."

It is said that the Kid responded by telling the judge, "You can go to hell, hell, hell."

Billy the Kid was the only man convicted of a crime committed during the Lincoln County War, which he believed to be patently unfair. His only hope, he understood, was that the governor would honor the agreement they had made. As he told a reporter, "I think he [Wallace] ought to pardon me. . . . Think it hard that I should be the only one to suffer the extreme penalties of the law." On April 16, he was taken by wagon to Lincoln, where he was scheduled to be hanged on May 13, between the hours of nine a.m. and three p.m. Among the seven men who guarded him during that five-day trip was an old enemy, Bob Olinger, who had fought for Dolan in the war and, from all accounts, was especially hard on the Kid. It was reported that more than once he poked him with his shotgun and dared him to try to escape so that he could shoot him in the back, "Just like you did Brady."

In Lincoln, the Kid was shackled to the floor on the second story of a merchant building, guarded by Olinger and deputy James W. Bell. On the evening of April 28, Olinger went across the street to get some dinner, leaving the Kid alone with Deputy Bell. People have always said Bell was a decent man who was just in the wrong place at the wrong time. There are several versions of what happened next, but they all usually begin with Billy asking the deputy to take him outside to the privy. Perhaps Billy shoved Deputy Bell down the steps, then hobbled into the gun room and grabbed a pistol. Maybe he bludgeoned Deputy Bell with his chains and grabbed his gun. Or perhaps Billy never touched Deputy Bell but instead retrieved a pistol that had been planted for him in the latrine. However it happened, Billy the Kid added to his legend by obtaining a gun and shooting Deputy Bell, who staggered into the street and died. Then, still in chains, Billy managed to get into the armory and grab Olinger's double-barreled shotgun, the very gun with which he had been poked and taunted. He then stood at the window, patiently awaiting the return of Robert Olinger.

It was not a long wait. Hearing the shots, Olinger raced from the hotel dining room. A passerby warned him, "Bob, the Kid has killed Bell." And, at that moment, Olinger saw the

Billy the Kid escapes from prison by killing deputy Robert Olinger.

Kid framed in the window only a few feet away, holding a shotgun. "Hello, Bob," Billy is reputed to have said.

Olinger accepted his fate and has been quoted as saying, "Yes, and he's killed me, too."

Billy the Kid fired both barrels; Olinger died without another word. With the help of people who were never identified, he was able to sever his chains, arm himself, and then steal a horse and ride out of town.

Pat Garrett had been in White Oaks when the daring escape took place. He assumed that Billy would head immediately for the Mexican border. So he bided his time, waiting until the following July, when he heard that Billy the Kid might be visiting a lady friend out at Pete Maxwell's place. He rode out there that night with his two deputies. Not surprising, there are other versions of the final confrontation between Pat Garrett and Billy the Kid. In one, Garrett tied up and gagged Paulita Maxwell, and when the Kid came in to see her, Garrett let loose with both barrels of his shotgun. There is no argument, though, that Pat Garrett shot and killed a man at Pete Maxwell's ranch on the night of July 14. The man believed to be Billy the Kid was buried by his Mexican friends on the Maxwell Ranch. A white wooden cross marked his grave, and inscribed on it were the words DUERME BIEN, QUERIDO ("Sleep well, beloved").

Almost immediately, souvenir hunters started pulling at the grave site, so within days, his body was moved to the nearby Fort Sumner military cemetery and buried next to his friends Tom O'Folliard and Charlie Bowdre. The inscription on their stone reads simply, PALS, then identifies the three men.

Pat Garrett did not receive the attention he had hoped for, and in fact, many people believed he had shot the Kid in the back in a cowardly manner. At an inquest, Garrett stated, "He came there armed with a pistol and a knife expressly to kill me if he could. I had no alternative but to kill him or suffer death at his hands." The coroner's jury ruled it a justifiable homicide. To profit from his success in tracking down the outlaw Billy the Kid, Garrett published a ghostwritten book in 1882 entitled *The Authentic Life of Billy, the Kid*. It was moderately successful but served primarily to embellish the growing legend of William H. Bonney. When Garrett ran for sheriff in the next election, he was defeated. In 1884, he ran for the New Mexico state senate, was also defeated, and left New Mexico for Texas. In 1908, he was shot to death outside Las Cruces, New Mexico, allegedly during an argument about goats grazing on his land without permission. His body was found lying by the side of the road.

In his twenty-one years, Billy the Kid was credited with killing twenty-one men, but as with so much else about his life, that number certainly is exaggerated. It is known that he

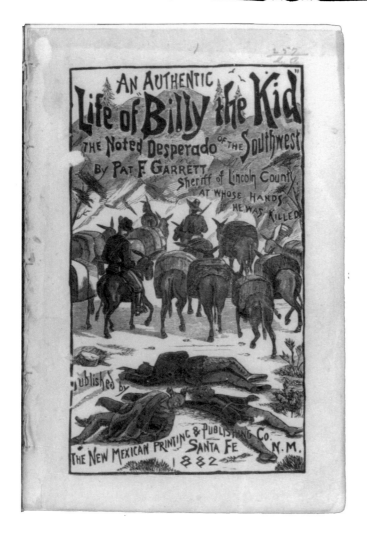

Months after he had shot Billy the Kid, Pat Garrett published this ghostwritten book, which did more to support the growing legend of Billy the Kid than benefit the sheriff.

killed at least four men himself and was involved in five more fatal shootings. That's nine. As for the others, no one will ever know how many notches were on his gun.

And as with other notorious outlaws, the story doesn't end in that hacienda. Legends take on a life of their own, and people wanted to believe that the Kid who'd pulled off so many daring feats and escapes had executed just one more. Rumors quickly surfaced that Billy the Kid did not die that night. To support these claims, people have pointed out that

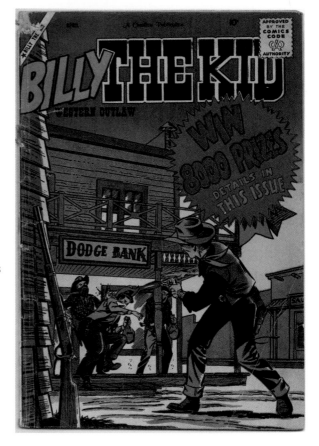

Although only twenty-one years old when he died, Billy the Kid had shot his way into American history. His legend has been celebrated in dime novels, books, comics, plays, songs, poems, and even an Aaron Copeland ballet. He has been portrayed more often in film and television than any other person, by actors including Paul Newman, Kris Kristofferson, and Marlon Brando.

no photographs of the body exist, no death certificate was ever issued, Pat Garrett was never paid the reward, and the three coroner's jury reports contained conflicting testimony and were signed by people who admitted they did not witness the shooting. In fact, beyond Pat Garrett's claims, there is little evidence that the victim was Billy the Kid.

Is it possible that Billy the Kid actually survived that night? According to one version, he was badly wounded, but the Mexican women of the hacienda saved his life, then substituted the body of a man who had died naturally that night; Bonney then lived the rest of his life peacefully under the name John Miller. Another version claims that Garrett and the Kid had become close friends years earlier in Beaver Smith's Saloon and that Garrett had helped set up this elaborate ploy, to enable Billy to live the rest of his life in peace. And from time to time, through the succeeding years, men would show up in the saloons of the Old West claiming to be Billy the Kid, saying they'd miraculously escaped death at the end of Pat Garrett's six-shooter that night—*And, by the way, would you buy me a drink?*

The most publicized claim was made in 1949, when a ninety-year-old man from Hamilton County, Texas, William H. "Brushy Bill" Roberts, stated that his true identity was, in fact, Billy the Kid. The man killed that night in 1881, he said, was a friend of his, known as Billy Barlow. He himself had lived in Mexico until things cooled down, then led a life of adventure. He'd served with Pancho Villa in the Mexican Revolution, worked in *Buffalo Bill's Wild West Show*, joined Teddy Roosevelt's Rough Riders and fought in Cuba, and even served as a US marshal while marrying four times and living under a dozen aliases. Although Roberts died of a heart attack in 1950, the book detailing his story, *Alias Billy the Kid,* was published in 1955. Although it was generally dismissed at that time, years later, the full transcripts of interviews conducted before his death seemed to make a much more convincing case.

Brushy Bill told an entertaining story. Although there was compelling evidence that "Brushy Bill" was actually a man named Oliver P. Roberts, who was born in 1879, other evidence seems to indicate that William Roberts had intimate knowledge of Lincoln City and many of the events that took place there. In face, there is more hard evidence to support the claim that William H. Roberts was indeed Billy the Kid than there is evidence that Pat Garrett actually killed the Kid the night of July 14, 1881.

In 2007, a legal effort was launched to settle the story once and for all by exhuming the remains in Billy Bonney's grave and attempting to match the DNA to that of his mother. That request was denied. Although it is still generally accepted that the legendary life of William H. Bonney, alias Billy the Kid, ended in the darkness of Pete Maxwell's bedroom, there remain enough unanswered questions to make this one of the Wild West's most compelling mysteries.

BUTCH CASSIDY

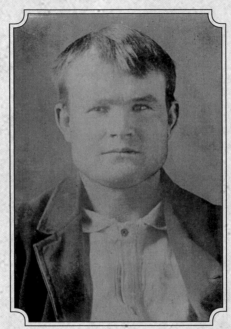

THE LAST MAN STANDING

utch Cassidy slowly pulled back a corner of the white lace curtain and looked out the broken windowpane. The plaza seemed deserted. But from behind every barrier, he saw the long barrel of a rifle pointed directly at him. Without counting, he figured at least three dozen Bolivian soldiers were drawing a bead on the house at that very moment. From the back of the darkened room, the wounded Sundance Kid asked evenly, "So, what do you think?"

"Looks like rain," Butch replied casually. "Now's probably not a good time to go for a stroll."

"Yeah, that's just what I was thinking." After a brief pause, Sundance said, "Hey, I got an idea; when it clears up, let's go watch one of those newfangled moving pictures."

Butch sparked at that thought, then smiled broadly. "Hey, maybe they'll make one of them about us sometime. You know, the story of two good-natured fellas just trying to make a decent living in a quick-changing world?"

Sundance laughed. "More likely, people'll be walking on the moon."

And then another shot shattered the remains of the window.

Did that conversation ever take place? Of course not. But it may be about as accurate as most of the stories that have been told about Butch Cassidy and the Sundance Kid and the gang they rode with, the Wild Bunch. Those oft-told tales, culminating in the award-winning 1969 film starring Paul Newman and Robert Redford, have ensured that the two robbers and the last gang to roam the Old West will live forever in American folklore. Although the movie purportedly told the "true story" of these outlaws, in this case, the word *true* was defined pretty loosely.

According to that history, after a successful life of crime in the United States, Butch and Sundance fled to South America, where they were eventually trapped by soldiers in a small house in San Vicente, Bolivia. The ambiguous ending of that classic movie left open the possibility that Butch and Sundance somehow managed to survive that last gunfight. And, in the century since that 1908 shoot-out, several intriguing stories would actually seem to support that contention. Although the fate of all the other members of the Wild Bunch is well known and accepted without question, some people do wonder if it is possible that Butch and Sundance somehow escaped.

Robert Leroy Parker was born in April 1866, the first of thirteen children, and grew up in Circleville, Utah. As a teenager, he worked briefly as a butcher, supposedly cutting up rustled cattle, then rode for a time with rancher and cattle and horse thief Mike Cassidy, which led to him being nicknamed Butch Cassidy.

Harry Alonzo Longabaugh was born a year later in Mont Clare, Pennsylvania. As a twenty-year-old, he was caught stealing a gun, a horse, and a saddle from a ranch in Sundance, Wyoming. While serving eighteen months in jail there, he picked up the nickname by which he gained fame, "the Sundance Kid."

A loosely knit association of various gangs, operating mostly out of the Hole-in-the-Wall hideout in Wyoming's Bighorn Mountains, the Wild Bunch pulled off the longest string of bank and train robberies in American history. In addition to Butch and Sundance, the primary members included Elzy Lay, Kid Curry Logan, News Carver, Tall Texan Kilpatrick, Matt Warner, Butch's brother Dan Parker, Flat Nose Currie, and Harry Bass. From 1889 through the turn of the century, the Wild Bunch purportedly stole the modern-day equivalent of about $2.5 million, before each of its members was caught or killed, one by one.

Robert Leroy Parker, who became the famed Butch Cassidy.

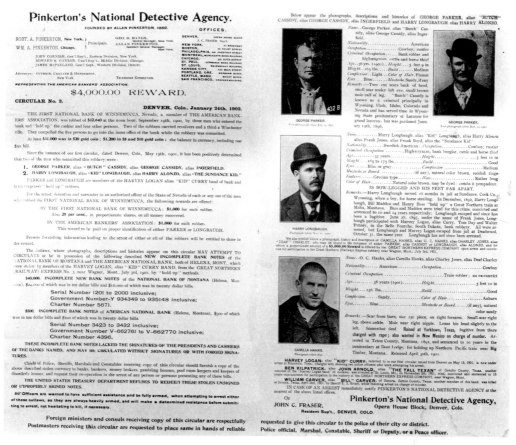

After Butch and Sundance held up the First National Bank of Winnemucca, Nevada, and got away with $32,640, the Pinkertons issued this Wanted poster, in which Cassidy was described as a "known criminal in Wyoming, Utah, Idaho, Colorado and Nevada," and it was pointed out that the Kid "is bow-legged and his feet far apart."

Butch Cassidy committed his first bank job in 1889, when he and several other masked men held up the San Miguel Valley Bank in Telluride, Colorado, riding away with about twenty thousand dollars. It was a transitional time for a region once known as the Wild West. Civilization was encroaching quickly, brought in by the 164,000 miles of railroad track that now stretched from the Atlantic to the Pacific, with trains that ran on a schedule. People were talking to friends miles away on the candlestick telephone. They were driving crazy fast in horseless carriages; in fact, only a year earlier, one of them had raced from Green Bay to

A 1901 formal portrait
of Sundance taken in
New York City

Madison, Wisconsin, in just thirty-three hours, almost as fast as the stage. In cities, people were speeding over paved streets on bicycles with pneumatic tires. And instead of living in fear of Indians and highwaymen, for only a few cents people could watch reenactments of Indian attacks on wagon trains and stagecoach robberies—and even behold the actual Sitting Bull and twenty of his warriors, when *Buffalo Bill's Wild West* and its "Congress of Rough Riders of the World," just back from Paris, came to town.

It took a while for Butch and Sundance to meet up, and by the time they did, both of them were fiercely committed to a life of larceny. Butch Cassidy had no formal education, learning the necessities of his trade from outlaw Mike Cassidy. By the time Mike Cassidy had killed a Wyoming rancher and taken off for parts unknown, Bob Parker could outride a posse and shoot well enough to hit a playing card dead center at fifty paces. It was said that he could ride around a tree trunk full tilt and put all six shots from his revolver into a three-inch circle. But in addition to outlaw skills, he also was said to have a pleasing way with words, a sense of fairness, and a quick wit. His first train robbery took place outside Grand Junction, Colorado, when his gang forced the Denver and Rio Grande Express to stop by blocking the tracks with a small mountain of stones. Guns drawn, the gang climbed aboard and ordered the guard to open the safe. He refused, claiming he did not have the combination. Butch's partner in that crime, a gunman named Bill McCarty, put his revolver to the guard's head, cocked it, and asked, "Should we kill him?"

After a pause, Butch suggested, "Let's vote!" He then persuaded the rest of the bandits to leave the guard alone. They collected about one hundred forty dollars from the passengers and rode away.

That wicked sense of humor was also present when he robbed the First National Bank of Denver. He approached the president of that institution and blurted out breathlessly, "Sir! I just overheard a plot to rob this bank!"

The bank president froze in his tracks. "Oh, Lord!" he supposedly said. "How did you learn of this plot?"

Cassidy smiled. "I planned it. Put up your hands!"

Sundance had spent several years working as a ranch hand, committing the occasional crime, when he joined Bill Madden and Henry Bass and held up the Great Northern westbound number 23 train near Malta, Montana, in 1892. This robbery was even less successful than Cassidy's attempt: Although he got away with about twenty-five dollars, his accomplices were caught and implicated him. Within days, the railroad issued Wanted posters bearing an accurate description of him and offering a five-hundred-dollar reward for his capture. A similar Wanted poster issued years later described his nose as "rather long," his hair as "brown, may be dyed, combs it pompadour," and notes that he "is bow-legged and his feet far apart." Madden was sentenced to ten years, Bass got fourteen, and Sundance spent the rest of his life as a fugitive.

It isn't known precisely when or how Butch and Sundance met, but in those days, after pulling a job, desperadoes were known to retreat to hideouts until things cooled down. As the *St. George Union* wrote in 1897, "The outlaws live among 'breaks,' the wildest, most rugged and inaccessible except to the initiated anywhere under the blue firmament. In recesses cut into the side of those yawning chasms, two or three men are able to hold an army at bay. To such places all who have stolen, robbed or murdered are welcomed so that the gangs are becoming augmented steadily as time goes on . . . There is no use attempting to dislodge them by force . . . the only way would be to starve them out and it is questionable if that is feasible."

These places had many advantages: They offered a clear view of all approaches, they were hard to find and get into, and if it became necessary, they were easy to defend. Pretty much anyone on the run was welcome in these hideouts. For example, young Bob Parker allegedly spent a lot of time in Brown's Park (or Brown's Hole, as it also was known), an isolated valley along the Green River, stretching between Colorado and Utah, when he was riding with Mike Cassidy. The Wild Bunch, or, as it originally was called, the Hole-in-the-Wall Gang, was formed by Butch Cassidy and his best friend at that time, rustler and holdup man Elzy Lay, while they were lying low in Robbers Roost, a hideout in southeastern Utah. (The gang also called itself, with a wink, the Train Robbers Syndicate.) When lawmen discovered the location of the Roost, the Wild Bunch departed for the famous Hole-in-the-Wall, a natural fortress atop a plateau in Carbon County, Wyoming, used by numerous gangs, a redoubt that could be reached only by squeezing through narrow passes and which was said to be so secure that a dozen men could defend it against a hundred.

Many plans were hatched and relationships formed along the well-known "outlaw trail." Membership in a gang was fluid; people would ride with several other bandits for a limited time or for a specific job, then move along. Several dozen men participated in at least one of the more than two dozen holdups believed to have been committed by the Wild Bunch. It's likely that Butch and Sundance crossed paths during one of these robberies.

By the turn of the twentieth century, it was becoming difficult to make a decent living cattle rustling or horse thieving, but it was a good time to be a bank or train robber. The West

Only outlaws on the run were welcomed at the easily defended Hole-in-the-Wall in Wyoming and at Brown's Park, or Brown's Hole, in Colorado (*inset*).

was being tamed. New towns were springing up all over the prairie; most of them had banks, while few of them could afford sufficient law enforcement. The iron horse was replacing the stagecoach, carrying money and mail vast distances, often with very little security on board.

Butch Cassidy was a new kind of bank robber. He treated robbing as his profession rather than as a dangerous hobby. Instead of just bursting into a place and waving guns around, he spent considerable time planning his jobs. Before proceeding, he gathered intelligence: By the time he was ready to move forward, he knew how he intended to get into and out of the town, how many lawmen might be on the job, and, most important, how much money was in the safe.

Even more crucial, he planned his escapes. For example, his men would climb poles and cut the town's telegraph lines to prevent the sheriff from contacting nearby law enforcement for help. They would leave horses waiting a good distance from a town, and if they were pursued by a posse of lawmen, they would ride hard to that place and change mounts, so that they would be riding fresh horses while the posse's would be wearing out. Sometimes all that planning wasn't really necessary. In 1896, Cassidy, recently released after serving eighteen months of a two-year sentence for stealing a horse, learned along with Elzy Lay and Bob Meeks that the town of Montpelier, Idaho, had only a part-time deputy who was paid a paltry ten dollars a month—and that he had neither a horse nor a gun.

But the town did have a bank.

They rode out of Montpelier with $7,165 in cash, gold, and silver—a fortune at the time—pursued by part-time deputy sheriff Fred Cruikshank, frantically pedaling his bicycle. When the word of that job spread, seasoned bandits began offering to ride with Butch Cassidy's Wild Bunch.

Sundance probably joined him right around that time. In April 1897, after cutting the telegraph wires in Castle Gate, Utah, the gang got away with the Pleasant Valley Coal Company's $9,860 payroll. In response, the company paymaster handed out checks to miners, informing them, "Paymaster Cassidy of Robbers Roost will honor the paper." As in almost all of Cassidy's heists, no shots had been fired. Butch Cassidy wasn't exactly nonviolent, but he definitely was averse to unnecessary bloodshed. He and his gang weren't in the robbing business to hurt people, just the banks, the railroads, and the large cattle owners who were putting up fences across the once-open ranges. The most dangerous member of the gang was Kid Curry, who was described by the *Anaconda Standard* as being "fond of dress and his taste in that direction is rather flashy. He is absolutely reckless and careless, and since he has been an outlaw has been known to take the most desperate chances. . . . A dead shot with a revolver and rifle, he will be a hard man to capture."

The "wildest of the Wild Bunch" was Harvey Logan, known as Kid Curry, who was credited with killing eleven men. He is shown here with his girlfriend, prostitute Annie Rogers, also known as Della Moore.

With each successful Wild Bunch robbery, Butch Cassidy's reputation spread. In 1898, a Chicago newspaper declared him "King of the Bandits," reporting that he was "the worst man" in Utah, Colorado, Wyoming, and Idaho. The article claimed that he had five hundred outlaws working for him, "subdivided into five gangs." The daring exploits and well-planned heists of the Wild Bunch made headlines and sold newspapers throughout the country. The gang did give newspapermen plenty to write about: They were committing crimes in five states, the named four plus South Dakota, in robberies that netted as much as seventy thousand dollars.

Although the size of the gang was obviously exaggerated, the "King of the Bandits" story was accurate on one important point: Butch did run the operation. He was known for teaching the other outlaws the proper way to plan and carry out a job and was the acknowledged mastermind behind many of the robberies—even if he didn't personally participate in them. Occasionally, something would go wrong. In July 1899, Elzy Lay was riding with a group of train robbers known as the Ketchum Gang. They held up the Colorado & Southern number 1 train outside Folsom, New Mexico, getting away with fifty thousand dollars. They didn't get far, though; the railroads had gotten a lot smarter and were hiring their own guns for protection. The Ketchum Gang was surprised by a determined posse, which lit out after it. They tracked it for several days, and in the running gun battles, two members of the posse were killed, including sheriff Edward Farr, and one man was wounded. One of the bandits died of his wounds, another man escaped, and Elzy Lay was wounded and captured. He recovered well enough to spend the rest of his life in prison.

The loss of his best friend left an empty saddle next to Butch Cassidy, and the Sundance Kid stepped up to fill it. For a time after Lay's incarceration, Butch Cassidy softened and considered leaving the profession. There are reports that he tried to make a deal with the railroads: If they agreed to let him be, he would leave their safes alone. He might even agree to consult for them as a security specialist—preventing train robberies. Any possibility of that deal ended near Wilcox, Wyoming, when the Wild Bunch took an estimated thirty thousand dollars in gold, cash, jewelry, and banknotes from the Union Pacific Overland Flyer number 1 train. According to a message sent by Union Pacific executives to the Laramie County sheriff, "[A] party of six masked robbers held up the first section of train number one . . . and after dynamiting bridges, mail and express cars and robbing the latter, disappeared." There is some evidence that this robbery served as the inspiration for the famous 1903 silent moving picture, *The Great Train Robbery*, and later for a memorable scene in the 1969 classic film *Butch Cassidy and the Sundance Kid*.

Blowing things up proved to be a bit of a problem for the gang. It turned out that the use of dynamite wasn't one of their areas of expertise. Because no crew member aboard this train was given the combination to the safe carried in the baggage car, the outlaws reacted by attempting to blow it open. Apparently they used considerably more dynamite than was necessary, blowing up the entire railway car, down to the frame. Some of the money was scorched in the explosion or stained by raspberries, also being transported in that car. Thus, the Wilcox robbery might be considered a failed experiment. As the *Rawlins Semi-Weekly Republican* reported, the robbers "wrecked the car, blowing the roof off and sides out, portions of the car being blown 150 yards." The safe, according to the *Laramie Daily Boomerang*, was blown "out of all semblance to the original self."

After the robbery, members of the train crew complimented the manners of the thieves, one of them telling reporters that he had asked for a chew of tobacco, which was given to him by one of the robbers. Another crew member said the bandits had reassured him, "Now boys, don't get scared. You're just as safe here as you would be in Cheyenne."

The robbers split up to make their getaway. Posses eventually including several hundred

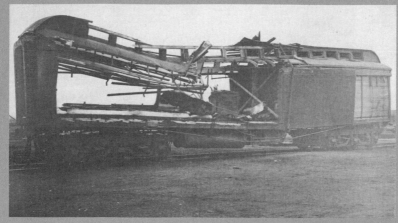

A classic scene from the movie *Butch Cassidy and the Sundance Kid* recreated the 1899 robbery of the Union Pacific Overland Flyer near Wilcox, Wyoming: Attempting to blow open the safe, the gang mistakenly used enough dynamite to blow up the entire railroad car.

In an attempt to catch the Wild Bunch, the Union Pacific created a special car for mounted rangers and their horses, enabling them to instantly pursue the robbers.

men, some of them using bloodhounds brought in all the way from Beatrice, Nebraska, for the task, pursued the bandits for several weeks. Converse County sheriff Josiah Hazen's posse eventually caught up to Sundance, Kid Curry Logan, and Flat Nose Currie near Castle Creek, Wyoming, and in a gunfight, Kid Curry shot and killed the sheriff. As the *Boomerang* related, "It was rough and broken country, and the outlaws had the advantage of knowing every inch of it. From behind boulder and brushwood they held off the posse—five men against two hundred. Hazen exposed himself and the next moment reeled back with a bullet through his heart. Darkness fell . . ." Eventually the bandits escaped into Hole-in-the-Wall territory.

The *New York Herald* reported, "They were lawless men who have lived long in the crags and become like eagles." Although in fact these were killers and robbers, people had already begun romanticizing the Wild Bunch. But this robbery put a quick stop to that.

Killing the sheriff and stealing gold that was to be used to pay American boys fighting in the Spanish-American War proved to be the beginning of the gang's downfall. The Union Pacific offered an eighteen-thousand-dollar bounty for the capture of the outlaws—dead or alive. It also hired armed guards, Rangers, to protect their trains, warning, "They ride on the engine. In the baggage car, on the dry coaches, or in the sleepers, being instructed not to stay always at one point of the train. Any gang of bandits attacking a Union Pacific train now will know it has to reckon on a stiff fight, for not only is each train guarded, but somewhere up or down the line is the patrol body of rangers, ready to be shipped to the danger zone as fast as steam can carry them."

Equally significant, the railroad also hired the Pinkertons to once and for all put the gang out of the stealing business. The Pinks represented the largest and toughest private security company in America. In fact, the Pinkerton agency was the only truly national law-enforcement operation; by the 1870s, there were more Pinkerton men than there were soldiers in the American army. They were known to be relentless in their pursuit, professional and thorough in their investigations, and as tough as necessary in their enforcement methods. Without question, they brought scientific detection techniques to American law enforcement, and they were the first to employ mug shots, fingerprints, and undercover agents. But they also were well known to rely on their own interpretation of the law to accomplish their objectives—even when it required bloodshed.

Following the Wilcox robbery, the Pinkertons picked up the trail of the Wild Bunch. And once they had it, they never let it go. By tracing scorched and stained banknotes, they tracked Kid Curry's brother, Lonnie Logan, and Bob Lee to Cripple Creek, Colorado. Lee eventually was captured and sentenced to ten years in prison. Pinkerton operatives caught

Hole in Wall S.H.

The Hole-in-the-Wall in the Bighorn Mountains of northern Wyoming, where the Wild Bunch was formed, was a full day's ride from civilization. Although outlaws were well protected, life was hard there. Each gang was responsible for its own cabins, livestock, and provisions. There was no leader, no structure—and almost no rules. Among the few prohibited acts were murder and stealing another gang's supplies.

up with Lonnie Logan in a rural farmhouse, and when he attempted to escape into the nearby woods, they shot him dead. Almost two years later, Pinkertons caught Kid Curry in Knoxville, Tennessee. After a trial, he was sentenced to 20 to 130 years in federal prison. He escaped less than a year later. In 1904, a posse caught up with him again after a train robbery near Parachute, Colorado. He was wounded in the shoot-out, and rather than surrender and be sent back to prison, he shouted to his companions, "I'm hit! Don't wait for me, boys. I'm all in. Good-bye!" Then he put his gun to his head and committed suicide.

Although the Pinks were successfully dismantling the Wild Bunch man by man, their real target remained the most wanted man in the West, Butch Cassidy. The reward offered for his capture or death was raised to ten thousand dollars. However, the fact that the greatest law-enforcement organization in the world was on his tail didn't appear to worry him much. On August 29, 1900, a masked robber boarded Union Pacific's Overland Flyer number 3 outside Tipton, Wyoming, put a pistol to the conductor's head, and ordered him to stop the train when it reached a campfire by the side of the road. The Wild Bunch had yet to master the art of dynamite and once again blew the baggage car to smithereens, causing a rain of bills estimated at fifty-five thousand dollars. The gang was polite about it, though: After the robbery, a member of the train's crew complimented the robbers on their courtesy, explaining that one of the holdup men told him the gang really didn't want to hurt anyone and had made a pact that anyone who killed without reason would be executed. And the bandits said "so long" as they rode away. In a sign of the changing times, a member of the train crew used a pay phone to report the robbery. A posse pursued the Wild Bunch for more than a week, but eventually, as the *Salt Lake Herald* reported, "All hope of capturing the four men who held up, dynamited and robbed the overland express train at Tipton three weeks ago has been given up . . . the route of the robbers was well chosen and was through a wild and uninhabited country. . . . The crimes go on record as one of the most successful and daring robberies in the history of the west."

Less than a month later, members of the gang were credited with looting the First National Bank in Winnemucca, Nevada, of $32,640. These robbers were not as polite, however, threatening to cut the cashier's throat if he refused to open the safe. Announcing their presence, one robber pulled a pair of .45s and warned, "Stick 'em up, Slim, or I'll make you look like a naval target," adding minutes later, "Just feel how fine and soft the atmosphere is above your head, feel it with both hands at once."

Although it's impossible to even roughly estimate the total amount of money stolen by the Wild Bunch—because no one knows how many robberies they actually pulled off—without question, they got away with today's equivalent of millions of dollars. Most of the

After Butch and Sundance stopped the Great Northern Express near Wagner, Montana, in 1901, they cut loose the express car, blew up the safe, and escaped with forty thousand dollars. In those days, different organizations offered rewards—including a percentage of the money recovered—so it's impossible to know the total amount of the bounty on the heads of the robbers.

money was spent on fast living, although stories are told about Cassidy handing out cash to people who needed it or refusing to steal money from civilians. He also was known to be meticulous about paying his debts. A man named John Kelly, who had worked with "Roy Parker" as a ranch hand, once lent him twenty-five dollars, "so he could get out of Butte, Montana." Several years later, Kelly unexpectedly received a letter from Parker, and when he opened it, one hundred dollars fell out. The enclosed note read, "If you don't know how I got this, you will soon learn someday."

It is possible that some of the loot ended up in the hands of women. Butch was a handsome man; his Wanted poster in 1900 described him as five feet nine inches tall with a medium build, a light complexion, flaxen hair, and blue eyes. His face was square and young-looking, and he bore a naturally inviting, bemused smile. When he was imprisoned in Wyoming, in addition to his physical description, his record noted, "Habits of Life: Intemperate." He appeared to enjoy the company of the ladies as much as they liked being with him, and it was said that he knew how to treat a woman properly.

Sundance was about the same height and weight, but on his Wanted posters, he was said to have "a dark complexion, black hair, black eyes" and "Grecian features." The Pinkertons added that he was a fast draw who "drinks very little, if any, and is believed to be involved with a school m'arm known only as Etta Place."

Little is known about Etta Place, not even her real name. Place was the maiden name of Sundance's mother. And Etta might actually have been "Ethel." It isn't even known if she really was a teacher; she also has been described as a saloon girl and as a prostitute who met both Butch and Sundance while working in a brothel, possibly Fannie Porter's Sporting Parlor in San Antonio. She was about ten years younger than Sundance and had, according to the Pinkertons, "classic good looks . . . and she appears to be a refined type." Other people described her as one of the most beautiful women they had ever seen, and men who later knew her in South America said, "She was a goddess—everyone was enamored of her." Whether Sundance and Etta were legally married isn't known, but she wore engagement and wedding rings, and they referred to each other as husband and wife.

It does seem that the core members of the Wild Bunch truly were friends in addition to being business associates. Less than three months after the Tipton heist, for instance, several members of the gang found themselves living the sporting life in the cattle boomtown of Fort Worth, Texas. For reasons that will never be understood, five members of the gang— Butch and Sundance, Kid Curry, News Carver, and Tall Texan Kilpatrick—walked into the photography shop of John Swartz, dressed in the dandy-wear of bankers and railroad executives, and posed for a formal picture. This iconic photograph eventually became known as "The Ft. Worth Five," the most famous mug shot in western history.

The proud photographer was so pleased with his work that he enlarged a copy and placed it on an easel in his front window as an advertisement. Among the people who admired the portrait was a Pinkerton agent who happened to be in town on an assignment and immediately recognized the gang. Within days, it was hanging in every post office, train station, Wells Fargo outlet, and law-enforcement office in the country.

Things were beginning to heat up in early 1901 when Cassidy and Sundance decided to make good their final escape. Although they had only done two or three jobs together, they had become close. Life on the run could wear a man down; as gang member Matt Warner once said, "You'll never know what it means to be hunted. You can never sleep. You've always got to listen with one ear and keep one eye open. After awhile, you almost go crazy. No sleep! No sleep! Even when you know you're perfectly safe, you can't sleep. Every pissant under your pillow sounds like a posse of sheriffs coming to get you!"

"The Ft. Worth Five"

Their challenge was to find a place where they weren't known. After the "Ft. Worth Five" picture had been circulated, no place in America was safe for them—unless they intended to spend the rest of their lives in some forsaken hideout. Fortunately, a lot of Wyoming ranchers were then moving to South America, in particular Argentina and Bolivia, where the weather was good, land was cheap and plentiful, and nobody asked a lot of embarrassing questions. Oh, and the nearest Pinkertons were more than five thousand miles away.

Obviously, they weren't in a big hurry. After welcoming the New Year 1901 in New Orleans, then traveling by train to Niagara Falls, Butch, Sundance, and the lovely and mysterious Etta Place visited one of the most populous places on earth, New York City. While there, Butch bought a gold watch and Sundance and Etta purchased a lapel watch and stickpin at the fashionable jewelry store Tiffany's, and the winsome couple posed for a "wedding portrait" at the De Young Photography Studio in Union Square. On the twentieth of January, Mr. and Mrs. Longabaugh, accompanied by her "brother," "James Ryan," set sail for Buenos Aires aboard the British steamer *Herminius*.

Without their leadership, the remains of the Wild Bunch scattered and by 1905 had passed into Old West history. Historians attribute more than twenty murders to gang members

during its roughly fifteen years in existence. Fifteen members of the gang died with their boots on, and another three committed suicide. Six of them were caught and went to prison—and were killed when they got out. Elzy Lay was believed to be the last survivor. He was pardoned and released from prison in 1906 for saving the warden's wife and daughter during a prison uprising and lived quietly in Los Angeles until his death—from natural causes—in 1934.

Retirement proved to be only temporary for Butch and Sundance. Upon their arrival in Buenos Aires, Sundance deposited $12,500 in an Argentinean bank. Then the three of them traveled by steamer to Cholila, a small frontier town in the sparsely populated region of Patagonia, where they lived for a time as Mr. and Mrs. Harry "Enrique" Place and James "Santiago" Ryan. Under the terms of an 1884 law, passed to encourage immigration, they were given fifteen thousand acres to develop. A portion of those lands actually belonged to Place, making her the first woman in Argentina to receive land under this law. They built a four-room cabin on the east bank of the Blanco River, with the snowcapped Andes in the distance, and started a ranching operation. It grew to a decent size, according to a letter Cassidy wrote to a friend in Vernal, Utah. The estancia had 300 head of cattle, 1,500 sheep, and 25 horses. Their closest neighbor was almost a day's ride away.

Sundance and Etta returned to the United States for brief visits in 1902 and again in 1904. During those trips, the tourists visited sites including Coney Island in Brooklyn and the St. Louis World's Fair, but they also saw several doctors, and the speculation is that both of them were suffering from venereal disease.

The Pinkertons had not let go of their pursuit. By intercepting letters Sundance had written to his family in Pennsylvania, they learned that the bandits were living in Argentina. In 1903, agent Frank Dimaio traveled to Buenos Aires and from there traced them to Cholila. Supposedly the onset of the rainy season prevented him from reaching the ranch, but there is a story that Butch and Sundance killed a Pink sometime that year and buried the body, which, in a quite embarrassing episode, was later dug up by Etta Place's dog while they were entertaining dinner guests.

Whatever actually took place, it did not appear to alarm the trio, because early in 1904, the territorial governor spent a night as a guest in their cabin, dancing with Etta as Sundance played a samba on his guitar.

Maybe their money was running out, or perhaps they just missed the excitement, but in February 1905, English-speaking bandits later identified as Butch and Sundance held up the

🖾 The "wedding portrait" of Harry Longabaugh, the Sundance Kid, and the beautiful Etta Place, taken in New York City in 1901, shortly before they departed for South America

Banco de Tarapaca y Argentina and got away with the modern-day equivalent of about $100,000. Supposedly Etta had assisted in the planning by talking her way into the vault to case the layout of the bank, and later in the actual robbery by dressing in men's clothing and waiting outside, holding the horses. A story often told in Argentina asserts that she was such a good markswoman that as they made their escape, she was able to split the telegraph wire with a single rifle shot.

There remains some question regarding whether they actually pulled this job. An official of the Argentinean government claimed to be with them on their ranch the day after the robbery, which, if true, was essentially an unbreakable alibi. True or not, governor Julio Lazana signed a warrant for their arrest, but they learned about it days before it could be executed and immediately sold part of their land for eighteen thousand pesos and ordered their foreman to liquidate the rest of their property, before sailing to Puerto Montt, Chile.

Sundance and Etta later left Chile for a trip to San Francisco, but upon their return, the three of them went back to work, holding up the Banco de la Nacion in Villa Mercedes, Argentina, and escaping with today's equivalent of about $135,000. When the bank manager resisted, he was, depending on reports, either pistol-whipped or shot by an unknown third "man." That third "man" could have been Etta, who had cut her hair short and had previously been described by a Buenos Aires newspaper as "an interesting woman . . . who wears male clothing with total correctness" and was also a "fine rider" who knew how to handle "all classes of firearms." Posses chased them into the Andes before losing their trail, but now they were on the run, and they would never stop.

At some point that summer, Sundance and Etta Place again traveled to San Francisco, but this time Sundance returned alone. There is some evidence that she had an operation in Denver for appendicitis or a gall-bladder problem, but the woman known in history as Etta Place was never heard from again.

The trail tends to get a little murky from then on. It's likely that Butch and Sundance found jobs at the Concordia Tin Mine in the Bolivian Andes—ironically enough, guarding the mine payroll. What better way for robbers to hide in plain sight than to protect a payroll? They probably were looking for the big score, that one legendary robbery large enough to support them for the rest of their lives. There were scattered reports of smaller heists that took place while they were living in that region, successful robberies attributed to "Yankees," but there is no real evidence linking Butch and Sundance to them.

Eventually they appeared to focus on the bank in the mining area of Tupiza. For several weeks, while casing the bank, they bunked with a British engineer named A. G. Francis in a small town about fifteen miles south of the city. Butch regularly went into Tupiza to study the bank operations. He discovered that a detachment of soldiers from an elite Bolivian unit was quartered in a hotel across the town square from the bank—much too close—and it didn't appear as if they were leaving anytime soon.

But while there, Butch discovered an even softer target, the Aramayo family mining interests. The family owned and operated several tin mines in the area, and the payrolls for all of them passed through their main office in Tupiza. Butch learned that an Aramayo manager named Carlos Peró would be transporting an eighty-thousand-peso payroll, about half a million in today's dollars, from Tupiza to Quechisla—by mule. On foot. Unarmed. And without any guards.

On November 4, 1908, as Peró, his young son, and a peon who was assisting him walked up Dead Cow Hill, they were confronted by two men. Bandanas covered their faces, and their hat brims were turned down so that only their eyes were visible. They were wearing dark-red corduroy suits and cartridge belts bulging with ammunition. Each man held a Mauser carbine and had a Colt revolver tucked in his holster. One of them stepped close and told Peró he wanted the eighty thousand pesos, and he wanted it quick. Peró apologized profusely. That payroll was being carried the next week, he explained, but this week he had only fifteen thousand pesos (about ninety thousand dollars). Obviously Butch and Sundance would not be coming back the following week, so they took the smaller payroll and a dark brown mule, then disappeared into the Bolivian wilderness.

Within a day, *la guardia*, military patrols, and armed miners were watching every town and village, every ravine and culvert, every train station and horse ranch, looking for two gringos with a dark brown mule.

Butch and Sundance had made it back to Francis's place. They leveled with him, then spent the night ruminating about what might have been. Francis recalled Cassidy telling him that he'd wanted to live a law-abiding life, but that each time he tried, the Pinks had shown up and forced him to return to the outlaw road. Cassidy told him he'd never hurt or killed a man except in self-defense—making him unique among western outlaws—and had robbed only rich corporations.

Fearing that an army patrol would find them, Butch and Sundance departed very early the next morning, taking Francis with them as a guide. A day later they released him. At sundown on November 6, they rode cautiously into the mining village of San Vicente, one of them astride a dark brown mule. The *corregidor*, a local magistrate named Cleto Bellot, welcomed the strangers and inquired as to their business. They were on their way to Santa Catalina, they explained, and asked for supplies and directions. Bellot offered his assistance, then found them lodging for the night in a thatched adobe house at the end of a walled alley.

After Bellot left them there for the night, he went right to the place where a four-man posse, consisting of soldiers and *la guardia*, was staying and told them where they would find the outlaws. As the four men approached the adobe house at the end of the alley, a man later identified as Butch Cassidy stepped into the open doorway and began firing his pistol at them. The soldier Vincent Lopez was struck in the neck and would die there. The posse took up defensive positions and began firing into the house. One of them went to seek armed friends who would guard the rear and the roof to prevent an escape. Unlike in the final scene in the wonderful movie that would be made about the outlaws sixty years later, only a few anxious men surrounded the house. And there was no cascade of bullets, only several shots. Within several minutes, though, three loud screams came from the house, and then there was no more shooting.

In the early light of the next morning, the soldiers entered the house. Both Yankees were dead: Butch Cassidy was lying on the floor, a bullet in his arm and a bullet in his temple. The Sundance Kid was still sitting on a bench behind the door, his arms wrapped around a large ceramic jar, with several shots in his body and one shot in the center of his forehead. To knowledgeable people, it looked as if Butch had finished off his wounded friend, Sundance, then killed himself.

The payroll was still in their saddlebags. No one knew their names, but Peró identified them as the men who had held him up. They were buried in San Vicente.

That's the whole story, except that the ending has long been questioned.

Several different versions of the climactic shoot-out were reported to have taken place in several different cities. One such version, written by missionary and explorer Hiram Bingham, who had coincidentally arrived in Tupiza two weeks after the shooting, was published in 1911. Bingham wrote, ". . . a party of 50 Bolivian soldiers went on the trail of the robbers, who were found lunching in an Indian hut. They had carelessly left their mules and rifles several yards from the door of the hut and were unable to escape. After a fight, in which three or four soldiers were killed and as many more wounded, the thatch roof of the hut was set on fire and the bandits forced out into the open where they finally fell, each with half a dozen bullets in his body."

Although these bodies were positively identified as those of the bandits who had robbed the Aramayo payroll, there was no evidence that they were Butch and Sundance. The Pinkertons were not convinced of their identity; William A. Pinkerton himself dismissed "the whole story as a fake," and the agency never officially ended its search for the outlaws. In fact, Pinkerton supposedly confided to an operative, "The last we heard of Longabaugh he was in jail in Peru for an attempted bank robbery. Cassidy had been with him but got away."

Many people later claimed to have met or spent time with both men in many different places, long after their deaths had been reported. Even Bingham concluded his story by admitting, "We received a call from two rough-looking Anglo-Saxons who told us hair raising stories of dangers on the Bolivian roads where highway robbers driven out of the United States . . . and hounded to death by Pinkerton detectives, had found a pleasant place to pursue their chosen occupation. . . . We found out afterwards that one of our informants was one of this damn gang of robbers."

Cassidy's sister Lula Betenson claimed that her brother had visited her in 1925 and related yet another version of the story. Two men were indeed killed that night in San Vicente, but they were identified as Cassidy and Sundance by a friend of theirs from the Concordia Tin Mines named Percy Seibert, who did it to allow his friends to start a new life without living in fear of the law.

The bodies of the two men who died that night have been lost to history, so DNA testing can't be conducted, ensuring that the question of who really did die in that small Bolivian village will never be definitively answered. For the many people enamored with the romantic tale of the gentlemen train robbers and the beautiful Etta Place, who want to believe that Butch and Sundance lived long lives under assumed names, this is a perfect ending.

Paul Newman as Butch Cassidy and Robert Redford as the Sundance Kid depicted the legendary friendship between the outlaws in the classic 1969 movie. Nominated for seven Academy Awards, winning four, it guaranteed that Butch, Sundance, Etta Place, and the Hole-in-the-Wall Gang would live forever in the legends of the Old West.

A MOVING IMAGE:
CREATING THE WILD WEST
ON FILM

No medium has done more to shape our image of the Old West than the motion-picture industry. It was a fortunate coincidence that moving pictures became easily accessible to most Americans at just about the same time in our history that the Wild West became settled. Western stories were perfect for the rudimentary technology then available: The large cameras required a lot of light, so most films had to be shot outdoors. Because there was no sound, plots had to be uncomplicated, and it had to be easy for the audience to instantly tell the good guys from the bad guys. A new genre was created, a world of adventure and suspense in which a man's character could be determined by the color of his hat.

Movies were pure entertainment; they were not intended to be history. The real challenges faced and conquered by the explorers and homesteaders of the West lacked the instant excitement of stagecoaches being chased by outlaws, settlers fighting Indians, and quick-draw shoot-outs, so those and other similar elements were magnified and exaggerated and very rapidly came to define the West in the minds of moviegoers.

Although Edwin Porter's 1903 ten-minute-long *Great Train*

Robbery is usually cited as the first Western, in fact, Thomas Edison was experimenting with films such as *Sioux Ghost Dance* a decade earlier. Ironically, those early Westerns were filmed in New York and New Jersey and featured lush landscapes replete with lakes, streams, and forests rather than the vast plains that would later become the easily recognizable West. And in many of those early films, Indians were noble and trustworthy people who guided whites through perilous adventures, often having to save their lives; it would be another decade before Indians morphed into the cunning and heartless enemy. Brave cowboys such as "Broncho Billy" Anderson and Tom Mix, with his "wonder horse," Tony, were the first movie stars.

By the 1920s, Westerns had evolved from inexpensive one-reelers shown in nickelodeons to epic films. The most popular film of 1923, *The Covered Wagon*, was based on a dime novel. In 1924, director John Ford, who probably did more than any other person to create and shape the myth of the Old West, filmed *The Iron Horse*, which featured an army cavalry regiment, 3,000 railroad workmen, 1,000 Chinese laborers, 800 Indians, 2,800 horses, 1,300 buffalo, and 10,000 cattle.

It was the necessity of filming outdoors that eventually caused the motion-picture industry to move west for the year-round sunny skies of Hollywood. America's passion for movies sparked another kind of California gold rush, and the studios began producing countless low-budget B movies. Inexpensive western series and serials, with their

Since the founding of the motion-picture industry, the incredible true-life adventures of the men who tamed the West have served as source material— which was then turned into the larger-than-real-life legends we celebrate.

formulaic plots, usually including deception, betrayal, stampedes, and showdowns—and just a hint of romance—filled theaters around the country, spreading the gospel of the straight-shooting cowboy defending the weak and exploited against unscrupulous outlaws and untamed Indians.

In the 1950s, television created a whole new audience for these films, further guaranteeing the survival of this mythical vision of the West. When those studios moved from showing their old movies to producing new western TV series, they stayed true to the myths, portraying real men such as Davy Crockett, Wild Bill Hickok, Bat Masterson, and Wyatt Earp as mostly fictionalized characters. By 1958, eight of the ten most popular shows were Westerns, and the three networks were broadcasting forty-eight different western series, thirty of them in prime-time hours.

Unable to compete with the action-packed series, the movie studios began using the western backdrop to tell deeper human stories. In 1953, for example, the allegorical Western *High Noon* was nominated for seven Oscars, winning four of them. In movie history, only sixteen Westerns have even been nominated for Best Picture, and three of them—*Cimarron* (1931), *Dances with Wolves* (1990), and *Unforgiven* (1992)—have won.

Awards or no, the motion-picture industry molded the image of the Wild West that has become so much a part of American history.

ACKNOWLEDGMENTS

There are many people whose efforts made this project possible. I would like to express my appreciation to our editorial director, Gillian Blake, whose calm management of a complex project under difficult conditions has been superb. Literary agent Paul Fedorko of N.S. Bienstock brought all the disparate pieces together and was always there with a solution when difficulties arose. And as Paul will happily admit, he could not have done so without his assistant, Sammy Bina.

Coordinating this book with the television series being created by Warm Springs Productions of Missoula, Montana, has been made easy by line producer Bridger Pierce, whose enthusiasm for telling this wonderful story resonates on every page, and among the many people who have assisted him are Keith Palmer, Ajax Broome, and Jason Broome.

The beautiful illustrations that bring to life this colorful period in our history were cultivated and selected by Liz Seramur, Emily Vinson, and Adam Vietenheimer, along with Nancy Singer, who also created the book's artful and complementary design. The following people provided invaluable assistance in finding the images: John Waggener and Victoria Allen, American Heritage Center, University of Wyoming; Alyssa Bentz, Wells Fargo Corporate Archives; Jeff Corrigan, the State Historical Society of Missouri; Eileen Price, Center for Southwest Research, University of New Mexico; Hayes Scriven, Northfield Historical Society; Loren McLane, Fort Smith Historic Site; Stephen Spence, National Archives at Kansas City; Jacquelyn Slater Reese, Western History Collections, University of Oklahoma; Gregory M. Walz, Utah State Archives and Utah State History; Karen Douglas, Kit Carson Home; Thomas Haggerty and Wendy Zieger, Bridgeman Collection; Glenn Bradie and Alison Rigney, Everett Collection; Brandt Buell and Michelle Graham, Getty Images; Sarah Steele and Silka Quintero, Granger Collection; Ashley Morton and Joergen Birman, National Geographic Creative; Peter Rohowsky and Jennifer Belt, Art Resource; Dave Alexander, Legends of America. A very special thanks to copy editor deluxe Jane Hardick, whose passion for clarity and accuracy has made a huge difference.

Several people assisted me with my research, including Rob Farwell, Dusty Pendleton, and Steve Boynton, whose efforts I truly appreciate.

Completing a project like this requires continued support through long days and nights, which I always get from my beautiful wife (and America's finest yoga instructor!), Laura Stevens, and the small but confident dog who shared those hours with me, Willy.

And finally, I would also like to express my deepest appreciation to Bill O'Reilly for making it possible for me to participate in this project.

BIBLIOGRAPHY

The following books were excellent sources for general background on the Old West.

Calloway, Colin G. *New Worlds for All: Indians, Europeans and Remaking of Early America.* Baltimore: Johns Hopkins University Press, 2005.
Cody, William F. *An Autobiography of Buffalo Bill.* New York: Farrar and Rinehart, 1920.
Custer, George Armstrong. *My Life on the Plains; or, Personal Experiences with Indians.* New York: Sheldon & Company, 1876.
Howe, Henry. *The Great West.* Cincinnati: Henry Howe Publishing, 1851.
O'Neal, Bill. *Encyclopedia of Western Gunslingers.* Norman: University of Oklahoma Press, 1979.
Wright, Robert M. *Dodge City, the Cowboy Capital, and the Great Southwest.* Wichita, KS: Wichita Eagle Press, 1913.
Zinn, Howard. *A People's History of the United States.* New York: HarperCollins, 2005.

I have also consulted several websites to gather, compare, and confirm information. The following sites proved to be especially trustworthy and provided useful material, as well as directing me to additional sources:

Books.Google.com
EyewitnesstoHistory.com
History.com
legendsofamerica.com
PBS.org
Project Gutenberg (gutenberg.org)
Truewestmagazine.com
Wikipedia.org

The following resources provided information on the specific subjects profiled in this book.

Daniel Boone

Bakeless, John. *Daniel Boone, Master of the Wilderness.* 1939. Reprint, Lincoln: University of Nebraska Press, 1989.
Boone, Daniel. *The Adventures of Colonel Boone, Formerly a Hunter, Containing a Narrative of the Wars of Kentucky, Written by Himself.* John Filson, 1823.

Filson, John. *The Discovery, Settlement, and Present State of Kentucke.* Includes an appendix, "The Adventures of Col. Daniel Boon, One of the First Settlers." John Filson, 1784.
Fort Boonesborough Living History, "Daniel Boone and the History of Fort Boonesborough," http://www .fortboonesboroughlivinghistory.org/html/daniel_boone.html.
Hawks, Francis Lister. *The Adventures of Daniel Boone, the Kentucky Rifleman.* New York: D. Appleton, 1843.
Lord Byron. *Don Juan.* Reprint of the 1837 Halifax, Nova Scotia, edition, Project Gutenberg, 2007. http://www .gutenberg.org/files/21700/21700-h/21700-h.htm.

David Crockett
Akenson, Donald Harman. *Irish History of Civilization.* Volume 1. London: Granta Books, 2005.
Clarke, Matthew St. Clair. *The Life and Adventures of Colonel David Crockett of West Tennessee.* 1833.
Crockett, David, E. L. Carey, and A. Hart. *A Narrative of the Life of David Crockett, written by Himself.* Philadelphia: E. L. Carey and A. Hart, 1834.
de la Peña, José Enrique. *The Memoirs of Lt. Col. José Enrique de la Peña.* College Station: Texas A&M University Press, 1975.
Editors of *True West* Magazine. "How Did Davy Really Die?" In *True Tales and Amazing Legends of the Old West: From* True West *Magazine.* New York: Crown, 2005.
Jones, Randell. *In the Footsteps of Davy Crockett.* Winston-Salem, NC: John F. Blair, 2006.
Legends of America, "Davy Crockett," http://www.legendsofamerica.com/we-davycrockettoutlaw.html.

Kit Carson
Burdett, Charles. *Life of Kit Carson.* Philadelphia: Porter and Coates, 1869.
Frémont, John C. *Report of the Exploring Exhibition to the Rocky Mountains, and to Oregon & California in the Years 1843–'44.* Washington, DC: Gales and Seaton, 1845.
Peters, DeWitt C. *The Life and Adventures of Kit Carson, the Nestor of the Rocky Mountains, from Facts Narrated by Himself.* New York: W. H. Tinson, 1858. Published as *Pioneer Life & Frontier Adventures of Kit Carson.* Boston: Estes & Lauriat, 1883.
Sides, Hampton. *Blood and Thunder.* New York: Doubleday, 2006.

Black Bart
"Black Bart: California's Infamous Stage Robber," http://www.BlackBart.com.
Hoeper, George. *Black Bart: Boulevardier Bandit.* Sanger, CA: Word Dancer Press, 1995.
Jackson, Joseph Henry. *Bad Company: The Story of California's Legendary and Actual Stage Robbers, Bandits, Highwaymen and Outlaws from the Fifties to the Eighties.* Lincoln: University of Nebraska Press, 1977. First published 1949 by Harcourt Brace.
Nolan, Frederick. *The Wild West: History, Myth and the Making of America.* London: Arcturus, 2003.
Pryor, Alton. *Outlaws and Gunslingers.* Roseville, CA: Stagecoach Publishing, 2001.

Wild Bill Hickok
Black Plains Pioneer, August 5, 1876.
Cheyenne Daily Sun, March 8, 1876.
Hardin, John Wesley. *The Life of John Wesley Hardin as Written by Himself.* 1896. Reprint, Norman: University of Oklahoma Press, 1977.
Nichols, George Ward. "Wild Bill." *Harper's New Monthly Magazine*, February 1867.
Rosa, Joseph G. *They Called Him Wild Bill: The Life and Adventures of James Butler Hickok.* Norman: University of Oklahoma Press, 1979.
Topeka Daily Commonwealth, November 3, 1869.

Bass Reeves

Burton, Art T. *Black Gun, Silver Star: The Life and Legend of Frontier Marshal Bass Reeves*. Lincoln: University of Nebraska Press, 2006.

Fischer, Ron W. *The Tombstone News* (2006): "Bass Reeves: He Set a Timeless Example," http://www.TheTombstone News.com.

Generic Radio Workshop Script Library, "The Lone Ranger, episode 1," http://www.genericradio.com/show.php?id=1975f5a375929e64.

Legends of America, "Old West Legends: Bass Reeves; Black Hero Marshal," http://www.legendsofamerica.com/we-bassreeves.html.

Nelson, Vaundra Micheaux. *Bad News for Outlaws: The Remarkable Life of Bass Reeves, U.S. Marshal*. Minneapolis: Lerner Publishing Group, 2009.

United States Marshals Service. "U.S. Marshal Bass Reeves," http://www.usmarshals.gov/news/chron/2011/111611.htm.

George Armstrong Custer

Ambrose, Stephen E. *Crazy Horse and Custer: The Parallel Lives of Two American Warriors*. New York: Random House, 1996.

Bismarck Tribune, September 2, 1874.

Connell, Evan. *Son of the Morning Star*. New York: North Point Press, 1984.

Lehman, Tim. *Bloodshed at Little Bighorn: Sitting Bull, Custer, and the Destinies of Nations*. Baltimore: Johns Hopkins University Press, 2010.

Buffalo Bill and Annie Oakley

Boston Journal, March 4, 1872.

Bridger, Bobby. *Buffalo Bill and Sitting Bull: Inventing the Wild West*. College Station: University of Texas Press, 2002.

Cody, William F., and Frank E. Bliss. *Life of Honorable William F. Cody, known as Buffalo Bill, the Famous Hunter*. Hartford, CT: Frank E. Bliss, 1879.

Cody, William F., and William Lightfoot Visscher. *Buffalo Bill's Own Story of His Life and Deeds*. Chicago: Homewood Press, 1917.

Gilbert, Sara. *Annie Oakley*. Mankato, MN: Creative Education, 2006. http://www.annieoakleycenterfoundation.com.

Norfolk Journal, May 18, 1873.

Russell, Don. *Lives and Legends of Buffalo Bill*. Norman: University of Oklahoma Press, 1960.

Rydell, Robert, and Rob Kroes. *Buffalo Bill in Bologna: The Americanization of the World 1869–1922*. Chicago: University of Chicago Press, 2005.

Jesse James

Daviess County Historical Society. http://daviesscountyhistoricalsociety.com/modules.php?op=modload&name=News&file=article&sid=384.

Kansas City Times, August 18, 1876.

Love, Robertus. *The Rise and Fall of Jesse James*. New York: G. P. Putnam, 1926.

Stiles, T. J. *Jesse James: The Last Rebel of the Civil War*. New York: Knopf, 2002.

Sunday Times of Chicago, September 10, 1876.

Yeatman, Ted P. *Frank and Jesse James: The Story Behind the Legend*. Nashville, TN: Cumberland House, 2003.

Doc Holliday

Denver Republican, May 22, 1882.

Herda, D. J. *They Call Me Doc: The Story Behind the Legend of John Henry Holliday*. Guilford, CT: Globe Pequot, 2011.

Leadville Carbonate Chronicle, November 14, 1887.

Masterson, W. R. Bat. "Doc Holliday," *Human Life Magazine,* 1907.

Otero, Miguel Antonio. *My Life on the Frontier*. New York: Press of the Pioneers, 1935.

Rewin, Richard E. *The Truth About Wyatt Earp*. Bloomington, IN: iUniverse, 2000.

Roberts, Gary L. *Doc Holliday: The Life and Legend*. Hoboken, NJ: John Wiley and Sons, 2006.

Tombstone Daily Epitaph, October 27, 1881.

Washington, D.C., Evening Star, January 1, 1878.

Billy the Kid

Garrett, Pat Floyd. *The Authentic Life of Billy, the Kid: The Noted Desperado of the Southwest*. Santa Fe: New Mexican Printing and Publishing, 1881.

Las Vegas Gazette, December 23, 1889.

Metz, Leon Claire. *Pat Garrett: The Story of a Western Lawman*. Norman: University of Oklahoma Press, 1983.

Nolan, Frederick. *The Billy the Kid Reader*. Norman: University of Oklahoma Press, 2007.

Pryor, Alton. *Outlaws and Gunslingers*. Roseville, CA: Stagecoach Publishing, 2001.

Siringo, Charles. *History of Billy the Kid*. Taos, NM: Charles Siringo, 1923.

Utley, Robert M. *Billy the Kid: A Short and Violent Life*. Lincoln: University of Nebraska Press, 1991.

Butch Cassidy

Anaconda Standard, July 14, 1901.

Descriptions of outlaw hideouts, http://www.wyostatearchives.wordpress.com.

Editors of *True West* Magazine. *True Tales and Amazing Legends of the Old West*. New York: Crown, 2005.

Fulton County News, April 26, 1905.

Garcia, Vince. "The Wild Bunch Chronicles: A Timeline from 1890–1910." http://www.centralcal.com/timeline.htm.

Kelly, Charles. *The Outlaw Trail: A History of Butch Cassidy and His Wild Bunch*. Lincoln: University of Nebraska Press, 1996.

Laramie Daily Boomerang, June 4, 1899.

Ogden Standard, June 3, 1898.

Patterson, Richard. *Butch Cassidy: A Biography*. Lincoln: University of Nebraska Press, 1990.

Pointer, Larry. *In Search of Butch Cassidy*. Norman: University of Oklahoma Press, 1977.

Raine, William MacLeod. "Guarding a Railroad in the Bandit Belt," *Wide World Magazine*, November 1904.

Rawlins Semi-Weekly Republican, June 3, 1899.

St. George Union, April 24, 1897.

Salt Lake Herald, September 17, 1900.

CREDITS

Page iii: Background and title logo courtesy of FOX NEWS CHANNEL. Page vi: Chappel, Alonzo (1828–87) (after)/Private Collection/Ken Welsh/Bridgeman Images; Courtesy Library of Congress, LC-DIG-pga-04179; Courtesy Kit Carson House and Museum; Mary Evans Picture Library/Everett Collection; Private Collection/Peter Newark American Pictures/Bridgeman Images; LegendsOfAmerica.com. Page vii: Courtesy Library of Congress, LC-DIG-ppmsca-33129; Universal History Archive/UIG/Bridgeman Images; Private Collection/Peter Newark American Pictures/Bridgeman Images; Courtesy Library of Congress, LC-USZ62-3854; LegendsOfAmerica.com; Courtesy National Archives, Photo no. 406-NSB-011-Billykid; Courtesy Library of Congress, LC-DIG-ppmsca-10772. Page 4: Chappel, Alonzo (1828–87) (after)/Private Collection/Ken Welsh/Bridgeman Images. Page 6: Library of Congress, Prints & Photographs Division, HABS PA, 6-BAUM.V, 1–5. Page 7: Cole, Thomas (1801–48)/Mead Art Museum, Amherst College, MA, USA/Museum purchase/Bridgeman Images. Page 9: Baraldi, Severino (b. 1930)/Private Collection/© Look and Learn/Bridgeman Images; Lindneux, Robert Ottokar (1871–1970)/Private Collection/Peter Newark American Pictures/Bridgeman Images. Page 10: Bingham, George Caleb (1811–79)/Washington University, St. Louis, USA/Bridgeman Images. Page 11: American School (20th century)/Private Collection/Peter Newark American Pictures/Bridgeman Images. Page 13: MPI/Getty Images. Page 14: Baraldi, Severino (b. 1930)/Private Collection/© Look and Learn/Bridgeman Images. Page 17: Private Collection/Peter Newark American Pictures/Bridgeman Images. Pages 18–19: The Print Collector/Print Collector/Getty Images. Page 20: Courtesy Library of Congress, LC-DIG-pga-02659. Page 23: Daniel Boone, 1820 (oil on canvas), Harding, Chester (1792–1866)/© Massachusetts Historical Society, Boston, MA, USA/Bridgeman Images. Page 24: Courtesy Library of Congress, LC-DIG-pga-04179. Page 27: Private Collection/Peter Newark American Pictures/Bridgeman Images. Page 29: Courtesy Library of Congress, LC-USZ62-7368. Page 30: Granger, NYC—All rights reserved. Page 33: Courtesy Library of Congress, LC-USZ62-43901; Courtesy Library of Congress, LC-DIG-pga-02501. Page 37: Callcott, Frank C. (1891–1979)/Dallas Museum of Art, Texas, USA/gift of Professor Dudley F. McCollum/Bridgeman Images. Page 39: Stephen St.John/National Geographic Creative. Page 40: Private Collection/Peter Newark American Pictures/Bridgeman Images. Page 41: Wyeth, Newell Convers (1882–1945)/Private Collection/Bridgeman Images; Private Collection/© Look and Learn/Bridgeman Images; Private Collection/Bridgeman Images. Page 44: Courtesy Kit Carson House and Museum. Page 46: Granger, NYC—All rights reserved. Pages 48–49: University of Wyoming, American Heritage Center, Everett D. Graff Collection, Accession Number 4912. Page 51: 000-742-0217, William A. Keleher Pictorial Collection, Center for Southwest Research, University Libraries, University of New Mexico. Page 52: The New York Public Library/Art Resource, NY. Page 53: Courtesy Kit Carson House and Museum. Page 55: Courtesy Library of Congress, LC-USZC4-2631. Page 57: 000-742-0067, William A. Keleher Pictorial Collection, Center for Southwest Research, University Libraries, University of New Mexico; Vector Graphic by Retro Design Elements. Page 58: Courtesy Library of Congress, LC-DIG-hec-13449. Page 60: Granger, NYC—All rights reserved. Page 61: Return of scouts—Cheyenne 1910 (photo)/Universal History Archive/UIG/Bridgeman Images. Page 63: Denver Public Library, Western History Collection/Bridgeman Images. Page 65: Courtesy Library of Congress LC-DIG-cwpb-07381. Page 66: Courtesy Library of Congress, LC-USZC4-11256. Page 68: Courtesy Library of Congress, LC-BH83-1371. Page 70: Mary Evans Picture Library/Everett Collection. Page 73: Private Collection/Peter Newark Western Americana/Bridgeman Images; De Agostini Picture Library/Bridgeman Images. Page 76: Private Collection/Ken Welsh/Bridgeman Images. Page 78: Private Collection/Peter Newark American Pictures/Bridgeman Images. Pages 80–81: Courtesy Library of Congress, LC-DIG-pga-01018. Page 84: Wells Fargo Corporate Archives. Page 86: Granger, NYC—All rights reserved; Vector Graphic by Retro Design Elements. Pages 88, 90, 93: Private Collection/Peter Newark American Pictures/Bridgeman Images. Page 94: Private Collection/Peter Newark Western Americana/Bridgeman Images. Page 97: Stock Montage/Getty Images. Pages 98–99: Private Collection/Peter Newark American Pictures/Bridgeman Images. Page 101: Courtesy Library of Congress, LC-USZ62-50004. Page 103: Collection/Peter Newark American Pictures/Bridgeman Images. Page 107: American Photographer (19th century)/Private Collection/Peter Newark American Pictures/Bridgeman Images. Pages 108, 111: Private Collection/Peter Newark American Pictures/Bridgeman Images. Page 114: Peter Newark American Pictures/Bridgeman Images. Page 116: Courtesy Library of Congress, LC-USF34-016687-C. Page 118: LegendsOfAmerica.com. Page 121: Courtesy Everett Collection. Page 122: Courtesy National Archives, photo no. 111-B-3202 and record no. 6851120. Page 124: Western History Collections, University of Oklahoma Libraries, Twine Family 61. Page 125: Courtesy National Archives at Kansas City, Records of the Bureau of Prisons, RG 129. Pages 131, 132, 133: Courtesy the Fort Smith National Historic Site. Page 134: Courtesy Library of Congress, LC-DIG-ppmsca-33129. Page 136: Amos Bad Heart Buffalo (1869–1913)/Private

Collection/The Stapleton Collection/Bridgeman Images. Page 137: Kills Two (Nupa Kte) (1969–1927)/Private Collection/The Stapleton Collection/Bridgeman Images. Page 138: Courtesy Library of Congress, LC-USZC4-7160. Pages 141, 142: De Agostini Picture Library/Bridgeman Images. Page 144: Courtesy Library of Congress, LC-USZ62-114798. Page 146: Courtesy Library of Congress, LC-DIG-ppmsca-24021. Page 149: De Agostini Picture Library/Bridgeman Images. Page 152: Courtesy Library of Congress, LC-BH831-365. Page 155: National Museum of American History, Smithsonian Institution, USA/ Bridgeman Images. Page 156: Becker, Otto (fl. 1895) (after)/Private Collection/Peter Newark American Pictures/Bridgeman Images. Page 158: Private Collection/Bridgeman Images. Page 159: Miller, Alfred Jacob (1810–74)/© Walters Art Museum, Baltimore, USA/Bridgeman Images. Page 160: Peter Newark Pictures/Bridgeman Images. Page 162: Universal History Archive/ UIG/Bridgeman Images; Private Collection/Peter Newark American Pictures/Bridgeman Images. Page 164: American Photographer, (20th century)/Private Collection/Peter Newark American Pictures/Bridgeman Images. Page 165: Private Collection/Peter Newark Western Americana/Bridgeman Images. Page 166: American School/Private Collection/Bridgeman Images. Page 169: Denver Public Library, Western History Collection/Bridgeman Images. Page 171: Private Collection/Peter Newark American Pictures/Bridgeman Images; Private Collection/Peter Newark Western Americana/Bridgeman Images. Page 172: Newberry Library, Chicago, Illinois, USA/Bridgeman Images. Page 175: Courtesy Library of Congress, LC-USZ62-21207 and LC-DIG-ppmsca-24362. Page 177: Private Collection/© Look and Learn/Peter Jackson Collection/Bridgeman Images. Page 179: The Illustrated London News Picture Library, London, UK/Bridgeman Images. Page 181: Private Collection/© Look and Learn/Bridgeman Images. Page 183: Courtesy Library of Congress, LC-USZ62-46076. Page 185: Underwood Archives/ UIG/Bridgeman Images. Page 186: Private Collection/Peter Newark American Pictures/Bridgeman Images. Page 188: Courtesy Library of Congress, LC-USZ62-3854. Page 190: Private Collection/Peter Newark American Pictures/Bridgeman Images. Pages 191, 192: Used with permission of The State Historical Society of Missouri. Page 194: Used with permission of The State Historical Society of Missouri; Courtesy Library of Congress, LC-USZ62-3855. Page 195: Used with permission of The State Historical Society of Missouri. Page 197: Courtesy Library of Congress, LC-USZ62-3855. Page 201: Everitt, Elias Foster (1837–1928)/Private Collection/Courtesy of Swann Auction Galleries/Bridgeman Images. Page 202: Private Collection/Peter Newark American Pictures/Bridgeman Images. Pages 203, 204: Northfield Historical Society. Page 207: Used with permission of The State Historical Society of Missouri. Page 208: LegendsOfAmerica.com. Page 209: Private Collection/Photo © Barbara Singer/Bridgeman Images. Page 211: Private Collection/Bridgeman Images; Private Collection/Peter Newark American Pictures/Bridgeman Images; Courtesy Library of Congress LC-USZ62-4049. Page 212: Private Collection/Peter Newark American Pictures/Bridgeman Images. Page 214: LegendsOfAmerica.com. Page 218: Private Collection/Peter Newark Western Americana/Bridgeman Images. Page 220: The Stapleton Collection/Bridgeman Images. Pages 222–23: LegendsOfAmerica. com. Page 225: Private Collection/Bridgeman Images. Page 228: Private Collection/Peter Newark American Pictures/ Bridgeman Images; Courtesy Library of Congress, LC-USF33-012679-M4. Page 231: The Denver Post via Getty Images. Page 233: Courtesy Library of Congress, LC-USZ62-50009 and LC-USZ62-50007. Page 234: Private Collection/Peter Newark American Pictures/Bridgeman Images. Page 236: Courtesy National Archives, Photo no. 406-NSB-011-Billykid. Page 241: 000-118-0017 and 000-742-0111, William A. Keleher Pictorial Collection, Center for Southwest Research, University Libraries, University of New Mexico; LegendsOfAmerica.com. Page 242: 000-742-0151, William A. Keleher Pictorial Collection, Center for Southwest Research, University Libraries, University of New Mexico. Page 243: Private Collection/Peter Newark Western Americana/Bridgeman Images. Page 244: American School (19th century)/Private Collection/Peter Newark Western Americana/Bridgeman Images. Page 246: Wallace, Lew (1827–1905)/© Collection of the New-York Historical Society, USA/Bridgeman Images. Page 247: AP photo/Fray Angelico Chavez History Library. Page 248: Courtesy Everett Collection. Page 250: Private Collection/Bridgeman Images. Page 253: Courtesy Everett Collection. Page 255: Courtesy Library of Congress, LC-USZ62-87581. Page 256: Charlton Comics, http://digitalcomicmuseum.com. Page 258: Courtesy Library of Congress, LC-DIG-ppmsca-10772. Page 260: University of Wyoming, American Heritage Center, Everett D. Graff Collection, Accession Number ah101308. Page 261: Used by permission, Utah State Historical Society. Page 262: Courtesy Library of Congress, LC-DIG-ppmsca-10770. Pages 264–65: University of Wyoming, American Heritage Center, Everett D. Graff Collection, Accession Number ah01053_0946. Page 265: Courtesy Library of Congress, LC-DIG-ppmsca-11844. Page 267: Courtesy Library of Congress, LC-DIG-ppmsca-07624. Page 269: University of Wyoming, American Heritage Center, Everett D. Graff Collection, Accession Numbers ah00176_0285, ah00176_0283, and ah-2995. Page 270: Underwood Archives/UIG/ Bridgeman Images. Page 271: University of Wyoming, American Heritage Center, Everett D. Graff Collection, Accession Number ah01053_0918. Page 273: Private Collection/Peter Newark American Pictures/Bridgeman Images; University of Wyoming, American Heritage Center, Everett D. Graff Collection, Accession Number ah001401. Page 275: University of Wyoming, American Heritage Center, Everett D. Graff Collection, Accession Number ah002690. Page 276: Courtesy Library of Congress, LC-USZ620132506; Vector Graphic by Vector Open Stock. Page 281: ©20thCentFox/Courtesy Everett Collection. Page 284: Private Collection/Peter Newark American Pictures/Bridgeman Images.

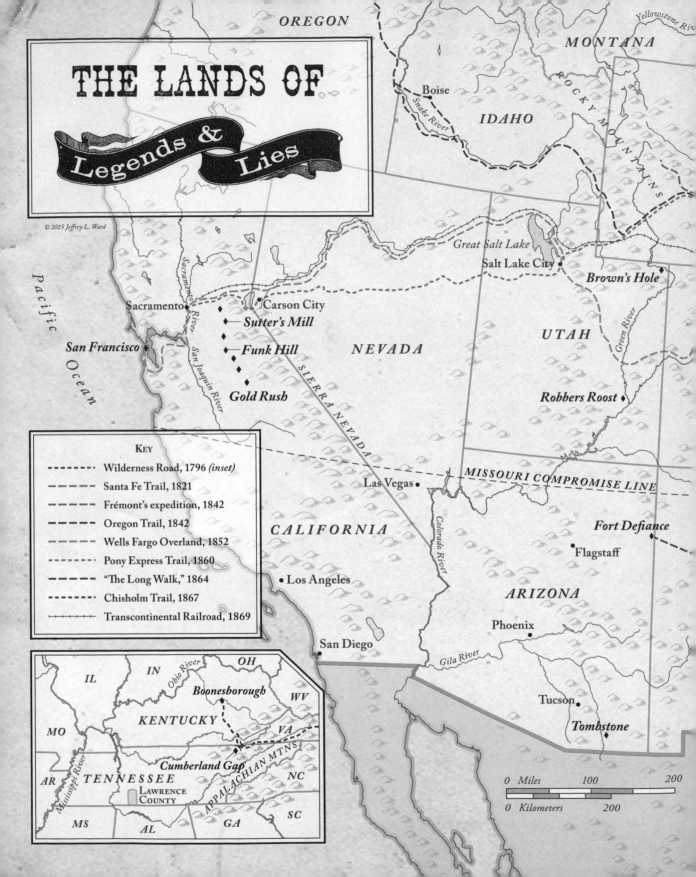

THE LANDS OF
Legends & Lies

© 2015 Jeffrey L. Ward

KEY

- – – – – Wilderness Road, 1796 *(inset)*
- – – – Santa Fe Trail, 1821
- – – – Frémont's expedition, 1842
- – – – Oregon Trail, 1842
- – – – Wells Fargo Overland, 1852
- · · · · · Pony Express Trail, 1860
- – – – "The Long Walk," 1864
- · · · · Chisholm Trail, 1867
- +++++ Transcontinental Railroad, 1869

OREGON

MONTANA

Yellowstone Riv.

Boise

IDAHO

Snake River

ROCKY MOUNTAINS

Great Salt Lake

Salt Lake City

Brown's Hole

Green River

UTAH

Sacramento River

Sacramento

Carson City

Sutter's Mill

Funk Hill

NEVADA

Robbers Roost

San Francisco

San Joaquin River

Gold Rush

Pacific Ocean

SIERRA NEVADA

Las Vegas

MISSOURI COMPROMISE LINE

Colorado River

CALIFORNIA

Fort Defiance

Flagstaff

Los Angeles

ARIZONA

San Diego

Phoenix

Gila River

Tucson

Tombstone

| 0 | Miles | 100 | 200 |

| 0 | Kilometers | 200 |

IL

IN

OH

Ohio River

Boonesborough

WV

MO

KENTUCKY

VA

Mississippi River

Cumberland Gap

APPALACHIAN MTNS.

NC

AR

TENNESSEE

LAWRENCE
COUNTY

SC

MS

AL

GA